Wickets in the West, or, The Twelve in America

The images appearing here are the best quality possible considering the condition and legibility of the original copy and in keeping with the filming contract specifications.

Les images suivantes ont été reproduites avec le plus grand soin, compte tenu de la condition et de la netteté de l'exemplaire filmé, et en conformité avec les conditions du contrat de filmage.

The last recorded frame on each microfiche shall contain the symbol →► (meaning CONTINUED"), or the symbol ∇ (meaning "END"), whichever applies

Un des symboles suivants apparaîtra sur la dernière image de chaque microfiche, selon le cas: le symbole →► signifie "A SUIVRE", le symbole ∇ signifie "FIN"

The original copy was borrowed from, and filmed with, the kind consent of the following institution

National Library of Canada

L'exemplaire filmé fut reproduit grâce à la générosité de l'établissement prêteur suivant

Bibliothèque nationale du Canada

Maps or plates too large to be entirely included in one exposure are filmed beginning in the upper left hand corner, left to right and top to bottom, as many frames as required. The following diagrams illustrate the method.

Les cartes ou les planches trop grandes pour être reproduites en un seul cliché sont filmées à partir de l'angle supérieure gauche, de gauche à droite et de haut en bas, en prenant le nombre d'images nécessaire. Le diagramme suivant illustre la méthode

1	2	3

1
2
3

1	2	3
4	5	6

WICKETS IN THE WEST.

THE TWELVE AT MONTREAL.
THE "MOUNTAIN" IN THE BACKGROUND.

yours truly

W. A. Fitz-Gerald

WICKETS IN THE WEST;

OR,

THE TWELVE IN AMERICA.

BY

R. A. FITZGERALD.

LONDON:
TINSLEY BROTHERS, 8, CATHERINE ST., STRAND.
1873.

LONDON :
BRADBURY, AGNEW, & CO., PRINTERS, WHITEFRIARS.

CONT NTS.

CHAPTER I.

CHAPTER II.

CHAPTER III.

CHAPTER IV.

CHAPTER V.

PAGE

CHAPTER VI.

CHAPTER VII.

CHAPTER VIII.

CHAPTER IX.

CHAPTER X.

CHAPTER XI.

IN THE STATES.

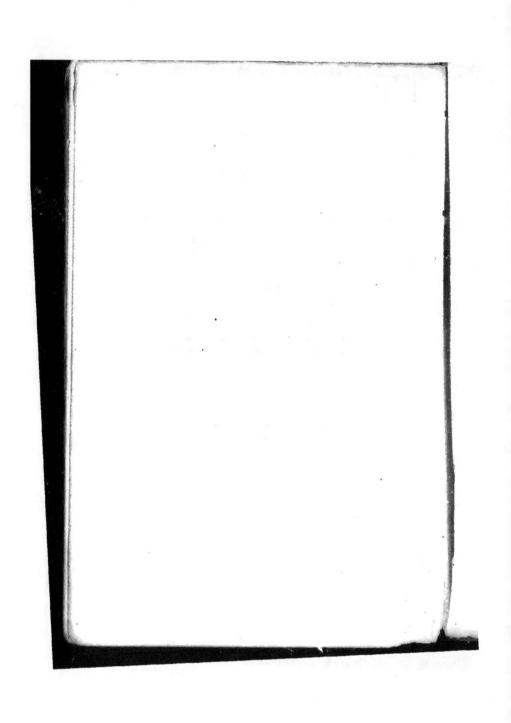

WICKETS IN THE WEST.

CHAPTER I.

PRELIMINARY CANTER.

KIND READERS (if any),

IT will be only right on our part to prepare you for disappointment. You may have supposed us capable of giving you much information about Canada and the United States; of at least amusing you with our adventures, or of interesting you in our cricket exploits. You might argue with reason, here is the last new light from Ame- The Lime. rica; now we shall know whether to plunge still deeper into Grand Trunk or North Pacifics. The satisfaction of the Yankees, whether real or feigned, at the so-called settlement of the Alabama claims; the delight or disgust of the Canadians at the San Juan

B

award; the probability of peace amongst Erie directors; the guilt, if any, of Mr. Stokes; the fate, if deserved, of Mr. Fisk; the actual depth of the central volume of the Niagara fall; whether the beauty of the " Horseshoe" exists only in Canadian imagination, or whether the grandeur of the American fall is more grand by being American; whether an Englishman diminishes daily in his own estimation as he travels through the States, through his admiration of republican institutions, and the manners of a free people. Whether the women of America are as beautiful as they are painted; whether they are painted at all; whether families of ten are prohibited by law; whether a people, hailing from one common parent, can really be so jealous of the elder branch, that it will not speak its language except with a different accent. These and other great questions of the day you might reasonably expect us to probe, for you know our little game—you can see nothing but the "stump" orator in a cricketer recording his impressions. You shall have the impressions; we can give you

Marginal notes:

Stokes. Fisk.

Beauty with or without paint.

The stump.

"proofs" before letters (though you may have them for the asking) of Transatlantic hospitality. Banish from your fevered mind all thirst for knowledge—we don't profess it. Don't make any great preparation to be amused, such invariably ends in disappointment. If you are a cricketer, you may smile (we don't object to that much) at some of the matches; if you are personally acquainted with any of the actors, you may possibly not recognise them under their altered circumstances. An Englishman abroad is not a Britisher at home. You would not recognise your retiring relation in the consequential stalker of the table d'hôte. You have heard him grumble at home, yet the confiding stranger, into whose ear uninvited he pours his abuse of things foreign, almost envies the home that sent forth so warm a champion. We do not wish to imply that any of *your* friends, who play their little part in this history, are undistinguishable thusly—we fervently hope none of us are or were. Our object is only to make you aware that Horace had America in his mental eye when he sang—"Cælum,

Horace.

non animum, mutant, qui trans mare currunt."
We certainly found a warmer sky, we
steamed on broader rivers and wider lakes,
we travelled through forests of unimagined
beauty and surprising extent, but we experienced the same welcome, we met with the
same kindness, that in our hearts we knew
to be English, though the hand that
pressed ours happened to be Canadian, or
the tone of voice that addressed us, to be
American.

You may be inquisitive to know the
" how " and the " why " we went across the
Atlantic. You shall be gratified so far.
But don't expect us to tell you anything
that you ought not to know; don't regard
The chan- us as a channel of investment or as the
nel. medium of intelligence unknown to the
columns of the *Mining Journal* or the *Wall
Street Gazette.* We shall hope to dispel a
few prejudices in respect of Americans, and
to establish a heartier feeling towards Canada
and Canadians. We do not deny that we
saw the colony at its best, that we heard its
prais ' sung by those who, loving it best,
might be expected without gainsay to laud

it most. The guest, who can disparage his
host after partaking of his hospitality, is not
a mortal to be envied; the tongue, indeed, The tongue.
that tastes, may be tied, and the evidence of
a full stomach may admit of qualification. The sto-
But we cannot forget that we were humble
strangers, our game was our best apology
for our visit, our flannel jackets were our
coat of arms, our bats our supporters, and
our motto a " fair field and no favour." We Motto.
were surprised at our reception from the
hour of our landing to the day of our
departure.

The true nature of the spirit that ani- Truth.
mated our hosts was not fully revealed to
us until we had passed through the Dominion.   We then learned that it was
not owing to any rivalry between town
and town, that we were made much of,
and more of, as we travelled west.   Our
cricketing exploits appealed to a comparatively small section, and if success in the
cricket-field had formed the sole basis of
sociality many of us would have gone sup-
perless to bed.

No! the spirit emanated from a higher

motive, though we are sensitive to a pin's point on the epidermis of our noble game. As we journeyed from Quebec to Montreal, from Montreal to Ottawa, and so on through Toronto to London and Hamilton, we were *made* sensible that our reception was mainly owing to the fact that we were Englishmen. The people were glad to see us, because they feel themselves to be no less Englishmen than ourselves; because they resent keenly the suspicion, which Heaven and the Home Government only know how, has arisen, of their loyalty to the Queen and affection to British institutions. Hence only could arise the united zeal in our favour that displayed itself in banquets, that danced

Pledges. itself at balls, that pledged itself at bars. Our expedition must not be looked at simply from a sporting view. That many enthusiasts really believed in the stir that we should give to their favourite pastime is undoubted. Whether that object of our visit

A private opinion. will be attained, is doubtful. We have our own opinions as to the practical results of matches between a trained eleven and an undisciplined twenty-two. We incline to the belief that the essential elements of good cricket can only be found in matches between foes of equal number. Should a 11 *v.* 11. visit of Englishmen on the same errand be repeated, we should feel more sanguine of its results than of our own, were the visitors even less distinguished than ourselves, so that the best *eleven* of the Dominion, instead of twenty-two, were pitted against them. We will not prolong this discussion further than saying that a "twenty-two" generally cuts Suicide. its throat in more than one place; that an "eleven" takes more individual interest in the game, and that the pleasure of the spectators is enhanced by "hits" obtaining their full value, rather than by the fall of the best hitter into the hands of an outsider. Hard Lines.

We have now taken you pretty well over the course; you will meet with a few obstacles erected, as you may suppose, by personal vanity, and your ears may be assailed by blasts of a brazen trumpet blown Our trumpet. too constantly by ourselves. We ask for your patience and kind forbearance. Our object is to place on record the details that made our expedition so pleasant, to do justice to our hosts, and to furnish, what we unhappily believe to be required, convincing proof of Canadian attachment to the old country.

Clear the
course.
The course being now cleared, the start need no longer be delayed, so with your permission—critics, "stand on one side, please"—we will attend to the race that is set before us.

CHAPTER II.

The " How " and the " Why " we crossed the Atlantic.

WE will take the "Why" first. In the summer of 1871, two gentlemen interviewed the Secretary of the Marylebone Club at Lord's Ground. The one, Captain Wallace, of the 60th Rifles; the other, Mr. J. C. Patteson, of Toronto. They there and then unfolded a cricket-scheme, pointing out to the Secretary where ·Canada was, and ex- Geography. plaining who the Canadians were. The precaution was necessary, as great ignorance prevailed in England at this time respecting its colony. The scheme amounted practically to this : Mr. Patteson was in- The invitation. structed on the part of the Canadians to invite an English Twelve to play a series of matches in the Dominion. The Twelve were to consider themselves as visitors, expressly invited by the several cricketing bodies in

Canada. The Canadians proposed to defray all expenses connected with the voyage out and home, and generally to provide for the comfort and passage of the visitors throughout the Dominion.

£. s. d.

It was hinted at the same time that the expedition might be extended to the United States, as Mr. Patteson expressed an opinion that a visit to New York, Philadelphia, and Boston, would be hailed with satisfaction by the cricketers south of 49°.

The scheme was left in a crude state throughout the winter, and in the spring, *Felo de se.* when to think of cricket is less like suicide, the Secretary took measures to ascertain the feeling of his young friends about crossing the water with their cricket-bags. It took ; he received flattering promises from more quarters than he expected ; he had at least sixteen promises to go anywhere and do anything under his guidance. This was flattering but perplexing. The invitation was limited to twelve ; his next step was to sound the note of public opinion, and though he met with objections in some quarters, he was advised generally, that an offer so made should not be rejected. He thereupon took it up in earnest. The cable announced his intention to the other side of the water, and a speedy reply expressed the satisfaction of the Canadians. The Secretary looked through his sixteen acceptances, and invited eleven of them to dine with him at Lords The Dinner. on July 2. All present swore a solemn The oath. oath—which we will not quote—that they would be true to the tryst; the day appointed for sailing was August 8. The original selection consisted of R. A. Fitz- The elect. gerald, W. G. Grace, V. E. Walker, R. D. Walker, C. I. Thornton, A. Lubbock, A. N. Hornby, A. Appleby, Hon. G. Harris, R. A. Mitchell, J. W. Dale, R. D. Balfour. This list soon eliminated itself.

Mr. Thornton saw a picture in a shop- A sea piece. window of a ship in distress, and read an article on sea-sickness, that did not convince him that he would be the lucky man in ten who escaped *mal de mer*. He excused himself accordingly. W. H. Hadow filled the gap. R. D. Balfour disappeared, and in his place C. J. Ottoway popped up; J. W. Dale then jacked up; and agony first fell upon the Secretary's mind. Bowling, it will be observed, was only represented by Appleby, and the more the manager *The dream.* thought of it, the less he slept; until one night he dreamed that W. M. Rose and lobs might be serviceable. He acted at once on the dream, and plucking the Rose from its blushing bride pinned him to the Twelve. C. K. Francis was next " added to the list," very luckily—as a young lady afterwards remarked. All went merry as a muffin's man's bell until August 5. *Dies iræ!* Ye Gods—three days only before starting and two vacancies suddenly occurred. The Messrs. Walker were struck down by illness. The Secretary has not much hair to lose, but he squandered that little in handfuls. What was to be done? Canterbury was at its height; there wasn't a day for weeks to come that hadn't its match; there isn't a cricketer, now-a-days, that is not claimed by at least three clubs. Into *Despair.* highways, into byeways, by dint of hansom cab, by wire and post, by everything that was sacred, in the name of everything unmentionable, drove, telegraphed, wrote,

ıg,
ed
;er
ne
bs
oɪ
its
'e.
he
:r-
a
'es
't-
d.
ɔy
.ir
in
r-
ɪy
ι;
is
:o
ɪɪ
ɪt
ɪ-
ɘ,

prayed, and swore the Secretary. His
prayers or maledictions were heard, Edgar
Lubbock and F. Pickering turned up
trumps, but the Secretary was not sure that Distrust.
two more might not turn up at Londonderry
after all. However fourteen were more to
be desired than ten. Much eased in spirit, on
August 7 the manager went down to Liverpool. The trysting spot was the Washing-
ton Hotel; twelve noon, on August 8, the
hour appointed. Right glad was he to see
half-a-dozen cricket bags in the hall, and Delight.
more to come, according to the porter.
Could it be? The Eleven were mustered.
Farrands, the umpire, answered to his
name, the expedition was a reality. The
twelve apostles of cricket were committed to The Apos-
their work; a friendly company insisted on   tles.
speeding their departure by a sumptuous
lunch at the Adelphi, the entertainers being
Messrs. Antrobus, Thornewill, H. Gladstone,
D. Cunningham, Phipps, Parr, and Wyatt.

One toast only was proposed, "Success to Dry toast.
the Expedition," followed by Speech No. 1 of
the Captain. These were very numerous in
the sequel, and very like each other, but sam-

ples will be given anon. Half-an-hour after, the pilgrims stood on the landing stage, each with a large easy chair under his arm, and parcels various in either hand. A cheer from the crowd, and they were off on *The tug.* the tug, and now we come to the "How" we crossed the Atlantic.

The How. The s.s. Sarmatian, the last new vessel of Messrs. Allan's fleet, lay in midstream; up her side soon clambered the passengers; a whistle from the boatswain, and the tug loosed off, the last tie that bound us to England was severed. From 3.30 P.M. to 9.25 P.M., the good vessel lay moored head to stream. The interval was employed in not blessing the delay and in shaking down into berths. Stock was taken of the passengers; ladies were in a minority; but the steerage afforded considerable amusement.   The *The Home* Brompton Home had consigned upwards of *at Bromp-* *ton.* 100 children of both sexes to a new life in a distant clime. They were under the charge of Miss Burt, sister of Mrs. Macpherson, the Lady Superior of the Home. At sunset the children were mustered on deck, and after being put through the manual and platoon,

which consisted chiefly in explaining to them
the difference between their right and left
hands, they began to sing, not exactly together or with one voice, but certainly with
one mind, some simple hymns. When all the
voices had ceased, Miss Burt delivered a very
stirring and touching address. Her words
affected more than one bystander. She told
the children to think of the little comrades
they had left behind them, of the Home
which had taken them from the gutters, had
sheltered and clothed them. She pointed to
the sun now setting in the West, whom they *Byron.*
would follow in his flight; they were leaving
the land of their birth for a land of new life
and of promise to all of them, and concluded
by exhorting them never to forget that they
were English boys and English girls.

There was not a sad face amongst them,
there was a strange half-lost look about many,
but the cheerful obedience and willing discipline that prevailed amongst these hapless *The gutter.*
waifs and strays of London streets spoke
volumes for the excellence of the short training they had received at the Brompton Home.
At midnight the bar was passed, and after a

pleasant run along the coast of Ireland, a delay of a few hours occurred in Lough Foyle, to take in mails and passengers. Here the Captain shewed signs of nervousness; some of his telegrams had directed their recipients to meet the s.s. Sarmatian here, and he narrowly scanned the new arrivals, but

Turn of the tide. the luck had turned and to his first disappointment there was not added an embarrasment of riches. The Twelve, at midnight of the 9th were sensible of the Atlantic swell. As many accidents occurred in the course of the trip, some of which will be mentioned, and others will not, we will record the first.

An accident. Animal spirits rise to the surface in smooth water; they sink, the steward knows where,

The Imp. in a swell. Nothing would satisfy the Monkey, as the ship lay at anchor off Greencastle, but to try his agility over as many chairs as could be collected on deck—from one chair, the obstacles increased to four and five. One fool makes many. We cannot say where the competition would have ended, had not "Alfred" landed on his little toe and partially dislocated it. The Captain then did interfere strongly, and for several days Alfred limped

like a hound with a toe down. The first day
in the Atlantic has a tendency to sober the
wildest, and the Twelve scarcely met each
other except spasmodically in the passages, Spasms.
and at service on Sunday, which happened to
be calm, until the 13th. By this time all little
difference between the stomach and the
ocean had been settled, and the party were
equal to that melancholy pastime called
" Shovelboard," varied by " ringing the peg." Shovelboard.
These are Atlantic institutions, and deserve
recognition, as they tend to break the monotony of the voyage ; but a better estimate of
that monotony cannot be afforded than by
the fact of such games interesting or exciting
anybody. Shovelboard consists of pushing
some flat wooden discs from one given point
to another, marked out in squares of different
numerical value. Its melancholy character
is sustained by the pusher losing all he has
previously scored, if he lands his last disc,
as he generally does, on the first square,
when the cry of " 10 off " is howled by the -10.
adversaries. Many a night did this fiendish
sound wake us from happy dreams of home.
" Ringing the peg " is an innocent amuse- Ringing the
Peg.

c

ment, and has the charm of occupying the body without distressing the mind. It consists of throwing rings of rope at an erect peg, you make the game what you like, and if you don't like, you let it slide. It is popular with the boys on board, but grave men sometimes stoop to it, in fact you must stoop to succeed at it, so it after all inculcates a moral lesson to the proud. Meals play an important part on the Atlantic. On the "Sarmatian," such as can, breakfast at 8·30 a.m., lunch at 12, dine at 4, tea at 7, and grog at 9 p.m. Starvation has a bad time of it on board. Those that prefer a horizontal situation, can breakfast in their berths. Conspicuous amongst these until entering the straits of Belle Isle was the Honorable George. He had the misfortune to share a cabin with Alfred the Lame. Now Alfred never missed a meal, and George never enjoyed one. Alfred's spirits were invariably high, George's proportionally low. Hence the opinion formed by the two, as to the pleasure or desirability of the expedition, differed *in toto*. To Alfred's cheery remark, as the good ship creaked and rolled, "She takes a little playing, George, this morning,"

Lesson to the proud.

Meals.

Audi alteram partem.

the
con-
peg,
you
vith
mes
eed
son
part
ich
12,
ar-
ose
ak-
gst
sle
is-
ne.
ge
erc
w.
to
on,
k,
he
."
,

or " She's a bit rough, and wants the roller,"
George was heard to mutter, " Shut up."
Alfred was cruel at meals, and the Captain
was obliged to interfere, on hearing him offer
to his sick comrade " Boiled mutton and Boiled mut-
capers, or stewed tripe this morning, George?" ton.
Gilbert the Great was bowled out very early,
and would have returned in an open boat
from Mid Atlantic, if such craft were in the
habit of plying there. We wonder they don't,
as more than half that cross would gladly get
back to land if they could. Still the voyage
was a pleasant one. The ship was admirably
officered and supplied. The steerage passengers led to walks of discovery, and Appleby
was seen in familiar conversation with a young
lady, name and destination unknown, whose A flirt.
unprotected state led to offers of consolation
on the part of our Bowler, which might have
been accepted, had not other of the Twelve
contested his right of " discovery." Whilst
they were all fighting, Helen eloped with Homer.
another Paris. Icebergs were sighted on the
morning of August 15, and several objects
very like whales, and pronounced to be such,
were seen. Soon a small patch of seaweed

c 2

floated by, and the sea-sick passengers imbibed
Colon. fresh life, like Columbus and his crew, as it
betokened land.   At last the welcome cry of
" Land on the starboard bow," brought everybody up from luncheon. Far down on the
Northern horizon lay a mysterious dark line,
broadening by degrees as the good ship kept
her course with undiminished speed.   Before
Belle Isle. dinner time, the Straits of Belle Isle could
be made out, and the forbidding shores of
Labrador, and not less uninviting Coast of
Newfoundland stretched far away on either
hand.   The welcome lighthouse of Belle Isle
was passed at 3 P.M.   The long rolling swell
of the Atlantic settled himself on the placid
Ducks. bosom of a duck-pond.   Talking of ducks, a
gentleman on board related the following
A tale. marvellous tale.   We only vouch for having
heard it.   According to our friend, a steamer
passing through the Straits of Belle Isle was
once obliged to " easy," and finally to stop,
in consequence of the flocks of wild ducks that
were floating ahead of it : they were gorged
Captain with herring-fry, and unable to fly.   The
Cook. humane captain, having consulted the sea-
cook, and discovered that a sufficient supply

ibed
ıs it
y of
ery-
the
ine,
cept
fore
uld
of
; of
her
Isle
vell
ıcid
, a
ing
ing
ner
vas
op,
ıat
ed
'he
ea-
ıly

of fresh meat was still in the larder, forebore The Larder.
from the plunder, for " he said 'twas a barba- Shenstone.
rous deed." He could not have proceeded
without making an unwilling " salmi." We
have searched the records of the Humane
Society, and, not finding any entry of a medal
being bestowed for saving life under " Ducks
and Drakes," the story must be taken, as we
took it—we smiled. Our Captain, otherwise The Captain caps it.
a silent man, burst into speech on hearing
this fowl tale, and said that he remembered a
ship sailing through a tunnel of ice, a stranded
iceberg having blocked the passage. You
see what straits travellers are put to in Belle
Isle, when such stories are rife. The tunnel
admitted the ship, mast and spars and all (if
you can swallow the ship, neither mast nor A swallow.
spar will stick in your throat). The hero of
the duck story, on hearing the Captain's tale,
went below, and did not join in general conversation for several days. He left the table
hurriedly another day when the steward,
instigated by us, offered him " Duck, well Stuffing.
stuffed, Sir ? "

Several icebergs were stranded on each
coast, one of huge proportions resembling the

statue of the Colossi in the plain of Thebes, another toppled over as we passed it within a few hundred yards. We had, indeed, been fortunate, 2,000 miles of our course completed without a gale of wind. Whist now set in with violence, and the gaps at table were filled. The Honourable George was now proof to Alfred's jokes, and retaliated with his own—these we must suppress for the present, as we wish to cajole the public into following us further on our way. It might be induced to stop here, if we were not cautious.

The therm. The temperature of the water on entering the Gulf of St. Lawrence stood at 58°, that of the air at 56°. Time, midnight. The nights at this season of the year are resplendent; the Northern Lights illuminate the sky, the lights, beyond the ken of man, that seem to hold mysterious communion with icy regions equally beyond his reach. As we progress across the Gulf, and sight the Island of Anticosti, we could readily imagine the feelings of the early discoverers of Canada. Oft on the evening breeze is wafted the incense of the pine forest, the shore is yet as untrodden by us as it was by them. We were safely out of the terrible deep, and the land now in sight presents the same appearance to us as it did of yore; only the beacon-light, so welcome to the wayfarer, betrays the presence of man; the bear is still the undisturbed denizen of Anticosti. We perhaps are more to be envied than Jacques Cartier, for it took him three voyages thus far before he discovered the mouth of the Great River. We trust to our helmsman to hit it off precisely. We are bound, nevertheless, on a voyage of discovery—we are pilgrims and pioneers. But our path is that of Peace, and the " weapons we wield leave no scourges, no record of anguish or pain." Here the parallel must end, as, with all our respect for James Carter and Co., we hope to leave a better impression on the white settler, than he and his lot did on the " red." Truly their game may be described in billiard parlance as " white " on the red, and black (old N.) was the player. At 7 P.M. on August 16 we were abreast of Cape Gaspey, and at breakfast time on August 17 we were fairly in the river. Such a river! land only just visible on either side,

Margin notes: James Carter. Zingari song. Pool.

The St.
Lawrence.

the outlet of half a continent. It was difficult
to regard that expanse of water as a river,
with our European types fresh to our eyes.
We have seen the Danube rolling its turbid
volume of water down to the Black Sea, and
have traced the Nile from Alexandria to
Wadee-Halfey; each was grand in its turn
to the traveller who judged of rivers by the
Rhine or the Thames; but this mighty stream
is well adapted to prepare the mind for the
New World, with its wealth of inland waters,
illimitable forest, cities of mushroom growth,
an atmosphere of expansion, the elbow-room
of millions. One thing struck us, if anything
invisible can strike, the absence of living

Profr.
Home.

thing upon the water—not a vessel, not a
bird—scarcely a dozen vessels were met with
on the passage. The wreck, indeed, of one
was seen. The land on the southern shore
soon gave evidence of civilization. The
wooden houses of the French Canadians were
scattered along the shore, and dotted on the
hills. The northern shore was of iron aspect,
iron to the core. At intervals a few trading
huts were visible on this side, but the aspect
of the interior might well father somebody's

idea that this was the chosen spot for the
penance of Pilate. Strictly speaking, we The Pilate.
have not that high opinion of early nautical
experience as to regard this as an historical
fact. But we are now off Father Point, a Off Father
general consultation of diaries on the part of Point.
the Twelve took place, and letters were
despatched by the pilot boat to meet the home-
ward-bound steamer. The "Prussian," of
which further anon, passed us a few hours later.
As evening gathered over the St. Lawrence,
a thick fog enveloped the "Sarmatian" for the
first time, the good ship ceased to throb—the
suspension of motion, after nine days' "plough-
ing," was like the stoppage of the heart's A shock.
blood at some sudden shock. As we warily
threaded our way in the dark, outlines of vessels lying at anchor betoken our approach to
the haven where we would be. Soon the
order to "clear away for the guns" stirred
the blood, and a loud report, twice repeated,
and a rocket soaring into the Northern sky,
told all that heard and all that saw that our
voyage was ended. The fog cleared, the
moon rose, and in silence, broken only by the
rippling of the strong current at the bows,

A point gained.

Crown jewels.

the good ship glided round Point Levi. There, on our right hand, majestically and solemnly rose Cape Diamond—the jewel purchased with British blood, one of the brightest in England's coronet of fame: Stadacona, Quebec.

At 10.30 P.M., the "Sarmatian" warped to the landing-stage. The cabins disgorged their living and impatient freight. The Twelve jumped ashore, making night hideous with their outburst of joy at finding themselves once more on land. The passage had been the fastest run of this year, and, in fact, has not often been beaten. The ship's log gave the daily run as follows :—

The log.

Aug. 9, 190 miles; Aug. 10, 230 m.; Aug. 11, 312 m.; Aug. 12, 305 m.; Aug. 13, 220 m.; Aug. 14, 292 m.; Aug. 15, 334 m.; Aug. 16, 320 m.; Aug. 17, 139 m.; total 2656 miles, in 9 days $1\frac{1}{2}$ hours. It was the second passage of the ss. "Sarmatian," and

Time.

she gave general satisfaction. English time was found to be $5\frac{1}{2}$ hours in advance of Quebec. After a wild career, on shore for a few hours, in which an acquaintance was first

The cock-tail.

formed with the cocktails of the country, the Twelve retired to their berths, it being too

'here,
mnly
1ased
st in
1bec.
1d to
;heir
elve
with
lves
1een
has
ave

m.;
13,
m.;
1tal
the
1nd
me
1e-
1w
rst
he
00

late to cross the river. It was a night to be
remembered. Moments well purchased by
any discomfort—the safe arrival, the accom-
plishment of a cherished wish—the sight of
the New World. To these certainties before
the mind, succeed the feelings of passing
doubt as to the reception, and the success of
the pilgrims. The Captain was the last to
sleep, as he revolved in his mind the various
chances of the game, but he fell asleep at Dreaming.
last like his less thoughtful comrades, and Waking.
dreamed that W. G. was not out, 1000, he
couldn't tell where, but he awoke refreshed.

CHAPTER III.

THE Twelve were met by Mr. Patteson and several influential members of the Toronto Club early in the morning of August 18. These gentlemen had kindly travelled a great distance in order to welcome the visitors, and to attend to their wants upon landing at Quebec.

All the good people were on their way to church and chapel as the Twelve toiled up the precipices, called streets, in Quebec, in search of a hotel. The St. Louis was full, and the Stadacona, if not full, was plethoric to a degree with voyagers and politicians. The elections were just over. The proprietor thought he might accommodate the party, if it was not particular. Now it happened to be particularly particular. It had flattered itself with the near prospect of a bath, and the comfort of a bedroom to itself. The chances of either appeared remote. The advent of several kind friends removed the difficulty. The Club took charge of some, Mr. Dobell captured the Captain, and finally shelter of some kind was found for the rest.

Twenty-four hours on shore put a new face and new legs on everybody. Alfred ceased to limp. George was brimming over with humour. The first appearance of Quebec is breath-taking, its streets are sides of mountains not made easy, and there is a venerable air of decay about the public buildings. Ladders are seen on every roof, and the first impression is that there has been a general hue and cry after a burglar on the house-tops, as he might traverse whole streets by the facilities of transit they offered. These ladders are an old institution by law to afford means of escape from fire. The great trade is "lumber." Our idea of "lumber" was anything of no use to anybody

Hue and cry.

Fire escapes.
Lumber.

which can be stowed away out of sight and
out of mind. Hide and seek in the " lumber-
room" is one of our earliest souvenirs. We
were amazed to find that "lumber" constitutes
a vast trade, and hails from remote forests,
that the polished floors on which we have
urged our wild career in casino and concert-
room at home, were once " lumber." That
the tree now standing 2000 miles away heed-
less of the coming axe, in the far forests of
the West, is living " lumber." That when
felled, and transported by the swollen streams
of spring, through an unbroken chain of inland
oceans, by canal, and in raft, it rests at
length after two years " in transitû " in the
coves of Quebec. It is then christened
" lumber."

In the bay of Sillery, Mr. Dobell showed
the Twelve his private collection of "lumber."
The enormous logs lie in the water for
several hundred yards. Here we nearly lost
A slip. our bowler. Appleby slipped off a log into
deep water. He luckily recovered his grasp
of the treacherous tree, but he had seen quite
enough of " lumber," and so said all of us.

Sillery is an interesting locality, as before

lumber was thought of, an early Jesuit
mission founded a chapel here, and was
scalped to a man by the Hurons. In the
immediate neighbourhood, Wolfe and his
gallant band scaled the heights of Abraham.
Not far from the St. Louis Road in a slight ^{Wolfe.}
hollow is the humble monument that marks
the spot where the hero fell.

The Governor-General hospitably entertained the Twelve on the evening of the 19th
at the Citadel.

In the earlier part of the day an excursion The Falls.
was made to the Falls of Montmorenci—the
crops had been carried, and the heavy rains
of late, succeeded now by tropical heat, put
an emerald sheet on the country. The Falls
were in good force, the day enchanting, and
whilst the more sentimental of the party gave
themselves up to the attractions of the
scenery, Gilbert and another would-be Izaak Izaak Wal-
Walton worried the wily trout with a worm. ton.
They captured a dozen, varying from an inch
to five inches in length. The worm looked
much more likely to swallow the fish, than
the fish to swallow the worm.

At midnight of the 19th, on returning from

and
ȷer-
We
ıtes
�280sts,
ave
ert-
hat
ed-
�480s of
ıen
ıms
ınd
at
the
ıed

ʋed
r."
for
ost
ıto
ısp
ite

ʋre

the Citadel, the Captain, W. G., Ottoway,
A calash. and Pickering chartered a " calash " and
The start. tandem, and started on an excursion into the
Bush. They were not very clear as to their
destination, and their driver, a French Kanuck, whose lingo was scarcely recognizable
as an European tongue, appeared to know
still less. He was, however, very cheerful if
unintelligible. The road for the first few
miles was a fair specimen of a country lane,
The bush. but on entering the " Bush " it was a mere
" track." For three mortal hours the Atlantic was a millpond compared with it. By
throwing all the weight on one side the
vehicle at times escaped destruction, at others
the hind-seat seemed to plunge into the
bowels of the earth, and the box-seat to
mount to the stars. Once the elastic Jehu
came to a sudden stop, swore a rich curse
and declared it impossible to proceed; hu-
mouring him with a dash of rye-whisky
and a cigar, he proceeded—no, that is too
mild a term—the gig of gossamer never proceeded—it swung to this side, it reeled to
that, it dived here and mounted there—
by the light of the stars, by the line

toway,
" and
ito the
o their
h Ka-
iizable
know
erful if
st few
r lane,
mere
e At-
. By
e the
others
o the
at to
Jehu
curse
; hu-
hisky
s too
. pro-
ed to
ere—
line

given by the tall pines on each side, the track could be maintained. The occupants were soon as disjointed as their rods. A slight descent encouraged the driver to quicken—"*en avant, capitaine*", smacking his whip and cheering the leader he rattled us along, holding on grimly, and trying to think it "sport indeed." A crash, a sudden full stop—*comment!* and a curse from Jehu meant a smash, or there never was one. It might have been serious. As it was the Ojibbeway narrowly missed scalping—a pine had fallen across the track, and a projecting bough, not allowed for or noticed by Jehu, struck the top corner of the trap—arrested its progress, and, as was observed above, was within a hair of robbing the Twelve of their wicket-keeper. After a succession of little lilts of a like nature, at 3 a.m. Jehu pulled up at a hut; he knocked at a window, a head emerged and answered to the name of "Dawson;" on hearing our errand, the head withdrew, and a hand opened the door; a light was soon procured, and the acquaintance formed with one of the honestest and best creatures that ever followed the "gentle

Lord Wm. Lennox.

The Red Indian.

Dawson.

D

sport." Dawson is of Irish extraction, but most of the Irish has been extracted by a long residence in the bush. He has a small clearing which keeps him and a wife—the latter, a pretty young woman from the village of Laval. His hut was built by himself, one room is devoted to the fishing interest, and fairly furnished and clean to a fault. Dawson is the Izaak Walton of the district, and by his intelligence and good-breeding, (his education has been of his own making, and his school the forest in which he was born) has won the esteem of all who visit the upper waters of the Montmorenci.

The rod.   Breakfast soon despatched, rods put together, W. G. and the Captain followed Dawson to the brink of the river. The Ojibbeway *The .un.* and youthful Pickering had designs upon the partridge, or any bird that came within range of their one gun. Sport commenced in the cool and fragrant hour of morning on one of the most picturesque streams ever whipped *Bites, fish, gnat.* by rod. The trout were not large, but willing victims; as the sun rose above the tall pines, the sandfly and gnat welcomed the fishermen to their favourite haunts. The

stream was rapid and deep; at times it was
necessary to seek a "portage" and force a
passage through the tangled forest. W. G.
detected the print of a bear, and the spirits Bruin.
of the gunners rose, as they had as yet seen
or heard nothing in the shape of fur or
feather. The solitude of the bush is indescribable. The strange noises proceed more
from inanimate nature than living beings.
An aged tree falls, or a bough cracks, a cas-
cade breaks into distant echoes, but no
joyous carol of bird is heard, no hurried flight
of wild fowl or pigeon. But to the new-
comer every tree is strange, every leaf is
new. The eye is busy if the ear is idle.
Dawson is a botanist, and took delight in Botany.
pointing out the various items that form the
wealth of a Canadian forest. The white oak,
the black oak, the pine of many kinds, the
button tree, the butternut tree; ferns were
scarce, though moisture was plentiful; his
quick eye detected the small white berries
clustering on a plant, that would have escaped
the observation even of Linnæus,—the Linnæus.
bush tea plant; the berries have a slight aro-
matic flavour, but the supply is too scanty

D 2

Bohea in the bush. for the lover of Bohea, and it would take a cartload to make a cup. Before noon the fishermen had filled their creels, 130 fine trout were scored. Meanwhile, the sportsmen with their one gun had wandered away to a clearing in quest of partridge. Their sport was interrupted by an aged female; they had innocently imagined themselves in No- Game Laws. man's-land, where game laws and rights of property were fabrics of an Eastern dream. Their innocence was rudely shocked by a A hag. half-clad lady of unprepossessing exterior and foreign but vigorous tongue. She threatened the youthful Pickering with a big stick, who wisely fled, his retreat in good order being The Ojibb. maintained by the Ojibbeway, the lucky hol- der, for the moment, of the gun. Their thirst f   ort was not quenched by the hag, as on return of the fishermen, they pointed in Gould's Birds. triumph to a small bird of the cockey olley genus, which one had marked, and the other shot sitting on a rock. It was with evident sorrow that the Captain noted their little spoil. It was the only bird that had crossed their path, and it was sad to reflect that the next comers to this enchanting spot would never see his like again. It was time to make tracks for Quebec. The sun was high in the heavens—the heat intense. Imagine the distress of the travellers on hearing from Bad news. Jehu, that "le Capitaine" had lost a shoe, and there was no anvil nearer than Quebec. It was a bad job for "le Capitaine," and very distressing to Jehu, but to return was imperative; so bidding adieu to the faithful Dawson with great regret, and to the banks of the beautiful Montmorenci, the homeward jolting was commenced. If the track appeared bad at night, when darkness robbed it in a great measure of its horrors, it was death and destruction to man and spring by day. Let us dismiss it. We did get out of the Bush alive, but with not much skin where skin is much prized. Jehu's addresses to "le Capitaine" were very affecting, and probably a more sorry lot never entered Quebec since its capture in 1759.

Loud reports were heard on approaching An engagement. the Stadacona Club, and an engagement was evident; a straggler reported that the first shots were exchanged at 2 P.M.; it was now 5 P.M. Hastily rushing to the scene of action,

ake a
n the
0 fine
tsmen
y to a
sport
they
i No-
its of
ream.
by a
or and
tened
, who
being
r hol-
thirst
as on
ed in
olley
other
ident
little
ossed
t the
ould

The action. the General soon came upon the débris of the contending parties. " Bones " of contention were visible on every side ; " dead

Bulletin. men " lay in heaps in every corner ; but one compact mass had held its own, and that was a British Round of Beef. A flank attack upon this was the work of a moment, and the places of the dead were rapidly filled by the stout waiter. Pop! pop! The firing recommenced, and it was not till 6 P.M. that the inside cried " enough ! " The members of the Stadacona Club had most hospitably entertained the Eight, and in the absence of the Captain and his three companions, a

Welcome. hearty welcome had been extended to the English Cricketers. The ramparts were handy, bat and ball were procured, a wicket

Practice. was pitched, and swiping of a mammoth character ensued. Accidents of course were

Hadow the rife. Hadow, whose misfortunes dated from
unlucky. to-day, put a finger out, trying to catch a " hot'un " of W. G. The fun was fast and furious. Stadacona gazed aghast. Alas!

Regrets. even thus early mingled regrets with joy ; grass grew rank in the Citadel square, no flag fluttered in the evening breeze, no sentinel

marked time with measured tread on the
ramparts.   The life and soul of a fortress,
won by British pluck, to be lost only by
British indifference, has fled.   The Citadel is *TheCitadel.*
the worthy home of a governor-general, with
every claim upon his countrymen's respect
and estimation, but the gallant defenders of
the country he represents no longer add an
attraction to his court, or aid by their presence in keeping fresh the memory of deeds
that added this great colony to the British
empire.

The first laurel plucked on Canadian soil *Racquets.*
was of intra-mural growth; it was won within
the walls of a racquet-court.   Hadow and *First win.*
Harris met and conquered the Stadacona
champions.   The Captain and Rose left cards
at the Citadel, on behalf of the Twelve, upon
the Governor-General and Lady Dufferin.
Before quitting the precincts of this interesting spot, it may not be beside our task to
mention a little improvement lately effected
by His Excellency's orders : his drawing-
room, late the ante-room of H.M. Regts. 1——
100, looks upon the St. Lawrence.   By at-
taching a balcony to the windows, access has *The Bal-*
cony.

A reverie. been obtained to the ramparts. To look
down at night upon the mighty stream,
reflecting the numberless lights of heaven as
well as those that can be counted of vessels
lying at anchor, would reward a daring
climber, could the cliff be scaled. To step
out from a drawing-room upon such a prospect on a summer's evening is to plunge into
Dreamland. You may sip your coffee, you
may puff your cigar, but mingled with the
fragrance of both comes the indefinable odour
of Jesuit MS., the savour that clings to Cape
Diamond, the one historical spot of Canada.

Cape Dia- Cape Diamond stands the advanced sen-
mond. tinel of the highway of the West. The
waters, curbed in their headlong career, rush
in a narrowed channel round its base. They
roll on for 700 miles to the Atlantic; they
bring with them souvenirs of Niagara, of
lakes, and forests, and streams, scarcely yet
History. acquainted with man. Beneath us halted
the first settlers in Canada; they started
hence on their perilous journeys westwards,
hither they returned as to their only strong-
hold; the bulwark of French fortunes, for
many a season, with its loss passed away

look
ream,
'en as
essels
aring
step
pros-
: into
you
: the
dour
Jape
da.
sen-
The
ush
hey
hey
of
yet
ted
:ed
ls,
g-
or
:y

the sovereignty which gave to the West the chivalrous Champlain, and La Salle, the *La Salle.* adventurous hero of the Mississippi.

We must be pardoned for lingering so long on the threshold, but here, and here only, are we chained to the past. As we advance to the West, commerce will be found to outstrip history; and in the busy streets of Montreal, little will be seen that tells of the varying fortunes of Hochelaga, nor up *Hochelaga.* Ottawa's stream, or in gay Toronto, shall we feel, as we do here, that a gallant race preceded ours, and that we are but accomplishing what others began.

At 8 P.M. on the 20th, the Twelve found *The other side of Jordan.* themselves on the other side of the St. Lawrence, prepared for a night journey to Montreal. They were not prepared for such comfort as was in store for them. Colonel Cumberland (whose praises will be sung hereafter) had placed his private car and "Parker" at their disposal—a pleasanter way of passing a night on a railroad cannot be imagined. You may well ask, Who's *Who's Parker?* Parker? "Parker" is to a private car on the Grand Drunk what the best appointed bar would be without a pretty girl to take your orders. We don't wish to imply that Parker is a Ganymede; but handsome is as handsome does, and, by that course of logic, Parker is an Adonis.

The car. The car itself is a study of comfort—easy chairs, sofas, tables; a room to sleep, a room to eat; there is a bar to drink—Parker keeps the bar; the bar keeps Parker perpetually on the move. There isn't a sly drink that Parker can't concoct; he can make a soft bed out of bare boards; he is butler, housekeeper, and housemaid combined.

Poor Haddock. Before the train started, the Twelve were reduced to eleven effectives. Hadow and bag met with an accident, serious to the one, fatal to the other. Whether it was the Stadacona luncheon, the stars, or the steps, never transpired; what he did, he could not explain; what he did not, was unfortunately clear—he did *not* land on the step of the carriage; when he stepped off the platform, he plunged into space; his nose and knee Losses. checked his course to the Atlantic, but his bag, containing, amongst other articles of

less value, his Diary and Thoughts on Sea- <small>Bag.</small>
sickness, fell into the St. Lawrence. It was
past recovery. Hadow the Unfortunate lost
what was valuable to himself and "beyond
rubies" to his companions, his bag and his
temper. He certainly had cause to be angry <small>Temper.</small>
—with himself; a very few inches—a little less
nose perhaps—and he would have followed
his bag, and the expedition would have
ended before it began. Parker did his best
to console the sufferer; and the party, by
means of potted whitebait, champagne, and
other sedatives, recovered its elasticity.

The Grand Drunk is well known to <small>The Grand Trunk.</small>
English speculators. If its shares have not
risen, it is not for want of spring in the
rolling stock, or from any disinclination of
the sleepers to give an "upward tendency"
to the whole concern. We don't believe in
"sleepers" on the Grand Drunk, whether <small>Sleepers.</small>
in a car or under it. Parker never sleeps on
the Grand Drunk—he is never so lively as
when on that track. Good days, nevertheless, are in store for the Grand Drunk; there
is every prospect of a dividend shortly;
there has not been a serious accident for

several months. The line itself, a single one, impresses the new comer with disappointment because of its singularity. The Grand Drunk gives one an idea of seeing double, and we travelled many miles on it ere we realized its single blessedness. It has cost a deal of money according to hearsay, but we are prepared to swear that there has been no extravagant outlay on bridges or boundary fences. The road is not luxuriously smooth, nor are the public cars patterns of profligate expenditure. We have been asked so many questions and so often about our experiences of the Grand Drunk, that we have been thus explicit. In conclusion, we will add that the Twelve were never more happy than when they were on the Grand Drunk.

The Tubular. The Victoria Bridge at Montreal is crossed in seven minutes. It is a triumph of engineering, and worthy of its great office, as the connecting link between two great countries.

Montreal. The Twelve arrived at Montreal at 7 A.M. on the morning of August 21. The cricket campaign will now commence, and from general we descend to personal observations. All that have accompanied us thus far are here requested to "take a drink." They have had some dry reading to digest, and there is a terrible desert before them; a vista of "stumps" cannot be cheerful even to a Canadian, though his eye may detect a luxurious growth springing up betwee. them. The wickets are open, the ball is rolling, you have paid your money. Gentle readers, you may follow our game as long as you like; we may at least hope to attain one object, we may send you to sleep.

A vista.

CHAPTER IV.

Aug. 21. THE Twelve explored the town.
Business and religion are the external characteristics of Montreal. The streets are full
of life, Scotch life especially, as the names
import. Churches are innumerable. Every
shade of doctrine has its steeple. They
ought to be very good people in Montreal ;
they, at all events, do their best to impress
a stranger with that belief. All the churches
are well built, and the fine old English type
of architecture, known as Churchwarden, is
not known here. The merchants' houses are

goodly to the eye and well furnished. Everything and everybody looks solid and substantial. The heat was intense. The thermometer
marked 92° in the shade. The cricket- *The ground.*
ground was interviewed in the course of the
afternoon. It is situated in Catherine Street.
A new church, lately consecrated as St.
Cricket's-in-the-Fields, appeared in dangerous
contiguity to Long Leg at one end. Behind,
at a distance of half a mile, towers the
Mountain. The ground will not require a *The moun-tain.*
poet to describe—a civil engineer can alone
do it justice ; he would call it three-cornered,
but it would puzzle him to pitch a wicket
square to any side, or, in fact, to find a good
place for a wicket anywhere. Rubbish has *Rubbish shot here.*
evidently, in times not pre-historic, been
shot here. Villas may owe their erection to
the stone extracted from its quarries ; roads,
doubtless, have derived their substratum,
and could do so still, from its surface. We
must not be hypercritical—we believe we
have been ; let us rather praise the spirit
that can reconcile cricket to such natural
disadvantages. Practice was soon started.
The chapter of accidents received a fresh

Skull of St. Francis. paragraph. This time Francis suffered, receiving a blow on the head which laid him prostrate; his head, luckily, was harder than the ball, so the consequences were not serious. The Captain thought it advisable to sound a retreat before any body was killed. A wicket for the morrow was with some difficulty selected.

Cricket. *Aug.* 22. Heavy thunderstorms rolled over Montreal from daybreak to noon. The air was oppressive, the rain descended in the biggest buckets. Cricket was critical. At 1 it partially cleared, and a start was effected.

A dip. The fashion of Montreal at this season is dipping in the St. Lawrence at Cacoona, consequently very few spectators appeared on the ground; twelve carriages only could be counted :—a very thin line indeed, and that only at one end of the ground, impressed the Englishmen mournfully; and if it had not been for the Twenty-two, who in variety of costume and colour dotted the ground, the scene would have been the reverse of gay. The Captain won the toss, and at once sent W. G. and Ottoway to the wickets. Our intention is to adhere, as far as possible, to

the local reports. They will be found to be
more original than anything we can invent,
and present to the general reader an idea of
cricket, which, until we perused them, had
never occurred to us. Here begins the first
quotation. Mr. Grace "is a large-framed, To quote.
loose-jointed man, and you would say that w. g.
his gait was a trifle awkward and shambling,
but when he goes into the field you see that
he is quick-sighted, sure-handed, and light-
footed as the rest. He always goes in first,
and to see him tap the ball gently to the off
for one, draw it to the on for two, pound it
to the limits for four, drive it beyond the
most distant long leg for six, looks as easy
as rolling off a log." W. G.'s innings was
marked with luck, but there were some
splendid hits in it. Ottoway's defence was
superb. The bowling was remarkably good,
especially that of Hardinge and M'Clean.
Runs were obtained with comparative freedom, as at 5 P.M. 100 runs were telegraphed,
and no wicket down. Ottoway retired for a
most patient 24, and when Gilbert had
attained to fourscore his end was near.
Nobody would have guessed that a stout

E

gentleman with a pipe in his mouth, and
Little Benjamin. of the name of Benjamin, would have put
the *coup de grâce* to the Leviathan. He
The Leviathan. did. W. G. cut a very hot one into the
abdominal regions of Mr. B.; it stuck there,
and the lucky Benjamin bounded into the
air, and was carried in triumph by his com-
Ape. rades round the wickets. The Monkey exhibited his remarkable powers of hitting, but
fortune favoured him, as he might have been
landed several times. Alfred played with
Joke. judgment but not for *Lang*, that gentleman
bowling him out for 7. Three wickets were
down at close of day's play for 130 runs.
It must not be supposed that the Twelve
were allowed to subside into private life on
leaving the cricket ground; their real work
commenced with the last ball bowled.

Cards. Cards were found on the table when they
returned to their hotel, with the inscription,

BANQUET

TO THE

GENTLEMEN OF ENGLAND,

AUG. 22, 1872.

The banquet. It was sumptuously carried out. After
dinner, the President indulged in a speech,

the political bias of which provoked hostile demonstrations; and at one time the Captain, who sat next him, was in expectation of an apple or other missile intended for the worthy President. However, a calmer tone soon prevailed, and the toast of the evening, "The English Cricketers," met with the heartiest reception. The Captain delivered Speech No. 2. It was a comprehensive speech; it dealt with the past; it played with the present; it prophesied pleasantly of the future; it complimented everybody; it did not forget himself; it left out, as most speeches impromptu do, all the good points it had carefully prepared; it gave utterance to other good things it would never have thought of but for the champagne and company around. It had one great merit; it soon came to an end. Great confusion prevailed in the company as to the particular people who should reply to the toasts. Canada is evidently a country of orators. Everybody speaks at a public meeting, not unfrequently everybody at once. Appleby was called on to reply for the "Navy," we never discovered why, unless the slight connection be-

The toast of the evening.

Appleby for the Navy.

E 2

tween bowline and bowling secured him the honour. He unaffectedly alluded to his services on the sea, better known to others than to himself, and after gracefully quoting several of Dibdin's odes sat down amidst general applause. The speech of the evening was W. G.'s. It had been looked forward to with impatience, not to say a tinge of envy, by the Eleven. He replied to the toast of the " Champion Batsman of Cricketdom." He said, " Gentlemen, I beg to thank you for the honour you have done me; I never saw better bowling than I have seen to-day, and I hope to see as good wherever I go." The speech took longer to deliver than you might imagine from its brevity, but it was greeted with applause from all who were in a proper position to hear it. About this time the audience was becoming a little impatient of speech. A worthy gentleman attempted to propose " The President of the United States "—an excellent toast; that would have been well received had the proposer been sufficiently sober to do justice to the theme. He was crushed, but only to break out in the bar of

W. G.'s speech.

Demosthenes.

Ulysses.

the hotel a few hours later. The evening was cheerful, and the honour paid to the Twelve was highly esteemed by them.

Aug. 23. The match proceeded, but there Cricket. were absentees on the English side. The Captain was down by the head, a general shakiness distinguished the lot. Hadow was still a sufferer. The Monkey and Francisco put a lively face on the Bill of Health. The nimble one made 39—181 for 4 wickets. Francisco scored 11 ; Harris "was clean bowled George. by Green, leg-stump, the ball went outside the player's leg, but with such a twist as to take the inside stump "—George's account varied from this—193 for 6 wickets, "with every probability that the Canadian team would prevent their opponents securing 300 runs in the first innings, regarding which there was some speculation." Appleby played in grand form. Edgar, meanwhile, was not idle, till "Maclean delivered a ball To quote. directly, evidently at the outside stump." This terrible ball Appleby placed in the hands, of cover-point. Pickering, to quote again, "although a little under the weather, developed powers of hard hitting which may

some time rival Thornton's " played a slashing innings, and Rose " carried his bat out
with an air of consequence, which never de-
serted him under any circumstances." The
Ten between them amassed 255.

The Twenty-two did not make a distinguished début with the bat. We have every
desire to do justice to each individual, and
would stretch a point, if it was only to fill·
these pages, in favour of the foe. But
honesty compels us to admit that the exhibi-
Incipient paralysis. tion was feeble. Rosa paralysed them, the
batsman at the wicket was no longer the
stout lad we had seen swiping at practice.
Gilbert crippled their hitting by his activity
at point. Ottoway chained them to the crease
by the dexterity of his fingers. It was well
To quote. said by a local, " that the batsmen apparently
could do nothing to advantage. If they hit
a half-volley, they were caught in the long-
field; if they left their ground, they were
stumped ; if they stopped at home and
blocked, they were bowled." It certainly
did look like it, yet the same panic-stricken
strikers could hit a long-hop or half-volley at
any other wicket, at any other time. A bowl-

ing analysis as a rule is an uncertain guide,
but it may be quoted here as collateral if not
convincing proof of individual merit. Rose
bowled 27 overs for 29 runs and 15 wickets.
Appleby bowled 27 overs for 16 runs and 6
wickets. The sun was not allowed to set on
one completed innings. Before the stumps
were drawn. The Twenty-two had lost four
wickets for 15 runs of their second innings.
The members of the St. James's Club invited
the Twelve to dinner on Friday evening, Dinner at
August 23. The ten convalescents accepted, St. James's Club.
and a better dinner could not have been
given by any London Club. Each guest was
provided with a menu on white silk, his name
being printed on one side and the names of
those members of the club, who were the
hosts on the occasion, upon the other.

On Saturday morning, August 24, the game Cricket.
was continued. Francisco was permitted to
bowl vice Appleby. He was more remarkable for pace than direction, but he succeeded
in dismissing three victims, 15 again falling
to the insidious Rosa. The second total was First notch.
67. An easy victory in one innings and 140
runs was thus secured.

If you wish for further information, please consult the score.

ENGLAND v. MONTREAL.

ENGLAND.

W. G. Grace, c Benjamin, b Laing 81	A. Appleby, c Hardman, b M'Lean 9
C. J. Ottoway, b Hardman... 24	W. M. Rose, not out......... 15
A. N. Hornby, leg b w, b Green 39	F. P. U. Pickering, c Mills, b Laing 19
A. Lubbock, b Laing 7	R. A. Fitzgerald, unwell ... 0
Hon. G. Harris, b Green ... 4	B 12, l-b 8, w b 8...... 28
C. K. Francis, c M'Kenzie, b M'Lean 11	
E. Lubbock, c Jones, b M'Lean 18	Total.................. 255

MONTREAL.

	1st inn.		2nd inn.
F. Tetu, b Rose	0	b Rose	2
A. Murray, b Rose.................	0	b Rose	0
W. Mills, b Appleby	1	b Rose	0
W. Smith, b Rose	0	st Ottoway, b Rose...	0
W. Holland, b Rose	0	b Rose	0
Capt. Henley, c Harris, b Rose...	12	c and b Francis......	12
C. M'Lean, b Rose	4	b Rose	9
J. Hardman, c E. Lubbock, b Rose	4	b Rose	1
A. Laing, c Hornby, b Rose	4	c Harris, b Rose ...	2
R. C. Bucknall, st Ottoway, b Rose	5	run out..............	0
H. Green, b Appleby...............	3	b Rose	2
S. Hardinge, st Ottoway, b Rose	0	st Ottoway, b Rose...	0
W. J. M. Jones, st Ottoway, b Rose	1	st Ottoway, b Rose...	2
G. Campbell, st Ottoway, b Rose	3	st Ottoway, b Rose...	0
F. Fourdinier, c and b Appleby...	1	st Ottoway, b Rose...	0
J. Liddell, c Grace, b Rose	0	b Rose	7
W. M'Kenzie, c and b Appleby...	4	b Rose	0
W. Matthews, c and b Appleby...	0	c Grace, b Rose......	7
R. Harper, c Hornby, b Rose......	2	run out..............	4
L. N. Benjamin, not out	1	c Ottoway, b Rose...	2
F. Colston, b Appleby	0	not out	1
J. Laing, c Francis, b Rose	0	b Francis	1
B 2, w b 1	3	B 5, l-b 7	12
Total	—48	Total	—67

ANALYSIS OF THE BOWLING.

ENGLAND—First Innings.

	Overs.	Maidens.	Runs.	Wickets.	Wides.
M'Lean	54	19	60	3	0
Hardinge	17	5	25	0	0
Laing	37	10	44	3	0
Mills	5	3	8	0	0
Green	35	14	40	2	0
Hardman	21	5	38	1	0

MONTREAL—First Innings.

Rose	27	9	36	16	0
Francis	51	13	14	2	0
Appleby	5	3	5	0	0

The bowling of the Canadians in this match was far superior to either their batting or fielding. The Ten would not have been vanquished, even if every chance had been accepted, but a better face might certainly have been put on the match, had some of the palms been sticky to which catches fell. The gum palm.

Messrs. Notman, of Montreal, executed a group of the Twelve, which, for individual likeness and grouping, was much admired. Their kindness in presenting each member of the Twelve with a dozen of self-perpetuators must not pass unnoticed. Photos.

The hospitality of the Canadians was not the only pleasant feature of this first match; The private asylum. attentions to the sick, as exemplified by Mr.

Kay, the president of the Club, and other offers on the part of several distinguished citizens, impressed the Twelve, that though in a foreign country they were not amongst strangers of alien blood, but with distant connections of the mother country.

Murder. As sooner or later murder must come out, it may as well be related here that an acquaintance was formed with long and short drinks. The Twelve were on good terms with most, but perhaps "Dan Collins" was the most favoured; his simplicity is very winning, which cannot be said of some others who took advantage of the boys at unguarded moments.

Dangers. We append a list, in which all who run may read the dangers that beset the dry in a thirsty land.

Brandy Smashes.	Sudden Death.
Corpse Revivers.	Rattle Snakes.
Bosom Caressers.	Mint Juleps.
Eye Openers.	Stone Fence.
Dan Collins.	Earthquakes.
Joe Smudges.	Tom and Jerry.
Ladies' Fingers.	Whiskey Straight.
Ladies' Smiles.	

These are known by the familiar name of Cocktails. Cocktail, and their special recommendation lies in the fact, that they do you just as much good at daybreak as at any hour up to and after sunset. They are peculiar to the country; but strange to relate, the stranger insensibly merges into the native under their influence, and it would puzzle the most discriminating to say who looked the worst after a long acquaintance with any of the above, the native born Kanuck or the confiding stranger. It is a winning card "take a The trump. drink," but it is played too often, although the thirsty climate must bear its share of blame. Another feature of the country strikes a foreigner favourably. There is no imperial pint or thimbleful; the bottle is given to you and you help yourself, so that ten cents. may represent a tumbler or liqueur glass. Strangers like this at first immensely. A compound called "Rye" possesses the con- Rye. fidence of the public. It enters largely into every cocktail, and is at the bottom of every piece of mischief that is brewed in the country. The wines, as a rule, are not choice; champagne of European or American manufacture can always be had for the paying. It is expensive, but as you are bound to believe that it has crossed the Atlantic, you Hochelaga. drink it, without further remark. Hochelaga is Indian for Montreal. Pickering the youthful, believed he had found out why Laga Laga beer. beer was so popular here. He said it was an Indian beverage peculiar to the place from which it derived its name.

Montreal is proud of its Mountain. It The moun- may well be so. It was the Mountain that tain. made it Mont-real. The view from the summit is most extensive. 337 years ago, James Car- Jacques Cartier surveyed the same splendid ter. prospect. It is quite refreshing to stand so close to the earliest records of a great country. Art of Love, No gods and goddesses, no river nymphs to Ovid. shock the eye, no hoary mist of antiquity, no lies between us and James Carter, the hero of a mere three centuries past. He is said to have found 50 Indian huts here and a village Moses. called Hochelaga. Like Moses, he saw the Promised Land of his dreams from this mountain. The prospect is enough to provoke a saint's ambition. Vandals have encroached on the mountain's side, and villas threaten to destroy its primæval charms. The Muncipality has lately checked the brick-layer, and there is reason to hope that ere long the mountain will be secured to future generations as a public park. The 50 huts of James Carter had disappeared in 1603, when the gallant Champlain did, what we did, Champlain. ascended the mountain. Montreal's history since those days has been chequered. In 1642 it was consecrated as "Ville Marie." The red Indian haunted its outskirts, and scalped many a Frenchman, for many a day. The priest settled upon it; he gave to the savage Christian instruction in return for fur. The savage imbibed more whisky than religion, and often took " hair " in exchange for fur.

In course of time the settlement was surrounded by a wall. It sustained a siege. It retains little trace to-day of the eventful struggle of 1759. Its trade has developed marvellously of late years, and the town owes much to the enterprise of the great firm, of which Sir Hugh Allan is the well-known head. Allan Brothers. There are several good hotels in Montreal, the largest being the St. Laurence Hall. A

friend staying in this hotel was disagreeably
A surprise. surprised one evening upon opening a drawer
The baby. in his room to find a baby well wrapped up.
No trace of its parentage was discovered, and
the position of our friend might have been
perplexing, if the baby in question had lived
to father itself upon him. It was dead. The
proprietor shrugged his shoulders, and the
matter dropped.

Gas.   Englishmen are very apt to blow out the
gas in their bedrooms; this is a pernicious
Ring the habit. It is as well not to ring a bell in a
bell. Canadian hotel; it will save disappointment
as it is seldom answered. If you carry out
the instructions given to you, you convert
A sell. your room into a cell; keys and bolts are provided to every room. The impression is unpleasant; in every footfall at night you look
for a footpad. There is no object moreover
in saying "come in," if you should be fool
enough to ring and anybody kind enough to
answer, for you have locked yourself in, and
you must get out of bed to let anybody in; he
can't come in if you don't.

La Chine Appleby, Francis, Ottoway, Harris, E.
Falls. Lubbock, and Hornby got up early one morn-

ing, and before breakfast had some good sport. They shot the rapids of La Chine. They described it as all others have done before them, in glowing terms as a genuine sensation. Appleby's diary contains three pages of his feelings in prose and poetry, very beautiful, but too powerful for a light work of this nature.

Appleby's Diary.

Before leaving Montreal we must quote a few passages from the local prints. They are personal, but they prove the interest taken in the Twelve, and the state of public intelligence generally in matters relating to cricket.

A column, headed "The English Cricketers in America; who they are and what they have done," attracted us first. "In personal appearance there is nothing about any of the Eleven which would be called strikingly English. Fitzgerald, Rose, and Pickering are only of medium height, the remainder averaging about 5ft. 11in. Grace is a six-footer, with a full black beard. Ottoway, on the contrary, has no hirsute adornment, while the moustachettes of Pickering and Harris are in the incipient mood. Hadow would be

To quote.

called the handsome man, Edgar Lubbock
he homely one. It is either on that account
or on account of his style of play that the
Eleven familiarly call Edgar 'Nobby.' He
has a happy disposition, and is a genial
companion. George Harris will be Lord
Harris if he survives his father. He appears
a very sensible and clever fellow. Hornby
is a light-weight, active and jolly. Appleby
and Alfred Lubbock are finely built, and have
strong handsome features. All the men are
well adapted to captivate the ladies, but perhaps I am getting too deep into Jenkinism."

Where our talented friend got his information from we never learnt. He then proceeds
To quote. to criticize their performances. "Rose bowls
underhand shoddy, twisting to the off.
Appleby is swift, left hand, and three-fourths
of his balls, if unchecked in their career, take
the off bail." He has a cut at the Canadians
in another paragraph, alluding to the catch
which ended Gilbert's innings, as the "non-
chalance of the elegant Benjamin was a thin
assumption." Another critic describes a hit
of the Monkey's thus, "Hornby's last shot
was sending the ball right over the heads of

bowler and long stop." This was a boomerang feat in a vengeance, and might have occurred in New Zealand. Rose was " a low drop bowler," and criticism received its crown in the pithy sentence, " an extraordinary instance of careless or incapable play occurred, Francis, who should have been caught out, obtained some runs instead."

The cricket matches on the whole were well reported. Stiff and Strong were excellent reporters, each in his own way. " Stiff " knew a great deal about the game, and watched it with care, but he had his weak moments. " Strong " knew nothing about it and didn't watch it, but was very clever. Woe to " Stiff " if, in an unguarded moment, he left his note-book in the tent, to " take a drink." " Strong " was down on his notes in a moment, and the rival paper, next morning, had " Stiff's " best things in " Strong's " best style. They sat together till each found out the other often looked over his shoulder. They were great friends at night. We liked them both. " Strong " has a claim upon us. We assisted him one night to his hotel, a lamp post would get in

The Reporters. Stiff.

Strong.

his way, we took it from him and he was very angry. "Stiff," next morning, on hearing the story, stole a march upon "Strong," and reported him as —— and incapable. Coming from Stiff, the story proved "too thin, it wouldn't wash."

CHAPTER V.

AT 7 A.M. on the morning of Monday, *La Chine.* August 26, the apostles took the train to La Chine. Here they embarked on a steamer, landed at Cerillon, and after seventeen miles in a railway car, re-embarked in a fine river steamer, and so ascended the Ottawa. Pass- *The Ottawa.* ing St. Ann's, Appleby was heard muttering *St. Ann's.* to himself; he was evidently in pain—a cocktail was applied in the right place—he was composing—he was composed—he gave birth to a song. Tommy Moore was on *Appleby* everybody's tongue, but in nobody's pocket. *and Tom Moore.*

The following ode is, therefore, almost original, as the poet himself could only recall the chorus of the Canadian boat-song, " Row, Brothers, Row," &c., &c. :—

SONG OF THE FAST BOWLER.

ST. MARY ANN—1872.

Stand to your stumps ! the toss is won ;
I shall bowl you all out, ere the day is done ;
Breathes the Kanuk, who can withstand
The ball as it leaves my big left hand ?
Field, Brothers, field, my rapids are near
To the sticks, and the shooters a way will clear.

Rose may bowl at the other end ;
May the breeze I spurn his slows befriend ;
No matter to me, if against the hill,
I am told to bowl, why, bowl I will !
Field, Brothers, field, my rapids are near
To the sticks, and the shooters a way will clear.

Ottoway's fingers tingle now ;
Edgar to long-stop will show them how ;
Gilbert at point shall take his post,
Of chances offered he grabs the most.
Field, Brothers, field, my rapids are near
To the sticks, and the shooters a way will clear.

One on the knuckles ! the wicket's rough,
Another on the shins ; they cry enough !
Middle stump, off stump, into mid air,
I can drop her short, if to swipe they dare.
Field, Brothers, field, my rapids are near
To the sticks, and the shooters a way will clear.

Tormentor they call me, I know not why,
From my deadly length, or my wicked eye ?
Take me off, let another try ;
　　Jealousy passes an Apple-by.
Field, Brothers, field, my rapids are near
To the sticks, and the shooters a way will clear.

Let Francis hurl, with unbated zest ;
The worst ball sometimes bowls the best ;
You'll want me again, ere the day is done,
And thank me, too, for the victory won.
Field, Brothers, field, my rapids are near
To the sticks, and the shooters a way will clear.

The song was in the true spirit of pro- The pro-phecy. Appleby might have been an ancient
bard—but we must not anticipate his great
performances with the ball. The scenery of
the Ottawa river is too well known to need
our tribute of praise. The Bush, at this The Bush.
season, has but one drawback ; it presents
an unvaried aspect of beauty. There is too
much of it. It was a relief to strike the line
of fire that spread devastation in the summer
of 1870 for many miles. This fire almost
encircled the town of Ottawa. The fate that
threatened it would have outrivalled Chicago,
for not a house would have been left standing. It, luckily, was diverted by the river
and strong winds in a northerly direction ;

but the possibility of yet another similar disaster does not seem remote. As we approach the town of Ottawa, the river's bosom bears marks of the caresses it has received from the saw-mill. Sawdust floats down in immense masses. The air is pungent with the same; snuff-boxes are now at a discount; the nostril is sufficiently titillated otherwise.

Night came on ere our steamer easied under the high banks; a distant roar betokened the vicinity of La Chaudière Falls. Lights illumined the banks above. The frosty night was brilliant with stars; a crowd of curious natives awaited the arrival of the Twelve. Shatterydans of various kinds The Russell conveyed them to the Russell House, where House. good accommodation was provided by Mr. Gouin, the proprietor.

The first evening was spent in " the Bar," where numerous acquaintances were formed with new compounds, human and spiritual. The Twelve went to bed wondering what Ottawa would be by daylight. The streets had given a rough impression of it by night. They would not have disgraced a Marylebone Vestry, to judge, at least, by the holes

into which the omnibus dipped, and the un-
expected mounds over which it bucked.

Ottawa, Aug. 27.—The second match Cricket.
commenced under the most favourable aus-
pices—a lovely Canadian summer's day—
sky of piercing brightness—a fresh breeze
that tempered the great heat. Rideau Hall, Rideau
the seat of the Governor-General, looks Hall.
down upon the Cricket Ground. Cricketers
look up to Rideau Hall with grateful eyes.
It has given them a site worthy of the noble
game. As early as 10 A.M. an immense
stream of visitors set towards the ground,
and on the arrival of the Twelve every point
of vantage had been secured. It was a gay
and animated sight. The small boy was in Tommy and
great force, the elder sister in full fig, his sister
mamma and papa in ample proportions.
The Twenty-Two were hard at it, practising
to make perfect (one of the great mistakes of
the day); practice before a match should be
limited to a few minutes, to take the stiffness
out of the joints, and not persevered in at
the expense of strength and waste of breath.
To resume. The wickets were well prepared,
and the outfielding tolerable; but as there

Cicada.

were no snakes, the long grass did not so much matter. The grasshoppers *were* woppers, and butterflies, big enough to knock one down, constantly made you duck your head as they floated in the air in hundreds around you.

The toss. won.

The Captain won his second toss. At 11 A.M. W. G. and the Ojibbeway appeared at the wickets—Messrs. Brodie and Carter bowling. Both bowled remarkably well. Gilbert was enfeebled by internal disorders, but, nevertheless, soon showed his marvellous powers of defence and hitting. The O., as usual, patient as a pike-staff, and quite contented with his quota of 9.

To quote.

The local said " Mr. O. miscalculated one of Mr. Carter's balls, which took off the bail

The Monkey.

by a very fine touch." The Monkey followed, and, in a very merry mood, ran up a score of 27; he had as many lives as a cat.

W. G. in luck.

Gilbert, meanwhile, had his share of luck. According to the local, " he gave the fielders an opportunity of making good catches, but invariably off ' bum balls,' which, not being understood by the spectators, caused them to burst with rapture, so occasioned no little

disappointment when the truth became evident." He should have been caught more
than once. Three fielders once tried to land
him, and, to quote the local again, "the ball
came down like a gob of mud between the
three." The Monkey retired in the 46th
over for 27 runs. Lunch was discussed, and
afterwards Alfred the Great ascended the Reign of
Alfred.
vacant throne. His reign was of some duration, and some brilliant play distinguished it.
Gilbert was finally bamboozled by Boothroyd, an underhand bowler of the daisy-
cutting *. .. He-made 73, allowing for
his debility, marvellously well. The bowling was well sustained, and the field smart
in return, if not deadly as traps for the
skyers. Ninety-one overs had been bowled
when W. G. retired. The game proceeded
briskly up to 6·20 P.M., when time was
called, the visitors having obtained 201
runs. The small number of byes and wides
speaks well for Smith, the longstop, and the
bowlers.

Aug. 28.—Play was resumed at 11·20. Cricket,
2nd day.
Our task is light. No individual of the
Twenty-Two calls for any special remark.

If we are to make an exception, it must be in favour of John Brunel, who doubled the score of any of his compeers, landing 10 to his credit. It was a slaughter of the Inno-

cents. The butcher's bill reads thus :—Rose, 8 wickets for 35 runs ; Appleby, 12 wickets for 3 runs. The latter performance, even against a moderate 'team, is marvellous. Appleby was not permitted, from motives of humanity, to bowl throughout the second innings, retiring in favour of Alfred's peculiars, styled by the local " overhead and ears patent roundhand Law defying breakbacks."

Appleby's analysis for both innings reads thus :—

180 balls, 20 runs, 17 wickets.

We doubt very much if any bowler (roundarm) has ever bowled through an innings against a Twenty-Two for 3 runs only.

The Ottawa innings was prolonged to three-quarters of an hour, and the total was raised to 43.

It will, perhaps, excite little wonder, after the above tale of disaster, to hear that a similar scene was enacted after luncheon. To quote the local will save us a pang.

Latest.

"Ottawa, Aug. 28.——The cricket match is being continued, and the wickets of the Canadians are going down rather more like shelling peas even than at Montreal."

This tells its own tale. We will but remark that in the course of another hour or so the Twenty-Two had gone to their long rest, leaving 49 runs behind them to show that they had been through the mill. We scarcely know what to call it; but having come a long way to do it, we trust we may be permitted to call it a victory—in one innings and 110 runs.

ENGLAND v. OTTAWA.

ENGLAND.

W. G. Grace, b Boothroyd... 73
C. J. Ottoway, b Carter ... 9
A. N. Hornby, b Swinyard 27
A. Lubbock, b Swinyard ... 28
Hon. G. Harris, st G. Brunel, b Swinyard 6
C. K. Francis, b Brodie ... 10
E. Lubbock, c Killaly, b Carter..................... 7

A. Appleby, c and b Carter 6
W. M. Rose, b Killaly 29
F. P. U. Pickering, c Phillips, b Brodie.............. 1
R. A. Fitzgerald, not out... 4
    B 3, l b 2, w b 2, n b 1   8
                              ———
    Total......... 201

OTTAWA.	1st inn.		2nd inn.
E. R. Benjamin, c Appleby, b Rose	1	c Fitzgerald, b Rose	0
J. Boothroyd, b Appleby	0	b Appleby	1
C. B. Brodie, b Appleby	0	leg b w, b Rose	4
J. Brunel, b Rose	10	c A. Lubbock, b Rose	3
G. Brunel, c Grace, b Appleby	1	st Ottoway, b Rose	3
W. Carter, c Grace, b Rose	2	not out	1
G. F. Hall, c Ottoway, b Appleby	2	c Appleby, b A.	
T. Halliday, c Ottoway, b Appleby	2	Lubbock	0
T. Miller, b Rose	0	b Rose	2
M. C. Herbert, c Ottoway, b Rose	2	c A. Lubbock, b Rose	0
Lieut. Henley b Appleby	3	c Grace, b Rose	5
A. Jones, b Appleby	1	c Grace, b Appleby	2
R. Killaly, b Rose	0	st Ottoway, b Rose	0
T. D. Paterson, run out	0	st Ottoway, b Rose	0
A. J. Paden, c and b Rose	0	b Appleby	0
Rev. T. D. Phillips, leg b w, b Rose	3	b Rose	1
C. S. Scott, st Ottoway, b Appleby	0	leg b w, b A Lubbock	6
D. Shaw, b Appleby	1	st Ottoway, b Appleby	1
Jas. Smith, b Appleby	0	c Grace, b Rose	0
Jas. Smith, not out	5	c Francis, b Rose	16
Dr. Spragge, b Appleby	5	c Fitzgerald, b Ap-	
Swinyard, leg b w, b Appleby	3	pleby	0
Byes	2	st Ottoway, b Rose	2
		st Ottoway, b Rose	0
		B 2, l b 1	3
Total	—43	Total	—49

In a great measure the hollow victory was due to the exaggerated opinion formed of the Englishmen's bowling; it would be unfair to deny a certain merit to Rose, and credit to Appleby, for their several performances. But it was past comprehension, Magic. unless we assume some magic influence, that young and stalwart cricketers should positively

refuse long hops and half volleys. The
Twenty-Two of Ottawa were a very fine lot
of young men, and that they could hit and
open their shoulders was very evident "at
practice." The match was played in the
best possible spirit; and from one and all
the Twelve parted with sincere appreciation
of the hearty welcome they had received.

As we have previously hinted, cricket
presented by no means the only field of
action where the Twelve exhibited themselves
and their prowess. "Knife and Fork" was Knife and Fork.
played at Ottawa in the Parliament Square.
The banquet was of the most *récherché* The Banquet.
character. Tables were laid in a capacious
tent. The arrangements were perfect, even
to the proverbial shower which always falls
on public dinners in the open air. The tent
let in a little rain, which soon evaporated in
steam under the warmth of British and
Canadian eloquence. Mr. Wright presided.
He gave the usual loyal toasts. The speaker
was fervid, and his periods were rounded—
too much so, perhaps, as his turn to speak
came round very often. The Captain was
emotional, but he spoke from the heart, and

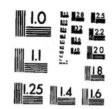

IMAGE EVALUATION
TEST TARGET (MT-3)

he may be excused a little warmth, as the ventilation was by no means good, and the occasion was a good one for a stump-orator. W. G. made his second speech; he said, " Gentlemen, I beg to thank you for the honour you have done me. I never saw a better ground than I have seen to-day, and I hope to see as good wherever I go." A similarity may be traced to his Montreal speech, but that does not affect its originality to a different audience. The chairman had got into a difficulty as to sex in a classical allusion to the three Graces. He did not bring it in very cleverly and Gilbert was puzzled how to reply, but taking the allusion as intended for the female portion of his family, he was understood to regret that his sisters were not present to return thanks for themselves. There was a call for Appleby to reply for the Ladies, upon George the Tourist declining the honour. (George would have replied but had been disappointed by Edgar of two stanzas which the latter had copied out, but forgotten to bring with him to the banquet).

Mr. Burrowes in proposing the Ladies

W. G.'s 2nd speech.

The Graces.

Appleby for the Ladies.

said he had the highest authority for connecting the fast bowler's name with the toast, for
it would be remembered by all that the *first* Eve.
lady in the land could not pass her "Appleby." The "unassuming" in his reply expressed his concern at having been connected
with the "Ladies," when there were so many
under the tent who had better claims upon
their favours—(cries of No, no)—"the honour No! No!
had been thrust upon him, and he would
trust on her as his guiding star." (Here the
dear boy began to ramble, and sat down on A ramble.
being asked to do so kindly by the Captain.)
A great many other toasts followed; toasts in
fact are not numbered in Canada by the glass
to the bottle.

An adjournment was effected to the coffee- A dance.
room of the hotel, where all that was beautiful in Ottawa was collected. The Canadian
young ladies are very collected. Their great
anxiety was to learn what the English visitors
thought of them, the prevailing impression
amongst them being that an Englishman
looks upon Canada as a "few acres of ice,"
and its inhabitants as mere consumers of
wood and ice-water. The Twelve wouldn't
tell them all they wanted to know, indeed,

it would be hard to satisfy the inquiring
mind of the fair Canadian.   Winter has a
long reign in these regions, but warm hearts
supply what the Hudson's Bay Company
fails to provide, and on the margin of the
forest the stranger will meet that hearty
greeting, which he may sigh for in a crowded
town amongst his own kith and kin.

A story.   It is recorded of the great Champlain
that at a feast in the far West provided for
him by some Jesuit priests, he was offered
by a Red Man a tender morsel, in other words
a bear-steak ; on tasting it he began to laugh,
and said, " If they only knew in France of
A bear- our eating bear's flesh they would turn away
steak. their faces from our breath, and yet you see
how nice and delicate this meat is."   " You
are always," said the Red Man, " saying
something humorous to us to make us feel
happy, and if what you declare should prove
true, we should be joyful indeed."   The ordinary reader will probably not comprehend
the nature of the Indian's joy, problematical
as it appears by his words.   Neither did we
previously to the banquet in Parliament
Square. There and then it flashed across us ;
amongst the delicacies of the season, the hind

leg of a bear (very rare) was offered to us; The hind
we brought all the pressure our teeth could leg.
muster upon it, and we can now appreciate
the irony of the Red Man—for if a bear's hind
leg could ever be proved to be nice and delicate there would be no bounds to our joy, or
rather bear within bounds might be our only
joy. Talking of the Red Man and his ex- Another
tinction or absorption by the white and story.
whiskey, an affecting tale was told us by an
amateur sportsman of Ottawa. Our friend
was in the habit every autumn of spending a
few weeks in the bush, shooting the wily
partridge in the tree and other wild animals.
He became acquainted with the chief of a The chief.
wandering tribe, with a very long name;
he was evidently proud of his name; translated into English it announced him to
be the Great Spirit Quencher, Smoke and
Snuff Consumer, The Terrible Toddy Mixer
of the Firewater, &c., &c. Our friend regarded him with veneration, as one who re-
called an early belief in Fenimore Cooper,
and juvenile worship of Catlin. His disen-
chantment was worked thusly:—a hard drinking Scotchman strolled into the camp one

Bruce.

day, and, to our friend's amazement, saluted the Red Man with "How are ye, Mister Bruce?" "Whish!" said the Red Man, eyeing our friend askance, terribly conscious of lies he had poured into a willing ear. "Bruce!" said our friend, "is it possible that the Terrible Toddy, &c., is not thy honoured name?" "Whish!" again whistled the Red Man, and dropping his voice, so that the terrible secret might go no farther than our

Tale of a grand-father.

friend's ear—"It's too true; my grandfather was a Scotchman." Our friend has given up sporting amongst the wild tribes. We tried in vain to extract other anecdotes of this interesting people, but to all our questions he answered "Nimium, puer ne crede colori!" Nobody has thoroughly done Ottawa, until Ottawa has tried its best to do for him in

The slides.

the well-known "Slides." The Slides are the fabulous dangers of Ottawa. They do not confer a diploma like the Cave of the Winds at Niagara (of which hereafter), but to shrink from the Slides is considered natural on the part of strangers. The ladies affect the Slides. The Twelve placed them-

Circe.

selves at the mercy of several Circes, and did

the Slides. It is an agreeable sensation; a lady clinging to each arm tightly, or if nervous yourself, clinging to a waist not loth to be pressed, a raft and rushing of water, a sudden dip, a stifled scream, a wild hurrah from a bridge, under which you slide, a succession of the above sensations in less time than you can say your prayers, a gradual unclinging and unfastening of waists, and the danger is done. All told, the peril is not equal to a real slide on a bit of orange-peel in the streets of London. A jolly slide.

It is good fun on a good raft with a merry party, but a real sensation must be sliding on a raft about whose construction you have your doubts, and in company with a Canadian raftsman, perfectly indifferent to your safety or his own. Having seen so much sawdust on our ascent of the Ottawa, it was but natural to see a saw-mill in full operation. Saw mills. To see huge logs converted into ball-room floors in a few whirrs of the untiring saw is very fascinating. To watch the nimble fingers of hundreds of girls and boys under the same roof, converting splinters of pine into matches with marvellous accuracy and rapidity is equally captivating. Lucifer.

Matches.   The matches of Canada are an institution.
None of your patent-safety lighting-only-on-
the-box affairs; the true Kanuk would scorn
any such civilized affectation. He lights his
match, *propriâ personâ*, on his coat sleeve or
such part of his trowser as he thinks proper,
even on your trowser if it looks more likely
to engender flame. Nothing brings strangers
nearer together than these primitive institutions. We felt at home at once with the
Canadian who lit his match on our leg as we
did with the American who pulled a crumb
Whiskers. out of our beard. At home such innocent
amenities would end in blood.

La Chau-   The La Chaudière falls are very beautiful,
dière.
a wild avalanche of waters; a little below
them upon the high rocks on the southern
side stand, in commanding relief against the
sky, the Parliament Buildings. These are
worthy of the great Colony. They consist
at present of a central building and two
wings unattached, a library is in process of
Public   completion, and when the Parliament Square
Buildings. is enclosed with iron railings, the whole
will form a group of building that may be
envied by any city. Yet here the magnifi-

cent architectural effect is presented to the
eye of the traveller, on the margin of the
primæval forest. Boundless woods stretch
far to the north and west. The great forest
fire of 1870 almost surrounded the city, nor
can danger be said yet to be far from the
gates. Houses appear to be built quite independent of any way to them, paved streets
are yet in their quarries. If the roads and
streets remind us of the Holy Land, the
public buildings and private dwellings and
churches evince a high order of architecture.
Villas here are not the cruet stands and Villas.
monstrosities that mark the outskirts of a
thriving English town. Elegant designs do
not, as at home, distinguish the Established
Church from the House of Dissent. Una-
nimity of style seems to reign amid a discord
of creed. The Twelve saw all that could be
seen in their short visit, their impressions of
the place and people, if superficial, were at
least agreeable. They left Ottawa much
gratified with all that had been done to welcome them in the cricket field, and fill up
the odd corners of time at their disposal.
The ladies of Ottawa patronized an im-

promptu hop in the coffee-room of the Russell House, that was kept up with spirit till 4 A.M.

The weather had been auspicious, and threatened only on days when cricket was not on the card. It did come down in earnest on the morning of August 30. The party *Prescott.* left at 7 A.M. by train to Prescott, a small town on the St. Lawrence. Here the first and last mistake was made by those who pulled the strings, we won't mention names. Considerable ignorance prevailed as to the locality of Belleville; an engagement, it appears, had been made by Mr. Pattison for the Twelve to visit Belleville. It had not been properly explained to the Captain. Nobody *Belleville.* knew where Belleville was, everybody *Brockville.* was loud in praise of Brockville; the road was clear enough to the latter, so it was decided *Explana-tion.* cided to go there. It is due to the good people of Belleville to explain that had the Twelve been aware of the preparations made to receive them there, they would have gone through fire and flood rather than disappoint them. Several hundreds flocked there to see *W. G.* "The Unapproachable." All kinds of games

were on foot, and the disappointment was
great. Our only apology is that it was un- Apology.
intentional on our part, and was much regretted afterwards.

The change of route led to one great
result, and the hand of fate was clearly in it.
Had it not been for Brockville the discovery
of America by the modern Columbus would The modern
Columbus.
never have taken place. Colonel Maude,
V. C., C. B., a distinguished ex - officer of The
Colonel.
Royal Artillery had been appointed military
and very civil commissioner to the Twelve.
The route was in his hands, the Twelve
followed him like lambs. The Colonel decided that they should spend the night at
Alexandra Bay, drinking a few bottles of Alexandra
Bay.
champagne at Brockville *en route*. The
Colonel believed Alexandra Bay to be on the
Canadian shore. On arriving at Prescott,
where a hasty breakfast was despatched, a
steamer took all on board bound for the unknown Alexandra Bay. Touching at Brockville, where rumour had drawn the champagne
from its bin, a deputation of three leading
citizens awaited the arrival of the Twelve; on
learning their intended destination a general

uproar ensued. It was then the discovery
took place that Alexandra Bay was on the
American shore. The Colonel's face dropped
into his waistcoat pocket. The discovery
was providential; the luggage was booked
fo A. B.; the captain of the Propeller
allowed thirty seconds for decision; in fifteen
the Captain determined that the baggage
and Farrands should go on together to the
new found land, and that the Twelve should
land to drink the champagne at Brockville in
honour of the modern Columbus. Off went
the steamer with Farrands and the luggage;
signs of discontent were not long in appear-

The carpet-
baggers.
ing. Rose and Hadow are much attached to
each other, but each is much more attached
to his baggage than to anything or anybody
else; frowns gathered ominously. The
Brockville deputation saw the storm brewing and checked it by a copious supply of
champagne; the difference was split; the

The dis-
contents.
discoverer and the discontents, by the kindness of the owner, steamed up to A. B.
in a launch and there rejoined their hearts'
treasure. The remainder spent a pleasant
afternoon amongst the Thousand Isles.

Rustic dancing was in progress, a picnic of Americans at its highest jinks; instruction in the noble game was given gratis with any implements that lay handy, a turnip and a broom handle the most conspicuous agents. Returning to Brockville, a dance was imme- *A dance.* diately set on foot; Messrs. Cook, Frazer, Gascoyne, and Jones hunted up the fair inhabitants. The rig of the English party was not *à la mode.*

> Some in high-lows, some in white shoes, *Poetry.*
> Some in every kind of boot ;
> Shooting coats and flannel trowsers,
> Adapted to an evening suit.

George and Edger retired early, Appleby and the Captain escorted some ladies home. It was very dark, and Appleby was sentimental, the Captain tender, and the walk *A midnight stroll.* was pronounced by all much too short. A bathe in the bright St. Lawrence the next morning braced up the nerves after the night's excitement. The arrival of the discoverer and the discontents from A. B., took all by surprise. The luggage came back with them. They reported very highly of the hotel at A. B., where they had spent a pleasant evening amidst the American cocktails.

The party once more united bade farewell
to the hospitable Brockville and their enter-
1,000 Isles. tainers at 1.20, on August 31. The course
soon lay through the Thousand Islands. The
Yankees are rapidly monopolizing the islands
—their villas and steam launches are numerous. They are welcome to the islands
so long as they do not claim the channel which
hugs the Canadian shore. After St. Juan,
it is possible they may have St. Lawrence
for the asking. The beauty of the islands
is exaggerated; it is cut into too many bits;
by the time you have passed a few hundred,
you begin to doubt whether the beauty you
have heard of has been passed or is still
before you, and when you emerge into the
broad bosom of Ontario it is with the sensation of a traveller escaping from a swarm of
insects; you never have an island out of
your eye for five minutes. St. Lawrence's
fine stream is chafed by them, and its majesty shorn by petty channels. Ontario received the Cricketers with a blessed calm;
on the previous day according to accounts it
had lashed itself to fury. Treacherous indeed are the smiles of the inland sea. King-

stop as passed at nightfall; the Monkey _{Kingston.}
& .: the Ojibbeway landed, the former wishing
to take the acquaintance of some young
lady, whose photograph he had once seen
in a brother's album. The Captain let them
go reluctantly, and only under a solemn vow
to turn up at Toronto, on Monday morning,
September 2. It was a lovely night on the _{Ontario.}
great lake, the air balmy, the northern shore
visible; a watery waste to the south, across
which at times a sail might be seen shim-
mering in the silver light; early next morn-
ing, September 1, Toronto was sighted, and _{Toronto.}
at 10.30 the party landed. Intensely hot.
Excellent quarters provided by Mr. Shears,
of the Rossyn Hotel. A week's cricket now
in store, the home of the game attained at
last; from Toronto sprang the first germs of
the expedition, to Toronto all looked forward as to a resting place, or at least, a
week's halt. Whether it may justly be considered a place of rest after such crowding of
events into the space of one week, as you
shall hear presently, if you have only patience,
we leave you, kind reader, to decide.

CHAPTER VI.

A BUSY week was indeed in store ; cricket
by day, dinners and dancing at night. We
do not pretend to be able to do justice to
our entertainers by any words that can
be written. We will simply record what
we did and how we did at Toronto.

Cricket.

Sept. 2, Monday.—The Twelve mustered
on the ground at 11 A.M. The first impressions were favourable; the wickets had evidently been watched for months, well watered
and protected from the sun; a green oasis
distinguished them from the outfielding,

which was brown as birdseye, but not bad.
Several flights of steps were erected on the
west side for the accommodation of 2000
spectators, tents for the scorers and players.
Mr. Blake, the proprietor of the ground, pro- Blake.
vided everything that could be desired, including soap and towels, for which we had
hitherto appealed in vain. Luncheon was
set out in the log-hut; a great attendance
on the first day was well sustained throughout the week. Royalty, in the person of the Royalty.
Lieut.-Governor and his Lady, honoured the
performances each day. Now to the crickets.
The Captain won his third toss. The day Cricket,
was hot, and cabbage leaves were at a pre- 3rd toss.
mium. W. G. and Ottoway appeared at
the wickets to the bowling of Blake and
Hemsted. In the fifth over the Unapproachable gave Blake warning to leave the ground
—a spanking hit for six, Ottaway scraping Out of the
carefully meanwhile, and 30 runs were ground.
scored off the first 10 overs. W. G. is
"reported" to have hit a shooter to square-
leg for two; we cannot vouch for this.
Wright supplanted Hemsted in the 16th
over; a shooter hit Gilbert in the chest

about this period—he deserved the rub.   In
the 29th over, 40 runs up, Gilbert might have
been lassoed, but was not.   The Ojibbeway's
time came when he had made 15, caught
by Spragge, the medico—point; he was well
cheered on leaving the wicket.   The Monkey
ran up 8 in two overs, and then climbed
down grinning at a ghastly shooter of
Wright's.   Alfred the Great joined Gilbert,
and the score reached 77 at luncheon, for

A kid.   two wickets.   After lunch Gilbert practised
a little kidding, which took in some of the
clever ones, and a general cheer was succeeded by a hollow groan, when it was seen
that the great man had no intention to leave
his wicket; it was the old kid—first bound
catch to point.   Alfred achieved 14, his
style eliciting hearty admiration; score 98.

Anna.   Anna went in, his advent was the signal
for Gilbert to open his shoulders, dreading a
rival—a magnificent drive for 6 to the railings—a 6 with 22 in the field is not often
obtained within bounds; shortly after his
life should have been taken by Brunel, who
spared him.   Anna "made a draw" for
2; Grace "legged a ball" for 2.   Whelan

here took Wright's place, who had bowled
well through the heat of the day. He soon
received notice to quit, a third sixer being
added to W. G.'s rapidly rising score. Anna
then retired, having in his fine free style
landed 17 ; score 167, 4 wickets. George
succeeded, and as if to warm him up, Gilbert
let out again and sixer No. 4 was chalked
up. His luck was not used up yet, as John
Brunel gave him another life, a gaper this time. J. Brunel a
To quote, " It lighted in John's hands, who, gaper.
alas for Toronto! dropped 't very quickly,
and it scored 1." In revenge W. G. went
over the fence again ; sixer No. 5. His
century was now obtained, but his bat was
broken in the effort. Gamble succeeded
Wright, and was successful in capturing
George, after making 11, with the assist-
ance of Armstrong at mid-wicket, where
he had fielded well. An immense roar told
the neighbourhood that the great man was
no more—the very last man expected to
catch him caught him—John Brunel was W. G.
a happy man; Gilbert's score of 142, out caught.
of 241, against a smart 22, barring a few
accidents, was a great performance, and

gave great pleasure to the spectators. A slight lull was now observable in the score. Francis was humane, but Edgar and Appleby between them caused some diversion.

Edgar the stylish. Edgar's "style" is provocative of merriment, but he generally turns the laugh to his own side. He was well caught by Baines for a slashing 21 ; time was called, Appleby not out, 7 ; total for 8 wickets, 273. The fielding of the Torontoes in the face of such heat and under such heavy fire was excellent, W. G.'s accidents excepted, but many of his hardest drives were admirably nipped in the bud. Hope at longleg was as good as could be ; Sproul, the longstop, and Whelan at point, and Spragge at mid-wicket, were very conspicuous. The bowling was also well sustained by Blake, Wright, and Swinyard.

Cricket, 2nd day. *Sept.* 3. — The game was renewed at 11.30. The Rose and the Apple-blos- *Flowers.* som flowered freely ; the Rose was plucked at 10, score 264 for 9 wickets. The *Pickweed.* youthful Pick. appeared, and the score mounted rapidly. He gave a chance to the worthy President, Mr. Heward, who

displayed some tergiversation in his attempt
to catch him, but he shortly afterwards fell a
victim to the same gentleman, who this time
showed a full front to the ball. The boys'
26 was warmly applauded; it included some
grand hits—one 4, two 3's, three 2's, and
singles. The Captain brought up the rear, The
and made the most of three balls, two sixers Captain.
and a single, when he was caught in the
long-field by Whelan—a good catch; Appleby carrying his bat out for an excellent
29; total, 319. At 12.45 the Torontoes
went in,—Rose and Appleby bowling; 8
wickets were down at luncheon time for 27
runs. Hemsted showed some form, but he
and others were all abroad to the insinuating
Rose. Some hospitable friend seduced five
of the Twelve from the field during luncheon; on resuming only seven appeared, Desertion.
the Captain was angry, but went on without them, consequently runs were obtained
with more freedom,—Francis bowling, *vice*
Appleby. Ottoway put a finger out, and the
Monkey donned the gloves; 9 wickets down
for 40. On Appleby resuming runs ceased :
17 wickets down for 60. Swinyard made

H

good his opposition, and, with Pattison, stemmed the tide that was setting against Toronto; they ran the score from 60 to 94. Grace took Rose's place, but was severely punished. Swinyard's 29 consisted of two 4's, three 3's, three 2's, and singles. The total amounted to 97. The innings concluded at 4.15, play resumed at 4.45 : Hemsted was soon busy; he made 28, including one 7 (two overthrows), two 4's, two 2's and singles—a dashing innings, though missed badly by Pickering and Edgar; 2 wickets for 38. Whelan took tea with Rose and led to a change,—Hadow going on at Appleby's end, and Appleby at Rose's; runs were creeping up till Whelan was c and b by Hadow; his 24 comprised two 6's, two 3's, one 2, and singles : a very hard hitter but not much judgment. The stumps were drawn at 6.30 : 12 wickets down for 83.

Light. The light in Canada never lasted to a later hour, and generally it was agreed not to play later than 6 P.M.

Some good fielding, on the part of George, Hadow, and Francis, and a few muffs, by way of contrast on the part of Edgar and

Pickering, distinguished the Englishmen. Time was not strictly adhered to, or the match might have been concluded; but the heat was inimical to strict cricket, and Heat. the Twelve found many friends at the bar.

Sept. 4.—The match was brought to a Cricket, termination before one o'clock,—total 118. 3rd day. The individual performances call for little remark; to quote from a local " The English majority is thus 104—very small when their high score is considered." We do not see the wit or wisdom of this remark; it was a good match to win and was well won. The Twenty-two did not bat their best: many of them showed good form against Appleby, who bowled undeniably well, but their weakness with William, who was as innocent as a new-born babe, was quite lamentable. There is plenty of cricketing stuff in Toronto and district; and with such bowlers as Blake, Wright, and Hemsted, and fieldsmen like Hope, Spragge, Whelan, and Sproule, a good eleven might soon be procured " with practice "—" there's the rub." The match was very pleasantly conducted, and the visitors could not fail to be gratified by the in-

terest shown each day by the enormous
crowd of spectators, including most of the
fair sex of the neighbourhood.

ENGLAND v. TORONTO.

ENGLAND.

Score.

W. G. Grace, c J. Brunel, b Swinyard 142	C. K. Francis, b Swinyard 1
C. J. Ottoway, c Spragge, b Wright 15	A. Appleby, not out......... 29
A. N. Hornby, b Wright ... 8	W. M. Rose, c Whelan, b Swinyard 10
A. Lubbock, c Armstrong, b Swinyard.................. 14	F. P. U. Pickering, c Heward, b Wright 26
Hon. G. Harris, c Armstrong, b Gamble 11	R. A. Fitzgerald, c Whelan, b Wright 13
W. H. Hadow, b Hemsted 17	B 7, l-b 5 12
E. Lubbock, c Baines, b Wright 21	Total.................. 319

TORONTO.

	1st inn.		2nd inn.
R. Parsons, c Appleby, b Rose ..	0	b Appleby............	9
E. Hemsted, b Rose	7	b Appleby............	28
J. Brunel, b Appleby..............	9	run out	3
N. Kirchoffer, c Grace, b Rose ...	1	b Appleby............	0
H. Totten, b Rose	0	c A. Lubbock, b Rose	4
J. Whelan, b Rose	3	c and b Hadow......	24
F. Armstrong, c Harris, b Rose...	2	c Grace, b Rose......	5
G. Brunel, c Lubbock, b Appleby	8	b Appleby............	4
R. K. Hope, st Ottoway, b Rose	0	b Hadow	0
J. Wright, c Grace, b Rose	5	b Appleby............	0
Dr. Spragge, c Lubbock, b Rose...	5	c and b Hadow... ..	0
R. G. Gamble, b Rose	0	b Appleby............	0
F. J. Gosling, b Appleby	4	b Appleby............	3
T. Swinyard, not out	29	c Appleby, b Rose...	1
J. O. Heward, b Rose	2	b Appleby............	3
R. B. Blake, c Pickering, b Appleby	2	b Rose	4

TORONTO—*Continued.*	1st inn.		2nd inn.
C. H. Sproule, st Hornby, b Appleby	1	b Rose	0
W. Hector, b Rose	0	b Appleby	0
H. Forlong, c Pickering, b Grace	3	b Appleby	0
T. C. Patteson, b Appleby	6	not out	3
G. P. Buchanan, b Appleby	0	c Hornby, b Rose	18
A. Baines, b Appleby	0	b Appleby	0
B 8, l-b 2	10	B 5, l-b 3	8
Total	—97	Total	—117

The following is the analysis of the bowl-ing. It must be observed, in honour to Toronto, that not one wide was bowled in the long innings of 319—an unprecedented fact :—

Analysis.

ENGLAND.

	Overs.	Balls.	Runs.	Maidens.	Wickets.
Blake	53	212	72	20	0
Wright	67	269	102	26	5
Swinyard	24	96	60	3	4
Hemsted	13	52	41	2	1
Baines	6	24	8	2	0
Gamble	8	32	14	1	1

TORONTO.
FIRST INNINGS.

Rose	32	128	57*	8	12
Appleby	30	120	22	23	8

SECOND INNINGS.

Rose	34	136	68	9	7
Appleby	33	132	30	20	10

During the progress of the match the Captain was interviewed by a deputation

The deputation.

from Oswego.   The deputation consisted of
a merchant tailor, a dentist, and a doctor,
from that thriving city.   The merchant
tailor was the spokesman; he shook hands

The Captain interviewed. with the Captain and then introduced himself and friends ; curiosity is a leading trait
of American character.   The deputation
were the gallant survivors of what would
have been a formidable hand-shaking fra-
ternity.   A lucky storm had frightened
four towns from joining Oswego in the
friendly mission to the English cricketers;
Utica, Syracuse, Troy, and Albany had
threatened, but it remained for Oswego
alone to carry out the programme.   There
was a mock air of gravity about the Merchant Tailor which was very killing; the

Pizarro. Captain might have been Pizarro and the
M.T. the last of the Mohicans, from the
solemnity with which the latter introduced

The original John Smith. the Dentist as "the original John Smith."
The Captain, struggling against a smile,
lisped his pleasure at meeting the original
of such a well-known and widely distributed

The Doctor. family ; the Doctor was introduced next, his
name and appearance were not so striking.

The Merchant Tailor produced a note-book
and solicited information of any kind
about the Twelve.   It was a fair opportunity
for the Captain, and Oswego, if it believes the
Tailor, will know more about the English *The Tailor.*
Cricketers than they do themselves.   The
Captain entered into weights, heights, number
of sisters, and when last vaccinated, together
with fabulous scores, feats of agility, sufficient
to fill several pages of the Tailor's note-book.
Joking apart, there was something friendly
about the deputation; it was not all "gas."
It ended with an invitation to "wine" with the
St. George's Society.   Unhappily other engagements prevented its acceptance; it
would doubtless have been a pleasant party.
Another instance of American enterprise was
brought before our notice : an invitation was
received to play at Chicago—time would not *Chicago.*
allow this to be carried out, perhaps happily,
as some days later, a native of Chicago
whom we met in the train, said there was no
cricket-ground to his knowledge anywhere
about the place, but, added the sanguine
citizen, "By the time you get there. I have
no manner of doubt they will have made

one." Judging by the remarkable rise of Chicago from its ashes, such a little matter as a cricket-ground, which takes seasons to perfect in England, would have been the work of a few days. There might have been occupation for the doctors, but nowhere on the globe is life less an object of living for than in America.

The Yacht Club.

The Twelve were invited to a grand banquet given by the members of the Royal Canadian Yacht Club. Their gallant Com-

The Commodore.

modore, Dr. Hodder, presided. He was a

The White Admiral.

venerable man — the White Admiral of the fleet. The club-house is on the shore of Lake Ontario. The evening was cheerful—speeches prolific—the Commodore very happy in his remarks—the Captain in voice, repeating all the good things he had uttered elsewhere; but warming at the sight of the neat naval uniforms worn by the members of the Club, expressed his conviction that so long as the Royal Canadian Yacht Club nurtured a gallant race of sailors, Canada need not fear for her inland waters. Seamanship of no mean order is acquired on these land-locked seas. And if Canada ever

looks in vain to England, which heaven
forefend! she will be grateful for the zeal
which the White Admiral for many years has
done his best to promote amongst the
yachtsmen of Toronto. W. G. was of
course called upon, and replied in speech No. w. G.'s
3 (see pages 52, &c., and for "bowling" and speech.
"ground" read "batting," and you have it).
George replied for the ladies, and had his
poetry in his pocket this time, thanks to The poet
Edgar, who sat near him. The party broke Harris.
up early in the morning. There were other
banquets in the course of the week: private
entertainments given by the worthy President,
Mr. Heward and Mr. Patteson, celebrated
for no speeches; rather disappointing to the
Captain, who had prepared an original one;
but an opportunity soon occurred for letting
it off, as an invitation was extended to the
Twelve by the President and members of
the Toronto Club. Mr. Cayley presided; The
a most excellent dinner was provided. It Toronto
Club.
opened the lungs, and gave voice to numerous orators. W. G. made his fourth
speech. He said (see above, and for w. G.'s
"ground," "bowling," "batting," read 4th speech.

"good fellows";) and he sat down amidst general applause. A humorous speech was made by Mr. Boultby, member for New-market. In returning thanks for the toast of the National Sports of Canada, he said he was only well acquainted with one of the national sports — viz., Poker: at this he could do more than hold his own, and he would be glad to instruct the Twelve at any time in it. Offer declined, with thanks. Mr. W. H. Smith, M.P. for Westminster, also spoke, and, of course, the Captain was on his legs; his great difficulty now being, after such constant practice, to pull up; his heart was full, his mouth was full; but yet he could not find words enough to express the feelings of himself and comrades at their reception in Toronto. It was not only to the members of the Club and to the leading members of society that the Twelve were grateful for the kindness shown to them, but they were also deeply sensible of the warmth and loyalty which had displayed itself on the cricket ground. He, the Captain, had at first regarded himself as another Barnum, travelling with a caravan of living curiosities.

Mr Boult-by.

Poker.

W. H. Smith, M.P.

Barnum.

He had, however, seen enough to convince him that it was not only curiosity that prompted many an honest artizan or back-woodsman to shake hands with Mr. Grace or any other of the Twelve. It was the hearty recognition of Englishmen from the Old Country by English settlers in the New. The Captain concluded by expressing his thanks for all the arrangements made by the Toronto Club committee of management, and especially to Mr. Shears for his great attention to them at the Rossyn Hotel. Dancing was not neglected during the week. A magnificent ball was given by the Lieu- The ball. tenant-governor and Mrs. Howland, at which the *élite* of Toronto were present. We must quote from the local report :—" Last night a large party assembled at Mrs. Howland's ' At Home,' given in honour of the English Cricketers. The excellent ball-room was crowded with votaries of Terpsichore, the splendour of the dresses and the beauty of the wearers being of a kind that cannot have failed to impress our visitors with a very favourable opinion of ' the dangerous Cana-dians.' Mr. Grace, who must now be known

by sight to more people in England than Mr.
Gladstone himself, was especially noticeable
for the skill and agility of his movements."
Our wish is to be impartial, and whenever
any of the boys distinguished himself, to do
him justice. Mrs. Howland, accompanied
by Lady M'Donald, wife of the Prime
Minister, showed great interest in the game,
and drove upon the ground each day. Before we proceed with an account of the
second match, we must devote a short
chapter to the most interesting day of the
whole week. You are not obliged to read
it; but pleasure as much as duty compels
us to record it.

CHAPTER VII.

" MR. AND MRS. CUMBERLAND request the *The invitation.*
pleasure of R. A. FitzGerald, Esq., and the
English Cricketers' company on an excursion to Lake Simcoe and Couchicing, on
Thursday, the 5th September, leaving Brock
Street Station, at half-past 10 o'clock precisely.

" An early answer is requested.

"*Pendarves, 20th Aug.* 1872."

An early answer was given in the affirma-
tive. The party numbered ninety souls or
more, amongst them many ladies, and the
route commenced within an hour after the
appointed time—a little law being required
for some of the fair, who had danced down

The journey.

the band at the Government House the previous evening. The railroad journey was of an hour and half's duration. The forest was soon entered, with its scanty patches of clearing, occasional glimpses of well-cleared farms and good out-buildings. Now and again a marshy bit, suggestive of wildfowl,— blackened trunks denoting the path of fire; the small fences zigzagging round small enclosures; several stations of neat designs were passed, the line itself well laid, and the handsome saloon carriages worthy of the line. It may be as well to state that this is the

G. N. R.

Great Northern Line. These first few miles of our route are also the first of that great artery of the Nor'-west, — the Northern

The Northern Pacific Railroad.

Pacific Railroad. The future success of this railway will mark an era in the history of Canada. The Home Government has voted a large sum towards its completion; a large portion of it has been surveyed, and it is advancing steadily on its mighty path to the west. Such an undertaking as this cannot fail to be interesting even to the traveller; to the people of Canada it is the El Dorado, the Great Unknown, the Profligate, the Far-

seeing, the Hope of the Future, the Curse of
the Present, just as their political bias in-
fluences them for the moment.   We constantly heard it abused as the worst of jobs,
and again listened to sanguine predictions
of the great blessing it must confer upon
the Dominion.   It is not for us to pretend to
decide upon so momentous a question.   To
our mind the idea itself sufficiently confirms The idea.
the experiment.   To penetrate vast regions
at present inaccessible, but known to be
favourable to grain and other produce ; to
connect the Atlantic with the Pacific shore ;
to bind the Dominion together ; to give it
what it has long needed, a spinal column,
with vertebræ of iron, and so strengthen its
dependencies on either hand, appeals most
forcibly to the imagination.   Speculation,
doubtless, looks further than the gradual
development of the regions through which
the line will run.   Her roving eye has
crossed the Pacific, and may fondly see in
the future the argosies of China and Japan
attracted to the northern port.   These and
other like dreams do not suggest themselves
to the simple traveller ; he can but judge of

things in a strange country from what he sees, and to some extent, with proper caution, from what he hears. The most careless observer in Canada cannot fail to perceive that there are signs of development throughout the country. The era of stagnation has passed away. There is a marked appearance of independence and self-confidence. The people believe in their future. The resources of the north-west are to a great extent unfathomed. All that is known conduces to a belief in mineral wealth, that may well excuse the daring fancies of the speculator. The wealth of the soil is undoubted. The forest, the rivers, the great lakes speak for themselves; food, fuel, and locomotion are within the grasp of all who penetrate these solitudes. Col. Cumberland, our host of the occasion, is the managing director of the Great Northern, and to him we are indebted for much information, as well as for hospitality on the route. To this we must now return. Belle Ewart received the inmates of the railway cars, by this time on a very good understanding with each other, to judge by the pairing that had

The pliocene.

Prospectus.

Col. Cumberland.

Belle Ewart.

already commenced. The "Emily May," an excellent propeller, took all "on board," whistled a parting note, and steered eastwards, so as to pass by the elegant residences of Messrs. Dodge and May—charming to the eye, and doubtless as good as they look. Comfort is a household word in Canada. The day was made to order—a bright sun and fresh breeze, sufficient to ripple the broad and gleaming surface of the lake, but not to agitate it inconveniently. The shores of Lake Simcoe are well wooded, and the scenery might be Italian: the pureness of the sky and the brilliant tints proclaim a southern rather than a northern hemisphere. The "Narrows" were soon reached. The lake is spanned by a long viaduct, of wonderful neatness and strength combined,—the first completed viaduct of the Great Northern Line. The steamer passes through a swing bridge, and cheers were given by the enthusiastic party to the success of the great undertaking. At three P.M. the picturesque town of Orillia was reached. Many charming villas peep out of the dark pine woods on the margin of the lake. The

Lake Simcoe.

The Narrows.

Orillia.

*I

town (so-called) is not important. The red
man is found here, paddling his own canoe,
carving uncouth instruments and toys, and
assisting the white settler in the consumption
of whiskey and all manners of stores. Orillia
smells of " lumber," and where wood is, there
is often fire.   A scene of late conflagration
was presented by a considerable portion of
The lovers. this thriving settlement.   The "Emily May"
nearly added to the colony a distinguished
pair, as she steamed away to some distance
before it was discovered that a youthful pair
had been left behind.   Unconscious of everything and everybody, they had strolled
through the town, and were much chagrined
on their return to the wharf, as they had to
run the gauntlet of invidious eyes, when the
steamer put back to take them on board.
Leaving Orillia, the steamer's head was
directed to Kempenfeldt Bay and the town
of Barrie. The bay is a small arm of the
lake, beautifully fringed to the water's edge
with the graceful pine and maple.   Most
charming sites for country residences are
occasionally aken advantage of ; and it was
hard to realise that the excursion was in

northern latitudes, and not on the shores of Devonshire. At Port Barrie, the party dis- Port embarked, and five minutes' journey by rail Barrie. brought them to Allandale.

A poet, a painter, is now imperiously de- Allandale. manded. Prepared we were for any surprise, after so enjoyable a day, amidst such enchanting scenery, in such pleasant company; but to describe properly the scene that met our eyes is beyond our *métier*. We will attempt it nevertheless; it will not die away from our memory, even if we fail to give any distinct impression of it to others. Allandale itself is a "bijou" station, of elegant design; it boasts of a flower garden and a fountain; a deep verandah runs round it; the clear waters of the bay ripple within a few yards below it. Col. Cumberland did not allow much time for rapture; he had better things in store than gape seed. Dinner was served "under a roof of pine." Dinner. The interior was decorated with flags, and inscriptions met the astonished eye—"Welcome to the English Cricketers. God save the Queen," the most conspicuous.

Long tables were arranged, and the viands

were of the most choice description. Ever-
greens of various kinds and wreaths of flowers
gave an agreeable aspect to the rude walls.
It was indeed an entertainment one would
have little expected at the gates of the backwoods. Not a hundred yards from where we
sit rise the tall pines that form the outposts
of many a league of forest. We were
hungry, and gave but little thought then to
the vicinity of anything that was not hidden
under piecrust or curbed by wire and cork.
If ever there was an occasion when you could
Speeches. not say too much, this was it. Speeches set
in with their accustomed severity. " The
Queen " was most warmly given and replied
to by the company and outsiders, of whom
The quite a number filled the door. The Captain
Captain. was not equal to the occasion ; he did not
express one-tenth of what he felt ; he intended to be very gallant to the Ladies, but
drew upon himself a severe castigation from
The M.P. Mr. Boultbee, the humorous M.P. for New-
for New-
market. market, who, in proposing the aforesaid
Ladies, observed that the English visitors
must not suppose this day's excursion to have
originated in any matrimonial speculation,

the Captain having remarked on the absence
of chaperons, and the advantages that might
be derived from the dinner, ball, and dark
drive home combined. The ladies might or
might not look upon it as suc ; he did not;
and he advised his young friends not to take
a leap in the dark. The Honourable George The Hon.
George.
replied (as the papers said) "with a happy
speech and a *soupçon* of poetry, as is his
wont;" and the party then adjourned to the
waiting-room of the station, where music
soon set the feet in motion. In the intervals
of dancing, promenades on the platform were Dancing.
taken; and perhaps a railway station never
witnessed so many flirtations. It might have
been a Junction, from all appearances, and
warm hearts were beating at the nearest
station in the world to the North Pole. At
a quarter to eleven the happy party was, to
some extent, broken up; it left Allandale
with a thousand regrets. The Twelve expressed their grateful sense of the trouble
taken by the worthy station-master, John
Cox, and his able assistants. Too much
praise cannot be given to Colonel Cumberland for the perfect organisation of the whole

trip; from first to last it was a success.
The party was only broken up, as a whole,
—on taking their seats in the comfortable
saloon cars, it broke into small items—a lady
in an arm-chair, a gentleman at her feet or
elbow, and so on, and off. It was a very
pleasant finish to an agreeable day. We
shall long remember it as giving rise to an
The muffin. explanation of the term "muffin." We had
incautiously used the term directly to, and
meaning thereby to distinguish, a certain fair
damsel. She rose at the remark, with an
appearance of anger, which was so well
feigned as to appear real to us. We were
alarmed; but, before apologising, requested
to know wherein our offence lay. We were
then told that the term "muffin" is not in
good odour at the present day; that no lady
will admit she ever was or ever could be a
muffin. "What," innocently asked we, "is a
muffin?"—supposing that our old acceptation
of the term must be incorrect. The lady
gave a very evasive answer. We returned
to the charge. We gave our authorities
(certain red men who once had a footing in
the land). We advanced with warmth our

belief in a muffin as in one of the institutions
of Canada, as inseparable from a cold climate
as a well-appointed sleigh, furs, and bells to
the horses. We quoted the well-known
instance of a brevet-major, who, landing late
in the autumn at Quebec, found all the
muffins gone, and had to take up with the
barrack-master's widow. Were the stories
of the red men wicked stories? Would the
lady deny or, blushing, own the fair impeach-
ment? The lady did not deny, nor did she
blush. With some difficulty we arrived at
the exact truth. Muffins there had been;
muffins there were not! No lady owned to
ever having been a muffin, at least not until
she knew her young man well enough to tell
him so. Muffins were not in favour with the
young civilian; they were crumbs of the
happy past (and here she sighed) when the
red man reigned paramount in ball-room or
sleigh. To have been a muffin was fatal to
many a beauty after the red man's exile.
The term was only uttered now *sottâ voce*. It
was still dear; but it was now better understood than often expressed. We pressed our
advantage. We were anxious to take a less

general view of the subject, to bring the muffin more home to ourselves. But the lady was on her guard. It resolved itself finally into this (and we believe this to be the existing social condition of a muffin): that the term might be applied *pro tem.*, but A whisper. not above a whisper. We asked for no more. A pleasanter relationship cannot be imagined than that which was formerly conveyed by a muffin. It could be entertained under no other climate than that of Canada, nor, from the fair types that we met of the *ancien régime*, can we imagine it to be better illustrated. It is needless to observe that the muffin has never attained the same dignity under the black-coat *régime* as it did under the red. We were very grateful to our fair exponent; and should this ever meet her eye, we trust she will acquit us of any intention other than that of presenting a muffin in her proper light. Where the argument would have led us *juste ciel* only knows; but a scream from the engine announced our Toronto. arrival at Toronto; and the hour, 2 A.M., will be a partial apology for this ramble into an interesting social question.

The day's excursion brought us in contact with many pioneers of the Canadian frontier; their conversation, coupled with what we saw ourselves on the shores of Lake Simcoe, assured us of the great want of Canada— English hearts and English hands to aid in the development of the country. Emigration *Emigration.* is the word in everybody's mouth. Send us men to work, for their own profit as well as our own. Canada is not the country for the loafer; but a loaf is at hand for as many *The loaf* as will ask, so that they are willing to put *and the loafer.* their strong shoulders to the common wheel. Saw-mills short of hands is the cry of Lake Simcoe. Wages which would be pronounced fabulous by the agricultural labourer of England are proverbial here. Why is the stream of English labour diverted from the English colony to the Western States of America? What advantages are offered by the Great Republic that are refused or withheld by the Dominion? We hazarded this question once in a motley crowd round our tent on the cricket-field. A voice from the crowd replied, " You can speak your mind in the States." " Yes," said another, " and it may cost you your life

to do so." This cannot be a sound answer
to the question. We certainly had but a
Liberty. short time wherein to compare the liberty of
thought and speech in the two countries, but,
from what we read in the local prints, and
what we heard, and more from what we daily
experienced in our tour throughout the
Dominion, we can speak with certainty as to
the freedom which characterises all classes
of society. Every working man is as good
as his neighbour. It was at first almost
strange to us, Englishmen with our insular
prejudices of caste or superior education, to be
greeted, as we were, in the familiar, but not
vulgar, manner of our brothers in Canada. It
took us a week or two thoroughly to under-
stand the relation in which man stands to man
in the New World. At first our hand did not
instinctively press the kindly fist held out to
us. The sympathetic chord is not struck at
The crust. the first touch. The hard crust of old English prejudice does not crumble without a
struggle in the operation. But it did
crumble ere we left the Dominion. It was impossible to resist the conviction that the hand
held out to the stranger was a proof of the

warm heart; and we needed no proof of the attachment of Canadians to the mother country. Canada is made of self-made men; the aristocracy is self-created; there are no obstacles to success save what man makes for himself. It is not the country for the aspiring clerk, the ambitious juvenile, The quill driver. discontented at home with his quill-driving salary—that class of emigrant is pre-eminently undesirable. It is the country for the strong man, with the head on his shoulders, the Hodge. muscle in his arm. Its wealth does not lie buried in the earth, where it may fall to the luck of the weak as well as to the strong; it lies within the few inches that must be turned by the plough; it is hewn by the axe. Still the stream tends to the prairies of the West, and why? Is it not owing to the neglect at home of our great colony, in some measure? Is not Canada lost sight of in the anxious watching of our ambitious cousin? Are not the crumbs doled to our blood-relations, and the pottage presented to our distant cousins, almost without their asking? The climate may influence some emigrants; Climate. and the horrors of a Canadian winter lose

none of their forbidding features on the
tongues of those agents who, in every part
of Europe, direct the stream towards the
States. There is no doubt that the organisation on the part of American agents is far
superior to that (if any) of the Canadian. So
far from the winter being regarded with
terror in Canada itself, on all sides we heard
its Christmas carols sung. It is the season
of locomotion; places inaccessible in summer
are brought within reach by the level highway of snow. Food is plentiful and cheap;
fuel, if increasing in price, is not scarce.
There is plenty of employment. In the
backwoods we were told by a hardy settler
that he looked forward to the winter, as he
could then travel speedily to Quebec; in the
summer the state of the roads prevented any
communication on wheels. Domestic servants can almost demand their own price.
What's to become of the missuses? is a
serious question now, and not a funny
picture from *Punch*. Nowhere is labour
brought so near to capital; the two converse
familiarly together; and if the voice be
raised, it is generally the former that gains a

hearing. We cannot pretend to any theory that may place emigration to Canada in at least as favourable a light as emigration to other States. We are simply recording our impressions of what we saw and heard from various sources. We can securely state that Canada is in great want of labour, and that she holds out the most honest and equitable inducements to Englishmen in return for their aid. The expenses attendant upon sending out an agricultural family must materially deter private individuals from doing much to aid the cause. England is properly loth to part with her agricultural population; at the same time, we do think that when hundreds are induced to quit their native land for a foreign soil, it is but right that Englishmen should know what advantages are open to them across the Atlantic, in a country which is English to the backbone, albeit separated by a vast ocean. We are far from intimating that money is picked Money. up in the streets or found in the woods, and that the listless, the lounger, the lazy will improve their position by crossing the water —far from it. What we do not hesitate to

advance is, that labour will at once find its
Market. market; and labour combined with capital
can nowhere else meet with so speedy a
The Picca- return. The lounger of Pall-Mall, on a
dilly swell. fortune of £5,000, with a taste for field-
sports, which he can only gratify at the
expense of his washerwoman or through the
kindness of his tailor, is a pitiable being in
his own estimation. Let him take his £5,000
A scheme. to Canada, or, better still, let him previously
invest part of it in labour, by equipping a few
families for the voyage, and providing for their
passage. Let him apply for a grant of land;
his little band will be carried over its first
difficulties by his aid; he will be repaid by
its labour in due time. The mutual assist-
ance will enrich both sides. A clearing will
be effected, the labouring men, in their turn,
will save their wages, and so become small
capitalists, and purchase land of their own.

The mischief that follows in the wake of
emigration is caused by the dangerous belief that money is to be amassed without
work, that the emigrant on setting foot in
America is thereby relieved from wants that
pinched him at home. He can starve almost

as well in Canada as he can in his native
village, if he is unwilling to accept the terms
upon which his fortune depends. If he will
not work, he will do what hundreds, alas ! Drink.
do, he will drink and die; cursing the day Death.
that tempted him to wander from the
fatherly protection of his village union. The
advantages held out to emigrants are often
depicted in too glowing terms, and a useless Paint.
class is thereby induced to try its luck in a
strange land. It cannot be too strongly
urged or too widely known that work of a
severe character must be encountered in the
first instance by those who wish to exchange
a dependent for an independent station in
life; disappointment awaits most who have
formed too sanguine a view of the Promised
Land; on the other hand, to those who are
not so anxious to obtain independency, as to
secure good remuneration for bodily service, and a certainty of food and drink, the
terms offered by the agricultural employers
of labour, the railway companies, in fact the
wages to be obtained everywhere throughout the Dominion, by every class of servant,
cannot be sufficiently or too glowingly de-

scribed. In a country of expansion there is
naturally an impatience of servitude even of
the mildest type.   We never saw such

Mary Jane. deference shown to the neat maid or the
clever cook as we did in Canada; each well
knows her value, she is only too apt to over-
estimate it.   It was refreshing at the same

Flunkey- time to be freed from flunkeyism; six-
dom. footers and white powder flourish not on the
soil. If the Mrs. has her little difficulties,
the traveller is not made aware of them, he
sees only the neatly dressed and smart-
looking maid, who waits upon him with an
independent air that rather gives a zest to
his appetite than otherwise. We are talking of what we observed in private houses;
we must tell another tale in respect of the
hotels. There it is the exception to meet

Boots. with civil attendants. The sauciest of the
saucy, as a rule, are the chambermaids.

Jane. Woe betide you if you lie in bed longer
than the lady who rules your passage with
a broom and bunch of keys, considers your
quantum suff. You will be roused from
your delicious dreams by a hard knock, often
repeated; you will be told that you *must*

get up, you, the proprietor *pro tem.*, as you
foolishly imagine, of a bedchamber!—must
hasten to leave it, as you are trespassing
upon the time of the lady whose pleasure it
is to do her duty how and when she pleases.
No money passes in America between you
and the domestics. This is a great revul-
sion of feeling even to the most niggardly.
It is difficult at first to believe that money
will not brush your boots or fetch your hot
water. It will not guarantee your being
called, nor will it of necessity take your
luggage from or to your room. The al-
mighty dollar takes higher flights, it will
assist you to the most gigantic swindle, but
it will not truckle to any underhand ways
and means, which may tend to establish
your superiority socially over your brother
man. But we are lingering too long upon
social questions; we must return to the
track upon which we started. Our apology
for straying lies in the fact of our having
been taken into the parlour or bed-chamber
wherever we went, and so we were brought
into pleasant contact with cook and house
maid. We gained a little insight into Cana-

K

The cupboard. dian cupboards. Our view of Canada is taken generally from the cricket-field, but from the cricket-field to the cupboard was no long journey, and a very constant one; we can speak with equal warmth and truth of the public as of the private reception. We are loth to withhold our grateful estimation of the kindness hidden under the bushel, whilst we are lavish in our notice of that which met the public eye. Before quitting the sociable theme, we may be per-

Comfort. mitted to add our conviction that comfort forms the great aim and end of a Canadian home. Warmth, to meet the rigour of winter, is eminently cultivated, walls are thick, books are plentiful, the body is well housed, the mind is not neglected. We saw enough to convince us that a winter in Canada owes not all its charms to its crisp frost and clear sky, which give elasticity to the spirits, and make activity necessary to the body. There is a marked sociability and freedom of intercourse amongst the people, which might be envied in many a warmer clime.

12... 10 - 35 = 3 | 57 (7E

79..

CHAPTER VIII.

THE Committee of the Toronto Club were
very anxious to conclude the week's programme with a legitimate match, eleven a
side. The cricket was expected to be of a
high order, and the match as made was
looked forward to with interest. As is
generally the case when much is expected,
the result did not give great satisfaction.
There was not enough speciality in the
match to interest the individuals engaged
in it. It was a clever handicap, and it
ought to have been difficult to name the
winner. It was wisely arranged to throw
the strength of the batting on the one side,
the weig of the bowling on the other.

The Captain leaned to the bowling, and Gilbert, of course, was the champion of the batting side.

Cricket.

Butterflies.

Friday, September 6th.—Very hot day. Myriads of bright butterflies floated in the light northern breeze. We had noticed the migration of these beautiful insects at Ottawa; at this season of the year they are wafted southwards, to perish in Lake Ontario by thousands, all of the same species, of a rich reddish brown hue, and as large as crown pieces. They people the air, and supply the place of birds. The graceful night-hawk is often seen towards evening, swooping down on the butterfly; swallows are not numerous, in fact the appearance of a bird of any kind was generally hailed by the Twelve with a shout. Humming-birds at this season may be seen hovering over the flowers in private gardens, but they are few and far between, and are already on the move southwards.

Ornitho-
logy.

The match commenced late; at one o'clock, W. G., who had won the toss, went in with George to the bowling of Rose and Appleby. The Monkey put the gloves on;

a fair assemblage of spectators looking forward to a second display of W. G.'s powers. They were doomed to disappointment; at the second ball bowled the Unapproachable _{W. G.'s 2nd ball.} dashed out, missed a short one, and was stumped by the Marmoset, retiring for 0 amidst general murmurs. The Ojibbeway succeeded him, and with George ran the score up to 52; a change was then effected, Alfred the Great went on with his patents, and broke through the O.'s system of defence. He obtained 17 judgematically as usual. Hadow the Unlucky only scored one, and retired breathing thunder. Edgar _{Hadow angry.} shared his fate. The Tormentor, being on his mettle, bowled in rare form; four wickets down for 67 runs. George was batting splendidly. The youthful Pick. was very lively, but took great liberties, which were not resented, at least his chances were not accepted. At luncheon 90 runs were obtained. George's time came when he had made 65, _{George's innings.} by exceedingly good play; he was much cheered on leaving the wickets; 103 runs for 5 wickets. Henley and Pickering were not parted until 134 were scored, of which the Lad secured 25. Henley the Strong succumbed to Alfred for 22; the stalwart son of Mars and Bellona having played very well for his runs. The Canadian contingent now appeared. The Brothers Brunel both showed good defence, and should have been sent in earlier. The innings closed for 168. The Captain's side then struck up an acquaintance with those lovely and tempting bowlers, Gilbert and Anna. Rose and Hornby were the first to taste the sweets, and the former was soon nauseated. Alfred scarcely had a taste of either, as in his hurry to meet the alluring Anna, he forgot the Red Indian with the large hand behind the wicket, and fell a victim to his hasty passion. The Monkey meanwhile got on good terms with both bowlers. Whelan made a dashing 10. The Monkey tried his gambols once too often, and was run out for a very dashing 22; he did warm Anna, and no mistake; 45 runs for 4 wickets was not creditable or easily credited. The golden opportunity of a Mammoth innings was thrown away. The Tormentor and Francesco, however, got together and put a new face on the

The Captain's side.

game. They made it very hot. Edgar did the
hot chestnut business again, in other words
he dropped a hot one, his palm was always
ready to try, but not always firm to hold.
He tried his luck at under-grounders, but the
only result was that runs came faster.
George supplemented Gilbert, who was as
usual hard to be persuaded that he was
getting togo, and Anna stepped into Togo.
Edgar's shoes. George must thank Pickering for a wicket, he very cleverly caught
the Saint after a score of 45, the second best
innings made during the day.

Francesco deserved a few runs, as nobody Francis in
the field.
fielded better than he did in every match.
The game was now interesting. Appleby
carried his bat out for 35, and when score
was called, the score had reached 115 for
5 wickets down. The game was resumed
on Saturday morning at 11·45. Spragge,
M.D., joined the Tormentor. The Doctor
died early. The Captain lost no time in
getting 8, when he fell a victim,—scalp,
No. 2, to the Red Indian; 7 for 130. The
Tormentor was bowled by George for a
lucky but effective 39. Gamble and Street

kept the ball rolling, both batting very steadily. Street was the first to become a thoroughfare to George's vehicle of destruction. The young Goose joined Gamble, and made a splendid hit for 5. Gamble after an excellent innings of 16 succumbed at last to the poet Harris. Bickle didn't make

Gosling. an effort, and the Green Goose carried his bat out for 9. The total 105, being only three runs behind their adversaries' score. Anna and the Ojibbeway were the first to appear on behalf of the batting interest. The locals said " a deputation of ladies had waited upon Mr. Grace, requesting him not to go in till after luncheon."

The Monkey soon accounted for the Indian at his own game, stumping him for

To quote. 4. Anna was bowled by Appleby, " playing back at a terrific overpitched shooter," according to the local. Brunel scored 12 in very good style, when he fell a victim to Rose: 3 wickets for 27. George and Henley got together, and some splendid

Slaughter of the innocents. hitting ensued,—George nearly killing two infants on the raised steps, and frightening the nurses out of their senses. 60 runs

were telegraphed at luncheon. The mid-
day meal was too much for George, as he
retired to the second ball bow'ed by
Appleby for another brilliant innings of 32;
"an innings that, played with all the style *To quote.*
and freedom of his first essay, did one's
heart good to witness, comprised of two 4's,
three 3's, four 2's, and singles." Gilbert
now appeared according to request, expectation ran high; it was not much disappointed. Henley retired for 14, well got;
80 runs for 5 wickets. Edgar retired for 4.
G. Brunel came in and made 4, a fine leg
hit. Gilbert then showed his muscle by
hitting Alfred out of the ground for 6, following it up by 7—a fine drive in itself, but
only worth 3—4 being voluntarily added by
overthrows. The Captain was angry, and
Appleby to soothe him bowled Brunel.
Parsons distinguished himself by nearly
running the Leviathan out, he escaped that
distinction merely to confer the honour upon
Alfred in the very next ball, of bowling
the great man—l b w—much to the disgust *Gilbert,*
of Gilbert and the spectators. Gilbert *l b w.*
growled, but it was of no use, out he went,

for 27 obtained in seven hits. Nothing else occurred, of a striking nature at least. The total reached 119, at 4·15, the Captain's side went in as for an easy victory. The lot collapsed for 63 runs, of which the Captain, who deserved a better fate, contributed 26; he was the last to leave the wreck. It was a poor display of batting, and can only be attributed to the want of interest shown by the side. It was to be deplored, as there was a goodly array of spectators, and it was the last opportunity of displaying their prowess before a Toronto public. "Boys will be boys" was the only audible remark of the Captain. He was defeated, but not disgraced.

MR. GRACE'S TWELVE v. MR. FITZ-GERALD'S TWELVE.

Score.

Mr. GRACE'S TWELVE.	1st inn.	2nd inn.
W. G. Grace, st Hornby, b Rose	0	leg b w, b A. Lubbock 27
Hon. G. Harris, st Hornby, b Rose	65	b Appleby 32
C. J. Ottoway, b A. Lubbock	17	st Hornby, b Rose... 4
W. H. Hadow, b Appleby	1	b Appleby............ 3
E. Lubbock, b Appleby	4	b Appleby............ 4
F. P. U. Pickering, b A. Lubbock	25	b Appleby 4
Lieut. Henley, b A. Lubbock	22	b A. Lubbock 14
J. Brunel, not out	15	b Rose 12

GRACE'S 12—*Continued.*

	1st inn.		2nd inn.
G. Brunel, b Appleby	13	b Appleby	4
B. Parsons, st Hornby, b Rose	2	c Fitzgerald, b Appleby	0
A Cameron, st Hornby, b Rose	0	not out	2
H. Furlong, st Hornby, b Rose	0	c Rose, b A. Lubbock	5
B 3, w b 1	4	Byes	8
Total	—168	Total	—119

MR. FITZGERALD'S TWELVE.

	1st inn.		2nd inn.
A. N. Hornby, run out	22	c Furlong, b Grace	2
W. M. Rose, c Pickering, b Grace	6	b Harris	8
A. Lubbock, st Ottoway, b Hadow	0	c and b Grace	11
J. Whelan, b Grace	10	c and b Harris	0
C. K. Francis, c Pickering, b Harris	45	c J. Brunel, b Grace	0
A. Appleby, b Harris	39	b Grace	0
Dr. Spragge, hit w, b Harris	0	c Cameron, b Grace	7
R. A. Fitzgerald, st Ottoway, b Hadow	8	not out	26
W. P. R. Street, b Harris	8	b Harris	0
R. G. Gamble, c and b Harris	16	c Harris, b Grace	0
E. J. Gosling, not out	9	b Harris	0
Bickle, b Harris	0	leg b w, b Grace	1
L b 1, w b 1	2	B 3, 1 b 4, w b 1	8
Total	—165	Total	—63

ANALYSIS OF THE BOWLING.

MR. GRACE'S TWELVE.

	Overs.	Maidens.	Runs.	Wickets.	Wides.
Rose	43–1	11	102	7	0
Appleby	69	32	99	9	0
A. Lubbock	29	6	70	6	0
Francis	2	1	4	0	0

MR. FITZGERALD'S TWELVE.

Grace	40	76	76	9	0
Hadow	20	3	81	2	0
Harris	34	15	45	10	0
E. Lubbock	4	1	18	0	0

The match was interesting in one sense, in that it brought out the natives in close comparison with the visitors. It showed some good cricket to be existent in Toronto ; some excellent fielding, and we must name especially Street, the longstop, Whelan, and Dr. Spragge. The batting, as a whole, was superior to that shown in the

Blake.

first match. Mr. Blake's successful efforts in preparing a wicket during the trying week deserve recognition. The sun was tropical, and the difficulties natural to the place and climate were increased by the great attendance, and the desire to practise by the numerous aspirants. Cricket was never watched with more interest, and the arrangements gave great satisfaction to all concerned.

Presenta-
tion.

The Captain presented a bat and a ball to the President of the Club. He expressed a wish that they should be held as champion prizes, presenting them in the name of the Marylebone Cricket Club.

Before leaving the ground, a hearty crowd gathered round the door of the dressing-room, and the Captain was " on the stump."

He thanked the kind friends before him for their cordial reception of his team, and felt glad for the opportunity to acknowledge in public his sense of the spirit which had led the cricketers of Toronto to invite himself and comrades to Canada. He was grateful as an Englishmen to that kindly spirit. It cemented the ties between the Old and New Country, and he felt convinced that a visit of this nature was not to be judged merely by its cricketing results. The Twelve were most cordially greeted on leaving the ground. We are glad to think that financially the week was a great success. The manager was well repaid for his large outlay, and a handsome balance was handed over to the Funds of the Club.

The Captain on the stump.

" In summing up the events of the week," (to quote from the *Mail*), " we cannot do better than publish the words of the English Captain, as, in feeling terms, he took leave of the Toronto Cricket Club. 'Never,' he said, 'had he and his friends spent a happier or more enjoyable week than they had passed at Toronto, and he and they would ever look back to it, and he

To quote. "The Mail."

hoped many years would not pass before they revisited the scenes of their present victories and amusements,' said, as it was, with all the bluff heartiness and honest sincerity that characterize the Secretary of the M.C.C., no further comment is necessary upon the brilliant success of the week, to mar which not one single *contretemps* has occurred of more significance than the pitching of a fly on a cow's back and its speedy removal by a switch of the tail." One more entertainment was in store for the Twelve. The lessee of the Lyceum Theatre had placed stalls at their disposal on Saturday evening. The Twelve went in perfect innocence, and in the garb of the period; imagine, if you can, their feelings upon entering the house, when the performance suddenly stopped, the band struck up Rule Britannia, and the gods above and the goddesses below rose with one accord in a tremendous acclaim of greeting. The cheering lasted several minutes. The Captain and his crew were completely staggered by the ovation. The actors took part in the hullabaloo, and the prompter had some diffi-

The Lyceum.

Rule Britannia.

The Gods.

culty in recalling them to their suspended
avocation. It was a genuine surprise to the
Twelve. It was also a kind farewell.
Within a few hours they had left Toronto
to meet new faces on fresh fields. It was
like leaving home. They parted with many Last words.
many friends they may never meet again,
but the cheers of that last evening in the
crowded theatre, and the pressure of one, if
not more than one, warm hand, said all that
words could say, or the heart could feel.

We cannot part with Toronto without an
expression of our thanks to Mr. Shears, for his Mr. Shears.
great attention to us at the Rossyn House. Rossyn
This magnificent hotel will compare to ad- House.
vantage with the best hotels in America. It
is by far the best in Canada. Its long and
lofty corridors admit of speedy ventilation;
for cleanliness, good attendance, and comfort
it is conspicuous in a country, where we shall
not be found fault with for saying that such
are not the leading characteristics of hotel
life.

We had but one regret in common, and The Clubs.
that was our inability to acknowledge properly the honour paid to us by the Royal

Canadian Yacht Club, the Toronto Club, and other public bodies who united in giving us so hearty a welcome to their hospitable town. Time willed it otherwise, and we were bound to time.

CHAPTER IX.

A HOT night's journey was in store for the The Muses.
Nine leaving Toronto at 11. 30 P.M. on Satur-
day evening, they arrived at London on
Sunday morning, September 8, at 7 A.M.

"The Nine" involves an explanation.
Sing, ye Muses, the charms that detained
the three. Who were the three Graces, and The Graces.
who were the three absentees? Suffice it
to record that the amorous Appleby, the
Ojibbeway and San Francisco had applied for leave to spend the Sabbath in
the same pew with three of the loveliest
ladies of Toronto, and leave was granted on

L

condition of their turning up in time for the morrow's match.

The morning of Sunday, September 8, was sultry and oppressive. The Nine crawled into the Tecompsee Hotel languid and dusty after the night's journey. The hotel was not up, the rooms were not ready, there was only one bath in the house, and it was not very clear where or when that one bath might be available. A fiend in human guise suggested a stroll to the Sulphur baths. It did not sound savoury, but by this time the nostrils were seasoned to oil. We were now in the kingdom of Paraffin. We had struck oil long before arriving at London, it struck us as very beastly, but then it must be remembered we had no share beyond the smell in this flourishing department of trade. Oil is cheap, not to say nasty; we had long been acquainted with its marvellous properties, we had detected it in every room and smelt it in every passage from Quebec to London. It was brought home to us here, or rather we were brought to its home.

The bread tasted of oil, the beer was impregnated with oil, the ice was oily, the

the

was
wled
lusty
s not
only
very
ht be
sug-
It did
; the
; now
struck
struck
oe re-
smell
. Oil
; been
es, we
t it in
n. It
er we

is im-
y, the

attendants were oily. We thought a sulphur bath would at least be free from the all pervading element; but no! there was oil on the troubled waters of the sulphur bath! The stroll was a half hour's walk through wide streets, at that early hour, without signs of life. It was not the cool, nor was it the fragrant hour of morn. The sulphur bath is extremely cold, we dipped our toes in it, but could not be persuaded to venture further. The oil was preferable to the sulphureous exhalation. The Thames is not *The Thames.* a magnificent river. The stream was very low and its colour creamy. Westminster Bridge is not a gorgeous structure. We passed St. Paul's Cathedral on our return to *St. Paul's.* the hotel. We were not tempted to linger in its precincts. London is a loyal town, it has its Pall Mall and Piccadilly, and later in the day we were pleased to find it had its loungers. It is called the Forest City. The neighbourhood is indeed lovely. It is the centre of a rich agricultural district. The Middlesex farmers rank amongst the best in Canada. Already preparations are being made for an Autumn exhibition of agricultural produce. London was founded about the year 1824, by General Simcoe. It does not show any signs of such antiquity. It appears to have started into life within the last ten years and to be now growing fast. The visitors were very hospitably entertained by several of the leading residents. Amongst them must be mentioned Mr. Beecher, Q.C., Messrs. Harris and Griffin. The attendance during the match was very gratifying, and a more appreciative circle had never yet been formed. It might have been a match in the Midland Counties of the Old Country. So to the cricket.

Cricket.   *Monday, Sept.* 9.—The Three did not turn up in time. The ground, as usual, deserves a remark. We walked over it before we were aware that we had passed the wickets. These were marked out on a small plateau, the only one visible, in dangerous vicinity to a long range of wooden buildings, afterwards discovered to be "The Barracks."

Rifle pits.   Rifle pits abounded on all sides. The barracks at some recent period must have sustained a siege. However a fair wicket was obtained, dead from thunder showers and

l about
It does
ity. It
hin the
ng fast.
ertained
.mongst
r, Q.C.,
endance
g, and a
yet been
h in the
ry. So

did not
sual, de-
it before
ssed the
a small
angerous
uildings,
rracks."
The bar-
have sus-
cket was
ers and

evidently not a run getting one. The first
question that arose was "How many" to How
allow for a swipe into the bedrooms of the many?
barracks. Was it a lost ball in the scullery?
Might the long-stop lean against the palings?
These little questions were soon amicably
adjusted. It was agreed that no Scotchman
should stand long-stop, the temptation to
scratch his back being too tempting to resist.
The Captain (of course) won the toss and in
the absence of one of "the gentlemen in
waiting," W. G. and Hornby went to the
wickets. The sun was now shining and the
ominous clouds that had copiously discharged
their contents up to twelve o'clock rolled
away. Messrs. Gillean and Wright bowling,
both fast and straight. Nothing occurred
till the fifth over, when "Mr. Grace was
caught by Henley, but it proved to be a
ground ball." The crowd was delighted "as
the umpire decided not out." It may as well A sell.
be stated that a hit to the fence scored 3,
and over the fence 4. The Monkey was
bowled in the tenth over of Gillean for 14.
Hadow, the Unlucky, went in. To quote again,
"He made a fine cut for 1 which was well

fielded by Mr. Despard, of the Bank of Montreal, at long leg." His stumps were then
scattered by Wright. Mr. G. had made a
few, but not without luck, he "gave a
splendid chance to Wright, as he sent the
ball straight up, but it was beautifully
muffled," 44 for 2 wickets. Alfred succeeded
and runs came quicker. A change was now
made. Ebberts taking Wright's place. "His
delivery was from the shoulder, and he bowls
a swift destructive ball." Alfred was printed
"Tubbock" in the scores. "Mr. Tubbock
was run out for 9," his own fault; 52 for 3
wickets, of which Gilbert owned 30. George
went in and "slipped a ball for 1;" Gilbert
was now sent home for a lucky score of 31,
very well caught off a good hit at deep
square leg by Hyman. The "Gentlemen in
waiting" had now arrived, and C. J. Ottoway went in. Runs were hard to get. The
Honourable George "was driven to his tent
by Gillean, his wicket being entirely flat-
tened out;" 56 for 5 wickets. The Ojibbeway
only made 1. The other "Gentleman in
W.," took his place, love had less effect upon
him for he made 12. Shooters made short

Gents in
waiting.

: of Mon-
ere then
made a
'gave a
sent the
beautifully
ucceeded
was now
e. "His
he bowls
s printed
Tubbock
52 for 3
George
Gilbert
e of 31,
at deep
cmen in
J. Otto-
t. The
his tent
ly flat.
bbeway
man in
ct upon
e short

work of the rest. The Unaffected only
arrived in time to carry his bat out for 1.
The innings closed for 89. The bowling of
Messrs. Gillean and Wright was admirable,
the fielding was creditable, the long-stopping
of Mr. Fradd to the swift bowling was ex- Fradd.
cellent. The Londoners were much pleased
at the small score obtained by the visitors.
It was the smallest hitherto obtained by
them. It may be attributed to the bowling
on a dead wicket being fast and straight, as
well as to the accurate fielding, the " return"
being very noticeable, and making it difficult
to achieve the second run for a hard hit.
The Cockneys went in at 4 P.M. and at 5.30 The
were all out for 55. Hymen played reso- cockneys.
lutely, with some luck, as he was badly
missed twice ; he hit well to leg and faced
the Tormentor, who bowled superbly, with
great spirit. Eleven Londoners laid an egg Eggs.
a piece, and being market day it led to some
merriment amongst the farmers' wives, six
of them made 1 run apiece, 10 wickets fell
for 43, and the remaining twelve contributed
a dozen. If it was difficult to the Twelve, it
was impossible for the Twenty-two to score.

It was calculated that at least seven thousand spectators were on the ground, and the receipts must have amply rewarded the outlay.

Cricket.

Sept. 10.—The return match was resumed at noon. Very heavy storms had saturated the ground during the night, so that the chances of the Twenty-two dismissing the Twelve for another short innings improved. W. G. and Ottoway went to the wickets, W. G. not very fit and the Ojibbeway languid after his exercise at the ball of the previous evening. W. G. had wisely declined the hop and should have been fit to run for the Derby. Gillean and Ebberts commenced the bowling. The O. was given out l b w, having made 6 while W. G. made 2. This does not often

The Monkey.

occur. The Monkey went in and caused much amusement by stealing runs, and with Gilbert's aid the score rapidly mounted. Dr.

Bray.

Bray has a curious corkscrew motion of the arm and provoked some laughter at his bowling. W. G. at last h t a ball over the fence, Which was only thirty-five yards from the wicket ; the first hit out, which showed how dead the ground was as well as how true the bowling. It was soon repeated, however.

The Monkey was the next to go, bowled by a shooter of Whelan's; his 21 consisted of one 3, one 2, and sixteen singles, 98 for 2 wickets. Alfred to the wicket, and W. G. again hit over the fence. At two o'clock luncheon was called, 112 for 2 wickets being telegraphed, of which W. G. laid claim to 64. He had been badly missed at square leg. On resuming play Gilbert was the first to leave, caught at long on for a score of 76, 130 for 3 wickets. His score consisted of one 5, four 4's, three 3's, eleven 2's, and singles. Hadow maintained his ill luck, being bowled for 0; 4 wickets for 131. Alfred only secured 8. The Captain had intimated that it was desirable not to prolong the innings if possible, and consequently there was a little slogging which soon terminated the innings. George obtained 10, and the small offerings thankfully received raised the score to 161, of which the large number of 24 was given by extras. No time was lost and the Twenty-two were very busy in putting pads on and taking them off, until time was called. The result of this process was that 10 wickets were disposed of for 45 runs. This unfor-

W. G.'s score.

The slog.

tunately necessitated another morning for the conclusion, and as time was pressing the third day's play commenced punctually at eleven.

Sept. 11.—The remaining eleven wickets gave little trouble. Hyman and Henley were very free with Rosa, but Appleby was ticklish at all times and allowed no liberties. The cockneys improved on their first journey by 10 runs.   Total 65.

ENGLAND v. LONDON.

ENGLAND.	1st inn.		2nd inn.
W. G. Grace, c Hyman, b Gillean	31	c Cook, b Henley ...	76
A. N. Hornby, b Gillean	14	b Whelan	21
W. H. Hadow, b Wright	2	b Henley	0
A. Lubbock, run out	5	c Neville, b Whelan	8
Hon. G. Harris, b Gillean	1	c Ebberts, b Saunders	10
C. K. Francis, b Ebberts	12	b Gillean	3
C. J. Ottaway, b Gillean	1	leg b w, b Gillean...	6
E. Lubbock, c Wells, b Ebberts ...	9	b Saunders	6
W. M. Rose, b Ebberts	2	c Ebers, b Saunders	0
F. Pickering, b Gillean	5	c Danks, b Saunders	1
A. Appleby, not out	1	not out	4
R. A. Fitz-Gerald, b Gillean	0	c Ebberts, b Gillean	2
B 5, l-b 1	6	B 12, l-b 3, w b 9	24
Total	—89	Total	—161

LONDON.	1st inn.		2nd inn.
Street, c Pickering, b Rose	0	c Grace, b Rose ...	2
Dayrill, b Appleby	1	c Hadow, b Rose ...	3
Neville, c Harris, b Grace	0	leg b w, b Grace ...	4
Wells, c Grace, b Rose	7	c Grace, b Appleby	0
Whelan, b Appleby	9	c Hornby, b Grace	0
Henley, c Ottaway, b Rose	2	b Appleby	9

; for the
he third
eleven.
wickets
ey were
as tick-
berties.
journey

2nd inn.
y ... 76
..... 21
..... 0
elan 8
iders 10
..... 3
n... 6
..... 6
lers 0
lers 1
.... 4
ean 2
b 9 24
... —161

2nd inn.
... 2
... 3
... 4
eby 0
ace 0
.... 9

LONDON—*Continued.*	1st inn.		2nd inn.
Goldie, b Appleby	0	b Appleby	2
Hyman, run out	18	b Appleby	9
Wright, c Ottaway, b Rose	0	c Grace, b Rose	0
Bray, b Appleby	1	absent	0
Shaw, b Rose	1	c Francis, b Grace	0
Patterson, c Grace, b Rose	1	b Appleby	0
Rae, b Appleby	0	b Grace	7
Saunders, c Fitz-Gerald, b Rose	0	c Grace, b Rose	0
Cooke, leg b w, b Rose	0	b Rose	4
Ebberts, b Appleby	1	b Rose	9
Bradbeer, c A. Lubbock, b Rose	1	b Rose	3
Fradd, c E. Lubbock, b Rose	0	absent	0
Despard, c E. Lubbock, b Rose	0	b Appleby	0
Danks, c A. Lubbock, b Rose	2	c Hornby, b Rose	1
M'Lean, b Appleby	7	c Grace, b Rose	2
Gillean, not out	0	not out	0
B 1, l-b 1, w b 2	4	B 1, l-b 1	2
Total	—55	Total	—65

This was not a bad win—130 runs to the
good. The batting of the Canadians was
again tested by the slow and fast ordeal of
Rose and Appleby, and the same remark applies to the Middlesex lads as to their neighbours. They did not do themselves justice;
the same unwillingness to open the shoulder,
the same preconceived dread of the straight
long hop. The Twenty-two were fair specimens
of the youth of Canada, and their bowling
was quite first class. The ground militated
against a good display of cricket, the dead
wicket equalising the good and indifferent

The Barracks.

player to a great degree. The Barracks, where luncheon was provided, are a pitiable sight. Rats and vermin had long since left them, as much too comfortless. They are rotting surely if slowly. The absence of the soldiers is as much deplored here as elsewhere. Mixing as we did with every class and listening to varied expressions of opinion, it is worthy of mention that we never heard

The Red Man.

the departure of the Red Man mentioned except with disapprobation. We do not pretend to analyse the policy, we only record facts. The ladies, as may well be supposed,

A bull.

are to a man, as they say in Ireland, against the withdrawal.

Matrimony is at a discount, and a street full of marriageable girls taunts the bachelor on the way to church in every town. The

Love.

young Canadian is too busy to love—or at least to flirt. The Red Man was always ready for either emergency. There are no

Flirts.

picnics, no strolls in the forest, no lunch at the barracks, no nothings that often led to something in the good old time.

The Londoners were not in any way behind Toronto in their desire to make the visit of the Twelve memorable. They had not been many hours at the Tecompsee Hotel before an elegant card was left upon the A card. Captain, bearing the following not strange device :—

CRICKET CLUB BALL.

IN HONOUR OF THE ENGLISH CRICKETERS.

The Members of the London Cricket Club request the pleasure of Mr. Fitzgerald's and Gentlemen Players of England company at the City Hall on Monday evening the 9th September, at half past eight o'clock.

Lady Patronesses.

Mrs. Walker.   Mrs. W. R. Meredith.   Mrs. Hyman.
Mrs. Street.   Mrs. B. Waterman.   Mrs. E. S. Birrell.
                Mrs. H. Waterman.

R. R. BROUGH,
Hon. Sec.

It is needless to say that the Twelve accepted, and a capital dance it was. A few fri. ds had followed the fortunes of the rovers. Amongst them one young being, who had come from a considerable distance for another dance with Alfred the Great. Her name will not transpire; nor may she, perhaps, know herself who she is under the tender soubriquet of "The Fly." It is a The fly. touching little story. Alfred caught a fly in one of the pauses of his wild waltz, and the lady had begged him to give it to her as a memento—imprisoning the helpless souvenir in her locket—a fly-leaf in a love-story, which we may fairly claim as original.

Stiff and Strong.

It was during the London match that the little difference between Stiff and Strong, the reporters, took place. London was very hospitable, and the reporters fell in for their share of the general greeting. Hence the adventure in which Strong and the lamp-post were the central figures. The Te-

Tecompsee.

compsee Hotel was not equal to the Rossyn.

Mosquitoes.

Mosquitoes were abundant here; we cannot say the same for the provisions, although the landlord was very civil.

Thunder.

On the night of the ball an awful thunder-storm gathered over the town; it broke in a

Lightning.

deluge of rain, accompanied by lightning, which defies description. Sheets of electric light illumined the dark sky, revealing vistas of the surrounding forest, and forming a display of the elements at war, such as is never witnessed in Europe. Earth, air, and water are on a grander scale; the elements have more elbow-room for their effects apparently—at any rate they leave that impression. Fires destroy whole towns; hurricanes sweep every sail off the waters; everything partakes of the wholesale on the great continent. The human body does not increase in proportion to the room allotted it to grow in; on the contrary, it rather decreases in size.

Mr. Becher, Q.C., entertained several of the Twelve each evening of their stay; his house is situated overlooking the Thames, and it might almost be in Richmond Park; forest glades in every direction; forest trees of no mean dimensions. The humming-birds hovered over the flowers in his garden, evidently tended by fair hands, and bright with thoughts of English homes. Several birds of beautiful plumage were seen here. The vicinity of the forest city is very attractive—seen, as we saw it, in its summer garb. Mr. Harris was equally attentive to others of the Twelve, and the visit, though short, was prolific of friendship. The match concluded in time for the Captain to take up a challenge presented by two fair ladies of London. They were the champion croquet

The champion croquet match.

players of the district, and the Captain and W. G., with some trembling, took up the mallet. Victory inclined to the visitors, not without a good struggle; the Captain's object in visiting America was not to be beaten at any game; it will be seen hereafter whether he succeeded. It is satisfactory,

The junior mallets.

also, to record the success of the junior croquet game, in which Alfred the Great and George, by good luck, managed to get home first in an encounter with two young ladies just out of the schoolroom. But the scream of the approaching engine warns us to take our tickets for Hamilton. The platform was crowded with kind friends, and we were off at last with the warmest wishes for our success in the States.

ain and
up the
ors, not
in's ob-
beaten
ereafter
sfactory,
junior
eat and
et home
g ladies
scream
to take
rm was
were off
our suc-

CHAPTER X.

THE route from London to Hamilton was a
matter of four hours on the Great-Western
Railway. This is an important line, and of
rapidly increasing traffic. It leads direct to
the Pork Corner at Chicago. Barrels of pork Pork.
and bushels of corn beyond weight and
measure pass this way. The line is well
laid and fenced, and the carriages excellent.
We must not forget our indebtedness to the
manager of the Great-Western, as also to
the manager of the Grand Trunk, who
passed the Twelve over their respective
lines, and to whose courtesy the comfort of
the travellers owes more than we can repay

M

in thanks. The admirable system of checking luggage deserves a passing recognition. Our united baggage never amounted to less than fifty, and often as many as sixty pieces. Not one piece was lost throughout the tour that can be charged to any neglect on the part of the railway companies. Brass checks numbered are given for each article, a corresponding check being attached to it by a leathern strap. Baggage is given up to anybody who presents the right number; but until that is done, the article remains in the custody of the company. The system gives much trouble to the company's servants, but it is a great saving of anxiety to the passenger, who does not trouble himself about his baggage until he arrives at his hotel, when he sends a porter with his checks to the station.

Pulman.   Whilst we are on the line, let us say a word for Mr. Pulman. Many night journeys were before us; one was now behind us, so that we can speak from experience. The Pulman car is an ingenious attempt to reinstate Morpheus as the God of the Sleepers. It has partially succeeded. When   the

sleepers under the carriage are indisposed to
activity, and the sleepers in the carriage are
inclined to sleep, Morpheus can, indeed, hold
his court. Pulman has the monopoly of his
carriages on every line in the States and
Canada. He receives so much per head, an
extra charge being made for each passenger
that takes a bed. An attentive official in a
very short time converts the seats into beds.
It is hard to say where the linen comes from,
but a clean bed is the work of a moment;
curtains are let down, and the snoring that
follows too surely announces that the occupants are at their devotions to the sleepy
god. The beds are on two tiers. There is
not much choice between them; if you
prefer the upper, you must take your chance
of the dust; if you lay down in the lower,
you must make up your mind to be a trifle
short of air. It is simply a choice of two
evils. We cannot say that you will awake
refreshed; dusty and dry in the mouth was
our experience; but as reading is impossible, owing to the bad light afforded by the
railway-lamps, we think that the alternative

presented by Pulman on a long journey is a boon to the traveller.

No smoking.

Great decorum prevails in the railway cars. Much to our surprise, smoking is strictly prohibited, save at the tail end of the train; we tried it on often, but never succeeded in cajoling the stern conductor. Women are especially protected; they probably assert their rights more strongly than in England; but we were struck with the deference shown to them, not only in the railway cars but in other places.

Cricket.

Thursday, Sept. 12.—A good night's rest at the excellent Royal Hotel sent the Twelve as fit as five-year-olds to the ground. The late rains had made the wickets dead—that was apparent to the eye—but great care had evidently been displayed. The out-fielding was excellent. The ground was not large, and could be got out of on three sides without much effort; but it looked like runs. The Captain won his fifth toss. W. G. and Ottoway to the front as usual——Messrs. Wright and Kennedy bowling. The fielding was of an improved order, and great vigilance was demanded by the batsmen. W. G. was

The fifth toss won.

stuck up by Wright, and nearly coopered
before scoring; he was the first to leave,
bowled by Wright, for 17. The Ojibbeway W. G. out.
batted very carefully, and, with George, piled
up the score, which had not been materially
assisted by the Monkey, Hadow the Unlucky, or Alfred the Great. Rain began to Rain.
fall at three o'clock, and several runs into
the tent had been made. The match was
eventually stopped at five o'clock, Ottoway
and George carrying their bats out, after a
fine display of cricket. Score, 101 for 4
wickets.

Sept. 13.—The game was resumed at Cricket.
11.15. The weather still looked doubtful,
and the attendance was not so great as
might have been expected. The wicket was
not improved by the night's rain. Ottoway
was soon caught. He was well applauded
on leaving the wicket; his 45 runs were not
all singles, and he deserved great praise for
his patience, as the bowling required playing.
117 runs for 5 wickets. The Saint was not San Fran
long "in waiting"; he made a fine hit to cisco.
leg, and was most unluckily caught. The
Unassuming gave an easy chance, which

was not accepted, at short-leg, following it up by an offer to wicket-keeper, also disdained. Encouraged by these slights, he began to hit, and a fine dashing innings he played. George, meanwhile, had gone to his rest, having achieved 38 "in his usual finished and graceful style." The Unassuming gave two more chances ere he was accepted, the last chance being the hardest; but he was caught splendidly by Spragge, M.D., in the long-field, running at full speed, and with one hand. The local said, "The great bowler has batted throughout the Canadian trip in a manner that would have justified his place in the team, quite independently of his left-hand peculiars." This is quite true. Edgar had been merry in his short innings of 10. The lad nearly killed the excellent umpire, Mr. Barber, hitting him hard in the breast, and thereby losing a 4 to leg. Slogging was the order of the day. Rosa was in luck and vigour. The Captain in vigour, but not in luck, as he was caught off the prize hit of the day, a veritable teapot,—a clever catch of Mr. Eberts, the long-field. The score 181, all told. Luncheon

Appleby.

*The lad.
Pick.*

Lunch.

llowing it
also dis-
ights, he
inings he
gone to
his usual
Jnassum-
he was
hardest;
Spragge,
ll speed,
l, " Th-
out the
ld have
e inde-
' This
r in his
r killed
ng him
a 4 to
e day.
Japtain
caught
le tea-
long-
icheon

was now discussed. At 2.15 the Hamiltonians commenced their innings. The first six wickets fell for 15 runs. Whelan then let go the painter, and Rosa's eyes sparkled with an unwonted glare behind his crystals. George went on for one over. This is too good to pass over slightly. Whelan made 12 runs off it—one " out of the ground," one An over, " 4," and one " 2." George recommended a 12 runs. change, and retired to the uttermost part of Poor George. the field. It was, perhaps, desirable. W. G. took the ball, and finally Whelan fell to the Tormentor; he made 31 runs in a short space of time by very free hitting. This was the largest score made by any Canadian. Largest score. Eberts played well for 9, and Spragge, Harper, and Shaw each contributed 7. " Praise undeserved is censure in disguise," so we will not butter anybody else. The total amounted to 86. Being in a minority of 95, there was nothing to be done but " to follow," much to the disappointment of the Hamiltonians, who had flattered themselves with achieving a more distinguished position. A few more Whelans, and they would have done so. The old story still in everybody's

Slocs bitter pill. mouth—a dread of the slows; the enigma not answered yet. On the second journey the first six wickets only realised 12. Whelan again showed his power, but no judgment; he hit one "out of the ground" in his score of 12. Seven wickets for 24. The *Skittles.* ludicrous part of the match now set in. To explain it, or rather to apologise for it, it is necessary to state that the Twelve were very anxious to conclude the match before nightfall. Niagara was in thrilling propinquity, time was short, and every moment precious that could be snatched from cricket and devoted to the Falls; hence it was arranged to play the match out, even if link-*Night.* men had to be employed. At 5.20 the light was diminishing, and the shadows growing long. The reporters were at fault. One said "We believe that about this period somebody made a 3, and somebody else a 2, but we saw neither performance." At 5.55 ten wickets were down for 43 runs.

The moon. The moon now rose, and lost balls no longer dreaded. However, the shadows deepened, and an occasional cloud passing over the moon, enabled the batsman to steal

enigma
journey
ed 12.
but no
md " in
t. The
1. To
t, it is
were
before
ropin-
oment
ricket
is ar-
link-
light
)wing
One
eriod
lse a
At

: no
lows
sing
teal

runs; in one case two were run to point. The spectators, much amused, encroached considerably upon the wickets. The field at this moment formed a tableau which should be perpetuated. They were obliged to stoop almost to the ground, it being impossible otherwise to follow the ball. The Captain made a catch " in oscuro," which was *The catch in oscuro.* scarcely credited, and is still a matter of doubt to all but himself. At 6.25 eighteen wickets were down for sixty. Mr. Harper came in, and, according to the local, " he was better up in lunacy than his brethren," as he stole several runs. " The Englishmen now crouched upon the ground to get a sight *A crouch.* of the ball—Hornby lying at full length, and the excitement was at its height, the last man being in, and darkness imminent." *An eclipse.* " Grace went on with fast underhand; in Rosa's next over Buckle made 3 to square leg—the field believing the ball to be in an opposite direction. The last wicket was hard to get, but it fell at last to an uncompromising sneak. It was skittles rather *A sneak.* than cricket, and was only justified by the necessities of the case. It must, however, be mentioned that the best wickets had fallen whilst there was still light, and the result of the match was never in doubt. The result was in favour of the Twelve by one innings, and 16 runs.

Presentation of bat.　The Captain presented Mr. Swinyard with a bat, to mark his sense of the trouble he had taken to promote the success of the expedition, as well as to testify to his successful efforts with the bat and the ball.—Score:

ENGLAND v. HAMILTON.

ENGLAND.

W. G. Grace, b Wright...... 17	A. Appleby, c Spragge, b Henley 35
C. J. Ottoway, c Eberts, b Kennedy.. 45	W. M. Rose, not out...... .. 6
A. N. Hornby, b Wright ... 2	F. U. Pickering, c Totten, b Swinyard.................. 2
A Lubbock, b Kennedy...... 13	R. A. Fitz-Gerald, c Eberts, b Henley 0
Hon. G. Harris, b Wright... 38	B 5, l-b 1, w b 4, n b 2 12
W. H. Hadow, c Swinyard, b Kennedy.................. 1	
E. Lubbock, c Shaw, b Henley 10	
C. K. Francis, c Shaw, b Kennedy..................... 0	Total................. 181

HAMILTON.	1st inn.	2nd inn.
Hebert, c Hornby, b Rose	3	c and b Grace 0
Street, b Rose	0	b Grace.............. 0
Spragge, hit w, b Grace.....	7	b Grace.............. 3
Henley, b Rose	1	b Rose 7
Crossthwaite, b Rose	2	b Rose 0
Kennedy, run out	1	st Ottoway, b Rose 2
Whelan, b Appleby.................	31	st Ottoway, b Grace 12
Swinyard, c Hornby, b Rose	5	c Pickering, b Rose 0

ets had
and the
doubt.

'elve by

rd with
ıble he
the ex-
uccess-
Score :

ge, b
.... 35
.... .. 6
ɔtten,
...,.... 2
berts,
.... 0
n b 2 12

.... 181
2nd inn.
.. 0
.. 0
.. 3
.. 7
.. 0
ᵉ 2
c 12
ᵉ 0

HAMILTON—*continued.*	1st inn.	2nd inn.	
Van Allan, not out	3	b Grace	0
Hope, hit w, b Rose	0	c Pickering, b Grace	12
Wright, st Ottoway, b Rose	5	b Rose	3
J. Smith, b Grace	0	c Appleby, b Grace	8
Clouston, run out	1	b Grace	3
Shaw, b Rose	6	c Pickering, b Rose	6
Cummings, b Grace	0	b Rose	2
Totten, leg b w, b Grace	0	b Rose	2
Eberts, b Rose	9	c A. Lubbock, b Rose	1
Harper, b Rose	7	c Fitz-Gerald, b Grace	8
Gough, b Rose	0	run out	2
Bickle, c Rose, b Grace	0	not out	5
Clarke, run out	0	b Rose	0
Woolverton, c Ottoway, b Grace	0	b Grace	0
B 4, w b 1	5	B 2, l-b 1	3
Total	—36	Total	—79

Mr. Swinyard entertained the Twelve at his house, and a large party assembled to do honour to the occasion. A few speeches were delivered, or it would not have been a Canadian banquet. W. G. uttered his fourth; this time in reply for "The Ladies." It was breaking new ground for the Unapproachable; but he acquitted himself with his usual brevity, and reading "ladies" for "bat, ball, and ground," and consulting his previous orations, you will have speech number four in its integrity :—The Twelve are greatly indebted to their worthy host; he had played against them in several

**IMAGE EVALUATION
TEST TARGET (MT-3)**

matches ; they appreciated his efforts to
promote the success of his own side, and
they recognised in the good cricketer the
kind host and zealous promoter of the
Canadian expedition. The Captain had an
agricultural acquaintance, to whom he had
written at Hamilton. He had emigrated
twenty years ago from a small village in
The Bucks Bucks. He is now a landed-proprietor of
farmer. thirty-five acres. The Captain knew him at
once by his family nose, and the worthy
man did not seem to be proud of his
heraldry. He is a fair average specimen
of the successful agricultural labourer. He
has married, and has a large family; he
has bought his farm, and is perfectly independent. He was quite angry at the
Captain refusing to stay with him; his wife
joined her protest ; they could not brook
the idea of anybody hailing from their native village taking shelter anywhere than
under their roof. It was very kindly meant,
but the necessities of the Captain's situation
prevented his accepting the offer. The
anecdote is mentioned by way of confirming
the attachment of the settlers to the old

country.   The farmer brought a load of
apples for the benefit of the Twelve : these Apples.
were very useful in preventing an inroad of
small boys over the palings into the tent.
Apples are very abundant, and peaches like- Peaches.
wise.   The latter are very poor to eat—
shrivelled and picked before they are ripe.
The peach and apple orchards are a feature
of this district.   The farming is of a very
high order, the soil prolific.   The Captain's
agricultural friend was in despair about his
apple crop.   He had more than he knew
how to dispose of.   A week with the Twelve
would have lightened his mind and the sur-
plus crop.

There is just a savour of Yankeedom in
Hamilton, sufficient to denote the vicinity of
the States, otherwise the tone of the place is
Scotch.   It is a very busy town.   The
barber is an institution of the country ; he The barber.
is attached to every large hotel.   The Hamilton barber was a very good specimen of his
class—as independent as Robinson Crusoe.
We generally found him smoking a pipe in a
shaving chair.   He cut your chin with quite
an air of condescension, and looked as if he

had shed his own blood, instead of yours, in a good cause. He hailed from the old country; but twenty-five years had put a lather on him of freedom that another fifty in his native land wouldn't wipe off. We met several notabilities here—amongst them M'Giverin, the humorous orator, Mr. M'Giverin, a great the orator. railway authority and the Joe Miller of Living- Hamilton. A brother of Dr. Livingstone—a stone. very strong likeness of the great traveller; he believes in Stanley, which was cheering. The chief During an interval of play on the cricket- of the two nations. ground, we were struck by the strides of a very tall man, crossing the ground in our direction. His appearance was very peculiar —very tall, in very tight trousers, and a low-crowned hat. Imagine if you can, our disillusion—he revealed himself to us as the Cooper-ed "Last of the Mohicans." We should never again. have guessed it. Stripped of his toggery, he was a Red Indian, the chief of the Iro- quois Nation; accoutred as he was, he is an The Solor. attorney of Hamilton—a strange combination of character under one skin. It is literally true. Our tall friend is the lineal descend- ant of the great chief of the Iroquois Nation,

who led his tribes from the unwelcome
thraldom of the young States to the Dominion
of the Great Father, who under the name of
George, then ruled over Canada. · The tribes George III.
own a large tract of land not many miles
from Hamilton : they are partially reclaimed
to civilization, but still retain many traces
of their original independence.   We cannot suppose that the chief who accosted us
sustains his almost regal pretensions in tight
trousers, there must be times when he ap- The chief
pears in his native tar and feathers.   We in trousers.
could not help recalling the story of Bruce. Bruce.
We are almost afraid that we did not pay
proper respect to the representative of the
Five Nations.   But it was impossible, with
our mind full of Cooper, the history of
Canada, Champlain, and La Salle, to look
upon a man in a low-crowned hat as having red blood in his veins, such as flowed ,
in the wild denizens of the prairie.   It was
wrong on our part, but the inclination to
smile was irresistible.   The chief was most
affable ; he extended the hospitality of his
nation to the Twelve, and was most pressing
in his offers to welcome them to his wig-

wam. There was no mistaking the cordiality of the red man, even in the disguise of a black coat. The Twelve very much regretted that their engagements would not permit of the excursion. The solicitor

Ugh ! breathed a deep guttural sigh, and strode away. An interesting episode in our tour was thus unfortunately lost. We watched his tall form for several minutes as he stalked through the crowd ; there was an air of disappointment about him, and his eyes gleamed with a spark of ancient fire. We never met a real Indian again, and we never met a

Red tape and red type. lawyer without thinking of the Red type.

General remarks. This chapter cannot be concluded without a few general remarks. Our Canadian tour proper was now completed. We had played five matches, and had been successful in all. We had expected to find stronger batting, but were not prepared to meet such good

Bowling. bowling. It is not too much to say that the bowling department, represented by Messrs. Maclean, Laing, Brodie, Swinyard, Wright, Gillean, and Eberts, was most effective ; any one of these gentlemen might bowl in a first-class match with a fair prospect of success. The fielding cannot admit of equal praise. There were many exceptions, if any must be named, let it be Messrs. Spragge, M.D., Hope of Toronto, Hyman of London, and Whelan. But many catches were dropped: in this particular the Twelve set a bad example on several occasions. To the demoralisation of the batting the defeat of the Canadians is due. It will be gathered from our history that it is difficult to explain. The Twelve, with the exception of Appleby, had not a first-class bowler amongst them. Rose bowled at times remarkably well, at others he was as plain as a pikestaff. Many wickets fell to longhops, such as would never have bowled a boy at a small school in England. The question remains to be answered, whether there will be any good practical result from the visit of the Twelve. We think there will be. We believe that the visit has given a stir to cricket; it has demonstrated the weak points, and has illustrated the strong ones. The bowlers as a class must feel proud of their exploits. Had they been backed by their field, the results would have been closer. W. G., especially,

Spragge, M.D.

The question.

N

W. G.'s.
luck.

was lucky beyond the ordinary lot of mortals. The batsmen will practise slow bowling, and will learn that it only requires patience and the proper use of the legs. Not to put them before the wicket, and run the risk of a blind umpire; but to have them ready to run to meet the *slow drop* ball; the batsman that is on his legs, not glued to his crease, will

The lob-
ster.

break the heart of the wiliest lobster. We are not preaching the doctrine of a swiper; the ball must be played hard and low, but to play a longhop or half-volley calmly to a field is to waste the energy of the cricketer and the time that can be devoted to the game. The game must be forced with slow

Hit! hit!

bowling. Hit with judgment, but always hit. Runs will be made through the best fieldsmen if you force them continually. We cling to a belief that a better match would have resulted in many places with less in the field. We almost wish that an eleven of Canada had been selected from the Dominion. With the one exception of a wicket-keeper, who never turned up, we saw the making of a good eleven out of the ranks of our antagonists. It must not be forgotten that the English Twelve had the Mammoth with The mammoth. them; his bat commands victory on the side for which it is wielded; his rapid scoring against twenty-two, allowing for luck, contributed vastly to the success of the Twelve. Many of the Twelve did not bat their best, and in some measure the crushing score already attained, made several players indifferent to their individual performance. This will account for the moderate scoring of several distinguished bats. The Canadians Types. must have learnt something from the terrific hitting of Hornby, Francis, and Pickering. The patient had his type in Ottoway; the unlucky could console himself by the example of Hadow; grace and elegance were represented by A. Lubbock and Harris; the man with a style too pronounced or too long persevered in to alter would take hope from Edgar.

The cricketer commencing cricket at a later period than most of his compeers, has Rose for an example; whist for the unassuming and hard-working, no better type can be afforded than Appleby, who bowled all day, went in when he was told, and obtained a

The
apostles.

very high average of runs. We may reasonably presume, therefore, that the apostles
were fitted to teach something, and that
some good must result from their mission. If
it tends to promote a love for the game, the
expedition will have been successful; if it
leads to another mission on less ambitious
terms, it will be of great service. No
pleasanter mission can be devised for the
autumn, and we feel confident that Canadian
cricketers would welcome again an eleven
from England. Let the next series of
matches be between foes of equal number.
The honours will be more equally divided.
It will be less disgrace to lose, it will be
equal honour to win. From a social point
of view there can be no question of the success of the expedition. All classes were
glad to greet the English Twelve. Their
mission as cricketers was duly acknowledged;
but the occasion was a fair one, and was
taken advantage of, to show the visitors that
the heart of Canada is not so much wrapped
up in love for the national game, as prompted
by the warmest attachment to English institutions.

The Twelve did not leave Hamilton without an opportunity of making the acquaintance of their fair entertainers.

They found a card on their table when The ball. they arrived.

PUBLIC BALL.
IN HONOUR OF THE ENGLISH CRICKETERS.

The pleasure of the English Cricketers' company is requested at the Royal Hotel, Hamilton, on Friday evening, 13th September, at 9 o'clock.

Patronesses.

Mrs. Buchanan.	Mrs. John Brown.	Mrs. Edward Brown.
Mrs. Irving.	Mrs. Mair.	Mrs. Ramsay.
Mrs. M'Givena.	Mrs. Swinyard.	Mrs. A. Macinness.
	Mrs. Villiers.	

H. G. RITCHIE,
Hon. Sec.

As at London, so at Hamilton, the fair Canadians did their best to make the Twelve quite incapable for exercise on the morrow in the field. The ball and supper were on the most handsome scale. It was the last opportunity, and many were the whispers and fond the farewells

CHAPTER XI.

THE Canadian tour had been brought to a
successful termination. The second great
object of the expedition was now attained.
Whatever might befal the cricketing programme, there was one thing always beyond
the freak of fortune. It had been one of the
mainsprings that moved the machine in its
earliest stage. The Captain had clenched
his bargain with the prospect of Niagara. A
cloudless sky and a hot sun ushered in the
morning of *September* 14. At 9 A.M. the
Twelve left Hamilton, arriving at Clifton at
11 A.M.; here they chartered carriages and
drove to the Clifton House. The road is
well known; the deep chasm, wooded to the

brink; the bright-green current freckled with foam, the gossamer suspension bridge spanning the ravine with its graceful length, bending and whispering to each breath of air. The increase of foam in the water beneath, the sullen roar that first strikes the ear, the feathery cloud floating into the clear sky from one point only in a spiral column, these first indications of the approach to Niagara are they not written in every diary? Our sentiments we cannot reproduce; the feelings on the first view of the Great Falls are beyond poetry; words do not rise spontaneously upon the lips, as, entranced with the majesty of the falling water, you gaze on the scene before you; words cannot describe all you feel when the first sensation has passed away. The feeling is that of absorption. It is fashionable to say that you are disappointed at first. There is this much truth in the allegation. You have been led to believe in the height rather than in the weight of water; your first view of the Falls is generally obtained from the high bank immediately opposite to the American Fall, and half a mile from the Canadian. You do not look up to either Fall, your eye crosses on the same level with the mighty mass of broken water; you must descend to the brink of the stream ere you can look up, so that it is on your second view and not on your first that you realize the height which your fancy has painted. If you are disappointed then, you had better plunge at once into the boiling stream, your life will have no nobler end in view. The roar is not so audible as many writers state; the Falls were almost in view ere we heard it. This probably depends upon the wind, but an air of exaggeration may reasonably be allowed to blow from *Hennepin.* such a source. Its first historian, Hennepin, sounded the gamut, and if the Great Fall does not gain by anybody's description, it certainly does not lose any material attributes. Hennepin describes it as 600 feet high, "as composed of two great cross streams of water and two falls, with an isle sloping along the middle of it. The waters which fall from this horrible precipice do foam and boil after the most hideous manner imaginable, making an outrageous noise, more terrible than that of thunder, for when the wind blows out of the south their dismal roarings may be heard more than fifteen leagues off." This is strong language, from a clergyman too, in 1679. Hear what Baron La Honten saith, in 1687 :—"As for the waterfall of Niagara 'tis 700 or 800 feet high, and half a league wide. Beasts and fish are drawn over the precipice and serve for food to the Iroquois, who take 'em out of the water with their canoes." In 1721, a more accurate account is given by Charlevoix :— "I am inclined to think we cannot allow the height to be less than one hundred and forty feet." That Niagara has presented various aspects during the short period of its acquaintance with white men may be gathered from the fact that Father Hennepin, its first story teller, ascribes three falls to it, and another reverend gentleman, the Abbé Picquet, who visited it seventy years later, mentions no less than six falls, three on each side of Goat Island. Large masses of rock have fallen within late years. The Table Rock has disappeared, the natural "detritus" must be constant, and geologists, who stick at nothing, go so far as to say, that some

Baron La Honten.

Charlevoix.

Abbé Picquet.

day the tourist who has paid his ticket to Niagara and ordered rooms at the Clifton House, will find the Great Falls removed for the season to some point more fashionable at that period and nearer to Lake Erie. A clever little book is sold at the Falls, from which we have drawn all our facts, and a little of our romance. From it we learn that Niagara has been spelt in forty different ways, beginning with Ouquihaara. We prefer the fortieth—Niagara, though all are not agreed on the proper accent to give that. The American Fall is ten feet higher than the Canadian; the depth of the central Horse-shoe Fall has been proved to be at least twenty feet. A vessel was chartered to make the descent in 1827. It had a few passengers of the brute creation on board.

The bear.
Bruin.
Several did not survive the passage: a few geese escaped, and a bear is reported to have seen mischief brewing and to have left the ship before it made its last dip, and to have escaped to shore. The ship's hull was known to be eighteen feet in depth, and she was completely submerged.

Cave of the Winds.
The Cave of the Winds is farmed by an

enterprising Yankee. For a dollar and a half
you can be made thoroughly uncomfortable,
and yet experience a novel sensation. As a
visit to the cave confers a diploma upon the
traveller, we will describe it. The cave itself
is formed by the wearing away of the shale
rock beneath the edge of the American Fall,
where it touches Goat Island. The water
that falls over this edge of the rock is of
less volume than the remainder of the cataract.
The space between the water and the rock at
the bottom may be some twelve or fourteen
feet. To arrive at this cave it is necessary,
in the first place, to descend by a winding
staircase to the foot of the Fall. The costume
of the visitor is very striking : felt sandals
for the feet, thick flannel suit for the body,
and nothing for the head. On emerging
from the staircase, the eye is blinded with
spray, and in two minutes the garments are
saturated ; descending still, the path is secured by a light handrail, and by the time
you are chilled to the marrow you have
emerged from the spray and are basking in
the bright sun at the margin of the river.
Looking up, you see the immense cataract

thundering above you; rainbows gather
round you; the prismatic colours enveloped
each of the party as they grouped together
shivering on the damp rocks. It was ludicrous and beautiful. The uncouth vest-
ments, the half-drowned look, the chattering
teeth, on one side of the picture; on the
other, the grand spectacle of Nature, the
mocking rainbow, the eternal roar. There
was little time for rapture. The guide took
the lead, and over the slippery rocks and on
to a narrow plank the party began the
ascent towards the Cave. A strong north
wind hurled the spray of the greater Fall
with terrific force against the face, the water
fell in drops of lead upon the bare head,
blindness succeeded to choking, choking
gave way to gasping almost for life itself;
the breath is suspended; a moment of relief
is gained when the Cave is reached, but the
molten shower still descends; a sense of ex-
haustion pervades the system. The beauty,
the grandeur, the novelty of the moment is
indeed intense, but your one wish is to get
out of it; your only anxiety how, and your
greatest pleasure, when you do. The Mon-

gather
eloped
gether
as lu-
vest-
tering
on the
e, the
There
e took
and on
in the
north
er Fall
water
head,
hoking
itself;
f relief
out the
e of ex-
beauty,
ment is
to get
id your
e Mon-

key was at the last gasp, he shot by those in advance, and before the door latch opened, which guards the entrance to this Inferno of water, he had clambered up it and was over it, and we found him chattering with cold, and were very glad to join him once more in the bright sun, in an atmosphere less like that of a milldam, and with a sensation of having escaped drowning by a miracle; such, at least, were the sensations of most of the party. George, curiously enough, liked it so much, as to repeat it the following day. Rose cautiously abstained from being washed in the shower.

The diploma is given by the proprietor. Diploma of He renews the ladders and platforms in the drowning. spring—they are destroyed by the ice every winter. On calm days the guide declared that ladies frequently remain for hours in the Cave and about it. Nymphs and Nereids might do so with pleasure, but our experience of water on the brain would not lead us to renew acquaintance with the Niagara shower-bath under a dollar a drop.

A copy of the diploma is annexed.

The certi-
ficate.

CAVE OF THE WINDS, AMERICAN SIDE.

This is to certify

that ———————————————— has passed through

THE CAVE OF THE WINDS,

at the Foot of Goat Island, and Behind the Central Fall.

G. W. WRIGHT, Lessee.

THOS. CONROY, Guide.

Given under this hand this

15th day of September, 1872.

The height of the Cave is 100 feet; the
diameter, 60 feet; width, 100 feet.

It is pleasant to look back upon, and un-
doubtedly no such intense conviction of the
weight of water that is hurled over the Fall
can in any other way be attained. One
glimpse at the avalanche of water, as our
faculties wavered between blindness and
drowning, will never forsake us. There is not
the slightest danger, according to the guide,
at any one point; if the foot should slip
off the plank, there are only a few inches
of water, and it is impossible for a human
being to be brought into the vortex, or even
near to the central volume of the Fall. We
cannot, at the same time, recommend the
Cave of the Winds to the weak of heart;

nor do we think there is much pleasure derived from the eyes being blinded with spray, or the lungs in distress, and blows raining as if from a prize-fighter's gloved hand upon the bare head. We advised everybody to try it if only for the diploma's sake, which confers a distinction on the traveller, and something less than a dollar and a half on two deserving guides.

A far more enjoyable sensation is that of *The Current Bath.* the Current Bath. These baths are so constructed that the water above the Fall on the American side is divided into sluices, which feed the baths; a small cabin is built over the water, the sluice is raised, and wading into the bath, and holding by a rope, the whole force of the stream can be enjoyed with a sense of delight; open bars allow the stream to pass through the bath at the farther end. The water was much warmer than might be expected; we had noticed the warmth of the St. Lawrence when bathing at Brockville, and were again struck with the high temperature of the river below the Canadian Falls; yet this rapid, turbulent cataract chafes beneath a coat of ice for many months.

To see Niagara in the summer, all allow is only to half see it. It has beauty at all seasons, at all hours; but it must be surpassingly beautiful beneath the magic touch of winter—arresting the spray on every branch, detaining the wave in fantastic curl, bridging the torrent that seems to-day to brook no restraint and yielding only to that irresistible current, which carries the waters of half a continent along with it.

The ball.   The Twelve gave a ball at the Clifton House. It was not a great success. They had hoped to induce a great many of their fair friends from the various towns of Canada to honour the farewell performance. Many things militated against it, and only a select few attended to the summons. These were amongst the fairest, so that there was little heartburning or despair. To swell the throng a general invitation was sent to the hotels on the American side. A very motley group was gathered together. The ball-room at Clifton House is handsome and capacious. The hearts of the Twelve sank on entering it; a solemn row of strangers lined the walls, enlivened only by an occasional eye-glass raised inquiringly as one after another the Twelve appeared. It required an effort to start it, but, thanks to a capital band, a little life was soon set going; a thaw set in, the ice melted, and the English and American elements combined cheerfully. A mistaken little Yankee annoyed the Captain by insinuating that the American ladies could not get partners; as the ladies he alluded to, by their appearance, should not have danced for many years, and as at that moment the Captain himself was three dances deep with one fair American, he treated the insinuation with disdain. The dance ended pleasantly, and the neighbourhood of the Falls led to moonlight rambles. Appleby was quite at home, though at one time it was feared he was lost in the Bush.

Appleby in the bush.

Mr. Bush and his daughter were most indefatigable in their exertions to promote the success of the evening; to the accomplishments of the latter a pleasant Sunday evening is mainly due. A drive to General Brock's monument is in everybody's programme who visits Niagara. The road lies through a highly cultivated country, most

o

excellent farming and substantial houses
meet the eye. The Whirlpool is another
grand feature of the spot. The river makes
a sudden bend a little below, the chasm
is narrowed, huge logs are whirled in
restless circles; human bodies have been
known to remain in the seething caldron
of waters for several weeks ere they are
rescued by some restless eddy and carried
down on the more tranquil stream; great
quantities of lumber float on the edge of
the whirlpool, waiting their turn in the giddy
dance, whilst the shores are strewn with all
manner of waifs and strays. The river be-
comes softer in its surroundings as the ravine
widens, and the view over the champaign
country to the shores of Lake Ontario is of sur-
passing beauty—richly wooded, dotted with
white mansions, the blue waters of the lake beyond. It is a scene that makes one comprehend the nature of the Red Man's long
struggle in defence of his native soil. It is
the garden of the West.

It was sad now to think that we were
leaving the Dominion—crossing the river
we were amongst cousins, not brothers.

Our welcome might be as hearty, and we had no reason to doubt of our reception by Americans; still we could not part with our kind friends without regret. Before the final adieu was said, the Captain composed an address, which expressed the sentiments, however feebly, of the Twelve towards their hosts and friends of the field. It was addressed to

THOS. C. PATTESON, Esq., Editor of the *Mail*.

" SIR,—

" I cannot leave the Dominion without expressing to yourself as the originator and manager of our expedition, and through you to the people of Ontario and Quebec, my grateful sense of the reception which has been given to my team of English Amateur Cricketers. *The farewell address.*

" We came to your shores as strangers, we have been welcomed as friends, we leave the Dominion as if we were leaving a second home.

" I am confident that our expedition will establish a more enduring result than that of simply promoting our national game.

o 2

"Cricket was the primary object of our visit, and if we shall have helped to encourage a love for the game and to promote a generous cause of emulation amongst your young athletes, our efforts in the field will not have been made in vain. I look beyond the cricket field and its generous influence. I cannot forget that we have been received on more social and intimate terms than a mere body of cricketers had a right to expect. Friendly as our relations have been with your cricketers of Montreal, Ottawa, Toronto, London, and Hamilton, they are secondary, in my estimation, to the loyalty and love for our common country, which, on many occasions, have prompted the backwoodsman, mechanic, or artizan to grasp our hands, and to welcome us as brothers. Our visit has been hurried, and our acquaintance with the vast resources of the Dominion is necessarily limited, but we have seen enough to justify a high opinion of Canada and Canadians, and we shall be failing in our duty if we do not share with others more competent than ourselves, in dispelling many existing misconceptions and prejudices at home. We can certainly report that if our eyes and ears do not misguide us, one common interest unites Canada and England, that a Canadian is American only by the intervention of a vast ocean, and that Englishmen have only to see the country and its people, to learn its value and their attachment to British institutions.

" To all with whom we have had relations, to our hosts and hostesses, to our brother cricketers, to the gentlemen of the press, who have so ably reported our progress, and to the Dominion generally, I beg most gratefully to return the thanks of the English Twelve.

" I am, Sir,
" Your obedient Servant,
" R. A. FITZGERALD,
" Captain of the English Cricketers.

" Clifton House, Niagara Falls,
' Sept. 16, 1872."

In the same paper appeared a letter, which well illustrates the state of public opinion in connection with the objects of the English visit.

TO THE EDITOR OF THE *MAIL*.

" Sir,—

" The English Eleven are about to leave
us for a short sojourn amongst our neighbours
before returning home.   We have endeavoured to treat them with the same hospitality as has been accorded to our representatives at Wimbledon, and if some errors of
judgment have occurred, we would fain
flatter ourselves that our friends have on
the whole been well pleased with our efforts.
What has been our gain?   The impetus
which the visit has given to the cricketing
spirit is undoubted.   There is scarcely a
vacant lot in the vicinity of our cities that
has not of late been utilized by our schoolboys for cricketing purposes, and if the game
grows more into favour with our youth a
great end has been gained.   Few people
now-a-days, even of the most prosaic, object
to a reasonable expenditure of time and
energy on the part of our youth in the way
of innocent amusements.   The ethics of
muscular Christianity seem to have pervaded the community at any rate to such

leave
ibours
indea-
hospi-
senta-
ors of
fain
re on
fforts.
ipetus
ceting
ely a
i that
:hool-
game
uth a
ieople
object
: and
: way
ics of
per-
such

an extent as to have created a sentiment
favourable to those recreations which tend
to develope the physical powers and recu-
perate the physical energies. Upon the
judicious fostering of this feeling depends,
more than many would be willing to allow,
the future well-being of our young nation.
There is abroad in the world too great a
tendency to utilitarianism. We are, with
the rest of the civilized world, too much in
earnest about life—life in its materialistic
sense—too eager to become quickly rich,
to forestall Providence, in fact. Everything
which fails to aid us sensibly and at once in
our short-sighted struggle is pushed aside as
valueless. Our boys, mentally half-fledged,
leave school for the counting-house and become men before they take leave of their teens;
and under the depressing influence of long
business hours their inclination seldom leads
them, even if physical strength should permit, to make good during their leisure the
deficiencies of their scholastic training.
Change and amusement of some kind must
be and will be had, and in the absence of
opportunities for the manly sports of which

cricket is certainly the king, many fall into
a confirmed habit of 'loafing,' a pastime
which, even if it does not involve positive
vice, is ruinous in its tendency to all the
higher aims of man.

"Any recreation which will call into play
those faculties which cricket cannot fail to
bring into action, while it at the same time
invigorates the physical energies, should be
welcomed by those who interest themselves
in our Canadian youth.   But cricket has
more emphatically its moral side.   We boast
of our freedom, and perhaps we are the most
really free people on the face of the globe;
but freedom without self-control soon de-
generates into license.   Liberty to do as
each one chooses, is simply another term
for anarchy.   Perhaps there is no
greater danger threatening this continent
than the growing unwillingness to put the
curb on the individual will for the general
good.   It is this tendency in democratic institutions which has so frequently in the
history of the world's republics led to their
downfall and decay.   This is the lesson of
the age, and no recreation is more capable

ll into
astime
ositive
ill the

) play
ail to
e time
ild be
selves
t has
boast
most
globe;
n de-
do as
term
no
tinent
t the
eneral
c in-
the
their
on of
pable

of teaching it than the king of games. There is an *esprit de corps* pervading every eleven of real cricketers which crowds out all selfish tendencies, while the quiet submission of individual opinion to the absolute ruling of the umpire or captain often calls for the greatest self-control. I cannot help feeling that Canadian cricketers have not yet learned this all-important lesson; and as during life they are likely to meet with many more grievous trials than that of being stumped by Ottoway, or being ruled out leg before wicket before a quarter of their anticipated score is gained, I kindly commend them to the influence of the manly game, and urge them in their future practice to bear in mind, that while it is important to guard their wicket, it is equally so to keep a constant guard upon the temper and the tongue. If our English friends have by their example in the field done aught to advance the morals of Canadian cricket, then their visit has been in the highest sense a success.

"I heartily wish them a pleasant trip south of 49°, and a safe return to merrie England.

"Leaving you, sir, to deal with the subject

of 'The English Cricketers in Canada,' in the spirit which characterises all the sporting utterances of the *Mail,* and hoping that my homily may not be without effect.

"I have, &c.,

"VIGILANS.

"Ottawa, Sept. 12, 1872."

The sound sense of the above letter will commend itself to the guardians of youth on each side of the Atlantic.   Before quitting the Press we must add a few extracts from the papers, in order to convince the Thomases at home that our utterances are not merely those of the fêted and clapped-on-the-back historian, but that they were shared by others more able to form a right opinion of the success or failure of the objects we had in view.

Thomas the un-believer.

To quote.

We will quote from one paper:—"It is not too early to say that the visit of the Englishmen to Canada has been a magnificent success, and that there is every prospect of all those ends being served which were the object of the visit."   Again : "We print in another place a letter from Mr. Fitzgerald.   In our opinion he does not exagge-

la,' in
orting
ıt my

ɴs.

r will
th on
itting
from
nases
ıerely
-back
ıthers
f the
ad in

It is
f the
agni-
pros-
vhich
' We
Fitz-
ɪgge-

rate the influence the twelve representative
Englishmen, of powerful, social relations and
alliances, can have for good, in narrating their
experiences of the colony.   No one or two
travellers or tourists could have seen the
country under such advantages as were in-
sured by the generous welcome accorded to
the English cricketers from Quebec to
Niagara.   They have seen, it is true, the
sunny side of Canada, and only its town
life ; but if proof were wanting of the happy
and prosperous lives led by our rural population, they had it at London, where the dense
crowd that lined the field reminded one of
the attendance at half-a-dozen English
country fairs rolled into one, and completely swamped the city element.   From
start to finish nothing has occurred to mar
the complete harmony that has prevailed."
Finally, " Real jolly good fellows our visitors
were, well-bred, single-minded, unassuming,
manly specimens of the English gentleman,
proved in many a hard-fought field and
schooled in the courtesies of geniality and
good-fellowship.   We only own to an honest
feeling of rivalry with the Americans, con-

sistent with all manner of cousinly love and affection; but at the same time we know right well that we echo the heartfelt wish of every cricketer in Canada who has shared in the honour of being well beaten by the Englishmen, when we say to them 'God speed, but at least lick your new opponents as handsomely as you have done us.' "

We may be pardoned any little appearance of bunkum in the above quotations. We are proud without vanity of our friends' good opinion of us. We are not ashamed to let it be known. We tried to gain it. We are happy to hear that we are allowed on all sides to deserve it.

Farewell to Canada. We must now bid farewell to Canada, and enter upon the second portion of our Transatlantic adventures.

IN THE STATES.

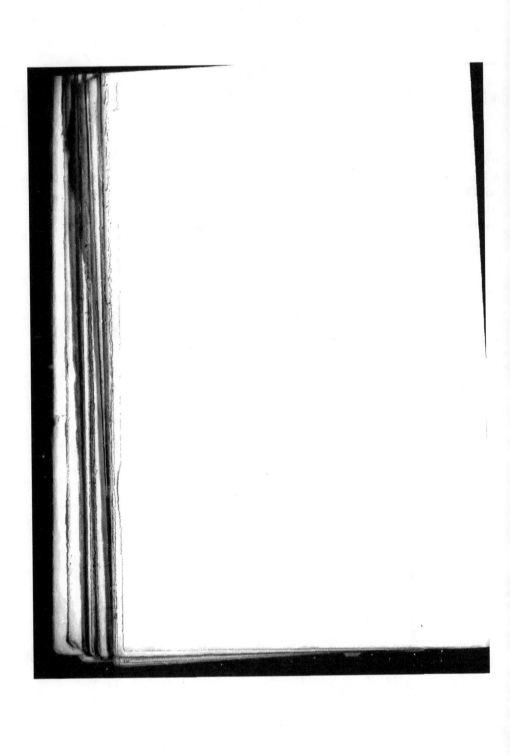

IN THE STATES.

CHAPTER I.

On Monday afternoon, September 16th,
at 5.45, the Twelve looked upon Niagara for
the last time. They were bound for Albany,
where they arrived at 7 a.m. on the 17th.
The Delavan Hotel provided them with an
excellent breakfast.

A good bath, rendered necessary by the
night journey, to wash off the American dust,
and a good meal, put the Twelve in good
spirits for their voyage down the Hudson.

This magnificent river shall not be shorn The Hudson.

of its attractions by any attempt of ours to
describe them. It is a delightful journey
from first to last. It never aspires to the
grandeur of the Rhine, but it is superior in
its wider range of view, and for the castles of
the middle ages it presents you with charming
glimpses of the modern villa, in every variety
of modern taste. Its stream is animated
with vessels, from the rapid propeller of magnificent proportions, to the picturesque sailer
laden with the produce of the rich country
watered by it. It is interesting at every
bend, as it recalls passages of the great
struggle which found it English and left it
American. Vines are seen at intervals on
terraces on the western bank. The Catskill
Mountains rise in their wooded heights far
Rip Van Winkle. away to the west. Rip Van Winkle opens
his eyes and believes it must be a dream,
when he sees the twelve cricket bags on the
steamer's deck. The villas are mostly on the
eastern side—some by the water's edge,
some on the gently rising slopes commanding
a more extended view, all pictures of elegance and neatness—gardens apparently well
kept, the graceful willow of astonishing size

weeping from head to foot—trees unknown
to English eye, towering amidst the well-
known cypress and pine. The first appearance
of New York does not come up to the idea of New York.
the merchant city—formed from newspapers,
panoramas, or Yankee tourists in Europe.
There are no docks comparable to Liverpool.
On landing, the Twelve found themselves in
the midst of busy traffic, crowded and narrow
streets—dirt indescribable, confusion con-
founded. The river trip took eleven hours,
a great rate of speed being maintained by the
" Emily Drew." The Brevoort House was Brevoort
reached at **7 p.m.** A dinner fit for gods was House.
prepared and despatched. Gods only could
pay the bill for any length of time. The first
evening was spent amongst the oysters. Oysters.
These luscious morsels were just in season ;
for size and flavour they beat anything in our
experience that ever revelled in a shell.

Sept. 18. The Hoboken ground. The Cricket.
cricketer of New York must be an enthusiast,
for to indulge in his favourite pastime he
must submit to great inconvenience. To say
nothing of finding your way to the Ferry, The Ferry
tramway cars, trucks of every kind obstruct-

P

ing the road, the route on the other side of
the river in the State of New Jersey, would
take an ordinary New York life to remember.
The Twelve were invited to breakfast on
The s.s. Baltic. board the Baltic, one of the magnificent
steam vessels of the "White Star Line."
Mr. Sparkes, the president of the St. George's
Cricket Club, was the host. The internal
accommodations of this fine ship are most
striking. A most sumptuous meal, at which
Reed Birds. we were first introduced to " Reed Birds,"
prepared us for the rough ride to the
ground.

The Hoboken ground is situated, we cannot
quite say where, but it is " out of humanity's
reach," approached by unfinished streets, and
surrounded by "carcases" of houses in an
advanced stage of non-completion.

Quite a number of people were flocking to
it, and at 12 noon, a good ring was formed.
Stubber. The wickets had been well prepared by Stub-
berfield, whom we regretted to see in bad
health. The Captain lost his first toss. The
ground played dead—one glance sufficed us
to prognosticate a few visits to the adjoining
gardens. It could be got "out of" on every

side. Rose and Appleby bowling. Four
overs were bowled before a run was scored.
A wicket was the first event. We shall
quote very freely from the New York papers
during the match. Their style is most ex-
pressive. The introduction of large type at
intervals enlivens the tale if it is apt to
mislead: for instance, we read—G. Wright
scored six before a ball from Appleby
knocked his leg stump "out of the ground." To quote.
"Treacherous slows," "A very pretty hit,"
etc., etc.—5 wickets fell for 19. Sleigh was
driven back to his coach-house by a magnificent catch of the Tormentor; so good was
this catch that it formed the subject of a picture in "Frank Leslie's Illustrated." Appleby is therein represented rushing midway Portrait
between the wickets with arms outspread like of Appleby
a winged Mercury—8 wickets for 30. Rose
was evidently too much for the New Yorkers.
Cox on his own dunghill played well for 10— Cocks on
13 for 46. Harry Wright, the civil Captain hill.
of the Boston Base Balls, was much cheered,
he had a slice of luck or two, Edgar and Rosa
both missing him, but he was well caught
by George—17 for 56. Luncheon ensued. Lunch!

P 2

One of our authorities represented this frugal
meal as served in a "pretentious edifice devoted to the retailment of sour lager and
stale sandwiches." He must have been
bilious, as he proceeds to describe the accom-

To quote. modation for the reporters as "under a canvas cover, with an apology for a table, and a
few worm-eaten benches upon which the reporters were invited to risk their precious
lives." The wickets fell freely after the re-
past. The "omega of the twenty-two was
Eyre, who walked valiantly away with an
indented bat, and no record to redound to his
credit." In English he carried his bat out for
0, not having had a ball to play. Total 66.

A flutter. There was a general flutter amongst the fair
sex as the Twelve shewed preparations for
the wicket. The first to appear (to quote

The Ojibb. again) was "Ottoway, a tall, lithe, sinewy
man, with a

SPLENDID REACH,

and an eye that can detect at a glance the
course about to be pursued by the invading
sphere of compressed leather." This descrip-

W. G. tion is worth $5 a line. "Then comes W. G.

s frugal
fice de-
ʒer and
e been
accom-
: a can-
ʼ, and a
the re-
ʼrecious
the re-
wo was
ʼith an
l to his
out for
ʼtal 66.
ʼhe fair
ʼns for
quote
sinewy

ce the
ʼading
ʼscrip-
W. G.

Grace—a monarch in his might—of splendid physique, he at once won attention by the
play of limb and easy exercise of

MUSCLE."

Brewster and Harry Wright bowling. The
latter was a humble imitator of our own Our Wil-liam's likeness.
sweet William—sweeter if possible—we will
give his analysis while it is fresh :

	Balls.	Runs.	Wickets.	Wide.
H. Wright	48	35	0	1

Gilbert was heard to smile—mischief was
pending, it soon came—No. 1, over the
telegraph wire into the heart of New Jersey.
No. 2, over everything within 100 yards.
Harry could not continue at this costly rate ;
he retired in favour of Norman. Brewster
meanwhile bowled admirably. 6 overs for
one run against such greedy ones is worth High life.
mentioning. Gilbert had a life off Norman ;
it was high and hot, and "if it had not been
that it fell to the luck of

A BUTTER-FINGERED GENTLEMAN

to stand underneath the ball, the lion of the
British Eleven would have been compelled

Small
change.

to retire." Changes in the bowling were
frequent.   No change took place in the
scoring, which continued to rise steadily.
The cricket was good—Gilbert in great form
—Ottoway shewing judgment and neat play
in contrast with his mammoth partner.   So
the sun gradually sank in the west without
any signs of weakness in the English camp.
Stumps were drawn at six.   Gilbert not out,
67. Ottoway not out, 27. Extra, 8. Total,
102.   Immense applause greeted the two

Ritorna
chi' ist'
ano.

heroes of the hour.   The Twelve returned to
New York in great spirits, prepared for any
light amusement that might crop up in the
evening : of these, more anon.

The attendance on the ground was worthy
of the occasion.   Many ladies, for whom re-
serve places were retained, remained to the
end of the day's play.   There was only one

Potter in
quod.

scrimmage in the crowd—one Mr. Potter,
who was in charge, knocked a gentleman's
hat off by accident in the discharge of his invidious duties, and was accommodated with
a night's lodging at the expense of the Jersey
State for so doing.   This was hard justice.
We pitied poor Potter.

g were
in the
teadily.
at form
at play
er. So
without
camp.
not out,
Total,
e two
rned to
for any
in the

worthy
om re-
to the
ly one
Potter,
man's
his in-
d with
Jersey
ustice.

Sept. 19. Rain had fallen heavily in the Cricket, 2nd day.
night, and the wickets were no longer in
good order for runs; Gilbert and the O.
followed each other's fate speedily. They
each added " 2 " to their respective scores.
Gilbert's 68 included three 6's, one 4, three
3's, two 2's, and singles. 1 wicket for 105.
Ottoway's 29—remarkable for singles. 2 for
105. The Monkey and the Saint put a lively
face on the game, and ran the score to 148,
when Francis was caught by Greig for 28.
A very dashing innings, including one spank
amongst the cottages for 6. The Monkey
was in luck, and as free as in his native
wilds. "He skied one of Greig's, which
Harry Wright carefully and deliberately

DROPPED,   A drop scene.

to the disgust of the spectators"—his 18 were
very quickly, if fortunately, obtained—4 for
158 runs. Alfred the Great was now " in," Alfred the Great.
and his elegant form was never seen to
better advantage. Edgar's eccentric style
being a good foil to his brother—the lad Pick.
having previously been dismissed for 3—he
was the only boy bowled. Luck clave to the

Twelve, as misses did to the Twenty-two.
Alfred had two lives, and Edgar one. The
former had made 15, " when Gibbes on the
long field

MUFFLED

him badly." It was an important error—as
he totalted half a century : changes were rung
in the bowling, and grateful were the field
when another bell rang for luncheon—176
The sand- up. After the sandwiches, the brothers ran
wich.
Ugh ! the score up to 216, when Edgar was thrown
Run out of out for 15, including two 3's. Haddock, the
Haddocks.
unlucky, was run out, having made one
grand hit for 3—another pile of agony for
the unfortunate being. Alfred saw George's
star set also—he was well caught by Lemon
Lemon —bitter cups for the youthful Harris : his 9
bitter cups.
included of two 3's—both good leg hits.
Alfred out. Alfred's 51 took him rather more than two
hours to make. It was marked by one 6
(over the fence), five 3's, and three 2's. The
remainder were in a hurry to finish the match,
and soon disposed of themselves. The total
amounting to 249, 228 being scored from
the bat, and 21 from extras. The bilious re-

ty-two.
. The
on the

'or—as
re rung
e field
—176
rs ran
hrown
k, the
e one
ny for
orge's
Lemon
his 9
hits.
in two
one 6
The
natch,
total
from ·
us re-

porter was again " nuts " on the lunch. He writes, " after a little practising to digest the sour beer and unpalatable viands, the contestants commenced again. John Bull's sons are generally

FOND OF GOOD CHEER.

They have a strange proclivity for taking their ease at an inn—and innate politeness forbade them from growling at the viands." We are not sure that it did, at least in a sottâ voce strain. The lunch was the only weak point on all the cricket grounds we had played upon.

Appleby and Grace were the executioners The in the second innings of the New Yorkers. Brothers Calcraft. The Tormentor is described as bowling with

TERRIFIC SPEED.

"He tore Hatfield's wicket down with a shooter, and a groan of distress went up, as one of the brightest lights of the Mutuals was drenched in a duck's egg." The Wright The Brothers played each a dashing innings. Wright. The fielding of the Twelve was at last what it ought to be. The Captain's heart was rejoiced. It was very brilliant—especially Harris, Hornby, and Francis. Eyre is reported to have received a hot 'un on the fingers, and to have

" WINCED AUDIBLY.

The next ball caused him wriggle, the next mowed down his wicket." What a picture of horror is thus represented. 7 wickets succeeded in scoring 0 each. "The majority falling victims to Grace's efforts to bowl for catches, and what Grace failed to do, Appleby secured with shooters." This well explains the result. "It was a complete slaughter of the innocents." "The fact is, Grace frightened them. They thought they saw some unknown and fatal influence in his bowling, and they simply played right into his hands all the time." These are not our words, but they tell the tale better, if more cruelly than we could. The innings commenced at 4.10, and was concluded at 5.30. Another report says, " The man who managed to save himself from the ignominy of having a cypher opposite his name was deemed highly fortunate by his fellows."

Innocents' day.

"The utmost good humour prevailed To quote. throughout the day, and even the hundreds of persons who had come from New York and other places to see the Old Country players get beaten went away heartily satisfied with the result. 2,000 spectators were computed to have been on the ground."

ENGLAND *V.* TWENTY-TWO OF ST. GEORGE'S The score. CLUB.

ENGLAND.

W. G. Grace, c Brewster, b G. Wright	68	W. H. Hadow, run out		3
C. J. Ottaway, c Jones, b Brewster	29	Hon. G. Harris, c Lemond, b Hatfield		9
A. N. Hornby, c Keiler, b Jones	17	A. Appleby, c Jones, b Torrance		5
C. K. Francis, c and b Greig	28	W. M. Rose, not out		9
A. Lubbock, c Bowman, b G. Wright	51	Fitz-Gerald, c Hatfield, b G. Wright		0
F. Pickering, b Greig	3	B 9, l b 4, w b 8		21
E. Lubbock, run out	15	Total		249

THE TWENTY-TWO.	1st inn.		2nd inn.
Bance, c Francis, b Rose	0	b Appleby	0
Jackson, c Grace, b Appleby	3	c Rose, b Grace	0
Fortun, c Harris, b Rose	5	c and b Grace	0
Jones, c A. Lubbock, b Rose	9	st Ottaway, b Grace	5
Cashman, b Appleby	1	c Harris, b Grace	2
Sleigh, c Appleby, b Rose	2	b Appleby	1
Moeran, c and b Appleby	0	c Hadow, b Grace	1
Keiler, b Appleby	6	c Pickering, b Grace	4
G. Wright, b Appleby	6	c A. Lubbock, b Grace	14
Lemon, c Ottaway, b Appleby	0	b Appleby	0

TWENTY-TWO—*continued.* 1st Inn.		2nd inn.	
Terranco, b Appleby	0	c Hornby, b Grace	0
Cox, c Appleby, b Rose	10	c Harris, b Appleby	0
Bowman, c Grace, b Appleby	2	b Appleby	2
Greig, run out	1	b Appleby	0
M'Dougall, c Fitzgerald, b Rose	2	b Appleby	1
Hatfield, b Appleby	2	b Appleby	0
H. Wright, c Harris, b Rose	5	c Ottaway, b Grace	0
Brewster, b Rose	4	c Francis, b Grace	2
Gibbes, b Appleby	5	st Ottaway, b Grace	1
Sparks, b Appleby	1	absent	0
Talbot, c A. Lubbock, b Rose	1	not out	1
Ayre, not out	0	b Appleby	1
B 1, w b 1	2		
Total	—66	Total	—44

We append the analysis, in order to compare the penetration of Gilbert with the insinuations of Rosa:—

FIRST INNINGS.

	Balls.	Runs.	Maidens.	Wickets.	Wide.
Rose	138	46	13	9	0
Appleby	137	18	24	11	1

SECOND INNINGS.

Grace	84	26	8	11	0
Appleby	81	18	10	9	0

This match was not of an International character—*pur et simple.* Cricket is not a popular game at New York. It has a struggle for existence, and is indebted for life to a few determined Englishmen. The sporting portion of Americans, with whom we came in contact, took very little interest in the proceedings, at the same time the greatest courtesy was shown by them, and the Twelve are much indebted to several influential members for an introduction to two of the leading Clubs in New York—the Union and the Travellers'. *The Clubs.*

Before leaving the scene of our exploits, it will not be much out of the way to recall the results of the previous matches at New York, in which Englishmen have taken part. The first visit was in 1859, when an Eleven, under George Parr, visited the Hoboken ground. It was played late in the season—on Oct. 3, 4, and 5, 1859, with the following result :— *Previous History.*

The St. George's Twenty-two,

38 and 54.

All England,

156.

Parr and Jackson bowled in the first innings; Parr obtaining 9, and Jackson 10 wickets. In the second innings, Wisden and Caffyn bowled; Wisden obtaining 4 wickets, and Caffyn 16 wickets. Not one wide bowled.

In 1868, another Eleven, under Willsher, played at Hudson City, on Sept. 16, 17, 18, 1868 :—

The Eleven,
175.
The Twenty-two,
61 and 88.

Willsher and Freeman bowled in the first
innings :—

	Balls.	Runs.	Wickets.
Willsher	119	23	13
Freeman	116	28	8

IN THE SECOND INNINGS.

Tarrant	65	15	2
Lillywhite	52	16	2
Freeman	116	30	4
Shaw	96	19	9

It will be seen that the Amateurs do not
lose by comparison with the formidable teams
that preceded them. Appleby's bowling is
especially noticeable by its results. The time
of game is given by the *New York Clipper*,
but we do not quite comprehend its meaning
—6h. 45m. is given for the duration of the
game played by the Amateurs, and 10h. 15m.
for that played by the Professionals, in 1868.
It must allude to the time consumed on the
last day's play, in one case, and to both days
in the Professional Match. The Press stated
that the fielding and bowling of the New

Time.

he first

Wickets.
... 13
.. 8

.. 2
.. 2
.. 4
.. 9

do not
le teams
vling is
he time
Clipper,
neaning
of the
h. 15m.
1 1868.
on the
th days
s stated
e New

Yorkers were decidedly in advance of either of the displays of 1859 and 1868. Fortun long-stopped well, and there was some excellent fielding displayed by the Wrights, Lemon, and Brewster.

The Match, if it cannot be considered an International one, gave the Twelve a very agreeable impression of Americans. They had to run the gauntlet of an American ground at least, and by one and all, both on the ground and on the way to it, if they were a bit prospected, it was in the best humour and most agreeable way. Running the Gauntlet.

The amusements of New York are varied. A dinner at the Travellers' introduced the Twelve to many of the leading sportsmen of New York. A very pleasant evening was spent. Hearty toasts were given and responded to. Conspicuous amongst these was an oration by the accomplished actor, Mr. Wallack. Mr. Hurst presided, and gave the toast of the evening, " Welcome to the English Cricketers," in a very stirring address. The Captain replied in a speech garnished with all the flowers of Western diction culled in Canada. He was plain on one point, Amusements. Dinner, Travellers' Club. Wallack. The Captain again.

which required no flourish—he could speak in grateful terms on the reception of his team in New York; also for a suggestion thrown out in the course of the evening, that Englishmen should make New York their rallying point in some future cricket campaign, to spend a few weeks longer than was intended this autumn, and thereby encourage more fully the dawning spirit of the game. The Captain explained that this visit to America was, in the first instance, due to Canada, and that the visit to the States must be considered supplementary. He hoped to be able, ere long, to promote another visit of longer duration, which would do more justice to the generous supporters of cricket in New York, Philadelphia, and Massachusetts.

W. G.'s last.

V. G. was, of course, put up once more. ...e was rather at a loss for something new, but luckily bethought him of the last thing in season—so for "Batting, Bowling, Ground, and Ladies," lead "oysters" this time, and

The Haddock.

Speech No. 5 lies before you. Haddock was in good voice, and favoured the company

The Cow.

with an agricultural ode in honour of a Cow. Mr. Wallack invited the Twelve to breakfast on board his fine yacht "The Columbia," and *The Columbia.* to take a cruise to Sandy Hook on the morning of Sept. 20. Only two of the Twelve were up to the mark at 9 A.M., and these two were in bed when Mr. Wallack's carriage called at the Brevoort House. Rose and the Captain shook off dull sloth, and the cobwebs of the previous evening. They were amply repaid—an excellent breakfast and a rattling breeze, testing the qualities of the taut "Columbia." It blew fresh from the north- *The Cruise.* east, and Sandy Hook was soon gained. The splendid harbour of New York was thus opened to the visitors. The Hudson is a Queen in a Republic of rivers—the splendid steamers arriving and departing daily ; a hundred yachts at anchor, or engaged in sporting rivalry, fortresses frowning on the sparkling waves ; nearer to the city the constant ferry-boats, plying from shore to shore, with human freight that scarcely yields to the approach of night; men of war, gunboats, and craft of all kinds. Truly, the waters of the Hudson are *the* yachting quarters of the universe— *Yachting Quarters.* wind enough and waves enough to test the stoutest—beauty on shore, life on the water.

Q

Rapidly sped the moments, but amongst the pleasantest of our recollections will be the hours so kindly filled for us by our host of " The Columbia."

The Central Park is a marvel of road-making and road-preserving. There is not a stone the size of a nut for a wheel to crack on the level surface of the road for several miles. New York is growing up to the Central Park—central is used prospectively —with a dip into the coming century. It is several miles from the centre of New York, though it will not be many centuries before it is the centre of the great city. Seeing such a road, you naturally imagine it is to keep pace with the rapid driving for which Americans are famous. Not so, you must creep like a snail on this even course, you may drive to perdition in the ruts and over the hollows of adjoining tracks. At intervals of a few hundred yards, officers, called Bobbies in England, preserve a minimum of curricular speed—at 6 miles an hour or so.

By the kindness of Mr. Travers, of the Union Club, we were enabled to test the watchfulness of the policemen, and to arrive

The Central Park.

Robert Le Diable !

ngst the
l be the
· host of

of road-
: is not a
o crack
several
to the
ectively
. It is
v York,
s before
Seeing
it is to
which
u must
se, you
d over
itervals
Bobbies
ricular

of the
st the
arrive

· at Fleetwood Park. We tooled Mr. T.'s Fleetwood Park. waggonette at the prescribed pace through Central Park. We could have wished almost to see one stone out of its place in the level road. There are no birds to throw at amongst the variegated shrubs, and the ducks don't look at home on the ornamental water. If we only did our mile in ten minutes on the waggonette, we made up for it in a trial trot behind a young one belonging to Mr. Florence, a sporting pub. It was the nearest approach The Pub. to Niagara for rapid-ity—luckily, without the Falls. We have always sat still hitherto, never moved a peg, not advanced a yard, everything in the shape of speed, time, eternity, comes back to us sitting on a racing-gig behind a 2′ 40″. A 2.40.

There is not too much to sit on, and for comfort the six miles an hour in the waggonette is preferable. It is a sensation of the first order, especially if your timepiece—trotters are known by the time they do the mile— breaks into a gallop. The trainers at Fleetwood Park did the honours of the establishment very agreeably. We were introduced The Stud Book. to several stars—Bismarck, foaled in 1867,

untried, a fine animal, standing 16h. 1½in. ;·
Gazelle, 7 years old, a noted trotter, purchased for $40,000 ; Lula, 8 years old,

The Gig. $25,000. The weight of the racing-gig is
52lb., and the driver gets up at 150lb.

Trotters. Trotters are considered in their prime up to
15 years old. The celebrated Flora Temple
was put to the stud at 21 years. The course
at Fleetwood is an oval. We were favoured
with an introduction to Jerome Park by Mr.
Travers, but we dallied too long with the
trotters to allow us to inspect the stables, so
we missed seeing Harry Bassett.

Hotels.   The hotels in New York are many and
sumptuous. The Brevoort is the most comfortable, and the most costly. If money is
no object, go to the Brevoort by all means,
say we. You can rub along there just comfortably, but not extravagantly, on the small
matter of £3 per day, your rooms will be
palatial, the attendance perfect. Dinners
equal to anything in Paris. If you prefer
ruin deferred to comfort and privacy, go to
the Fifth Avenue Hotel : here for 5 dols. a
day you can be as comfortable as it is possible
to be amongst several hundreds of your own

6h. 1½in. ;
tter, pur-
ears old,
ng-gig is
at 150lb.
ne up to
a Temple
he course
favoured
: by Mr.
with the
ables, so

any and
ost com-
noney is
 means,
ast com-
ic small
will be
Dinners
 prefer
, go to
dols. a
ossible
ur own

species. The etiquette observable amongst Americans in the presence of ladies is very remarkable. Englishmen have a belief in the freedom of America. There is not half the freedom that is taken in Europe in the presence of women. You are particularly *Woman.* reminded of your hat, which you as an *Your Tile.* Englishman invariably keep on your head, except in church, and then you are occasionally looking into it. You must pass through the saloons to your bed-chamber with your hat in your hand. You must not loiter in the coffee-room in conversation with a friend with your hat on, if there is a lady in the room. The American at home is very far indeed from our conception of him as we meet him abroad. We were prepared for all kinds of surprises under the red cap of Liberty, Freedom, and Equality. Our real surprise was to find if possible a more exacting code of manners than our own. One thing does strike the English eye, you never see a child, to judge at least by manners. The *No Child.* youngest young lady is a woman in disguise. We cannot recall a single boy or girl to our mind; we remember many advanced speci-

Advanced Youth.   mens of youth, boys and girls only in stature. Children by their early introduction to hotel life acquire a self-possession which never deserts them, and which in fact goes a long way towards the American character. Did

The Blush.   any one ever see an American blush?

Oysters.   We cannot leave New York without a word for its oysters. Appalled as we were at their size at the first mouthful, we soon recognised their transcending merits. It is a mouthful, not to say, two bites. But you miss the taste of the steel and the briny savour of the native. The American oyster meets its doom in more ways than one. It not only yields its last groan to the brutal knife; it is amenable to the influence of steam, it is broiled and baked; in colour it is creamy, and though of a size sufficient to cover the palm of your hand, its flavour only tickles the tip of your tongue.

Gaslight Views.   New York by gaslight presents many strange aspects. Broadway is a stream of light, many shops leave their windows exposed to view and illuminated internally by gas. Halls of Light are numerous. The good taste of the exhibitions of some of

these is questionable. Let us enter a
Hall of Light—a long counter with its
attendant genii, the spirits of the country,
numerous round tables, nymphs in no garb
of a later date than the palmy days of Lais
of Corinth — these advance as you beckon
and take your orders, execute them and return to your side to await fresh orders or
indulge in sprightly conversation. Their
looks are not seductive, nor does the spirit
you imbibe aid the charm. We thought we
might be prejudiced by the first hall we
entered, so we tried several others, but with
the same unpleasant result. The eye is not
pleased, the imagination is not fired, and yet
each hall was full too overflowing. There is
no want of decorum, and nothing to offend a
Quaker beyond a dearth of beauty. There
is no music to lend an enchanting air to the
Halls of Light. You are provoked without
provocation. You are disgusted in your delight. Standing in one of these halls of
pleasure and surveying the scene, which at
that moment presented only the ordinary
features of a drinking saloon—nymphs excepted—we asked an acquaintance if these

Marginal notes: A Hall of Light. Nymphs. A Scene.

gentle scenes ever ended in riot. "Your question is opportune," said our friend, "where we are standing, two nights ago, the amiable man behind the counter, with his sleeves tucked up, shot a man through the heart." We innocently expressed surprise at seeing the man-slayer behind his counter. We were not acquainted with the customs of the country. The intruder had endeavoured to force his way into the hall after the proper hour for closing, the proprietor objected, the intruder insisted; the argument was concluded in favour of the proprietor by a press of the trigger. Verdict, Served him right, and accepted by all who knew New York intimately. Our friend showed us the stairs where Col. Fisk met his death at the hands of Mr. Stokes. This leads us unconsciously to the Tombs, where Mr. Stokes now resides. We were furnished with an order to visit these well-known prisons. We met with a rebut at the door, our order was *en regle*, but the gaol official was *de rigueur*. We were denied admission flatly. We returned to the gentleman who had furnished us with the order, he countersigned it, and we returned to the

Argumentum ad hominem.

Fisk.
Stokes.
The Tombs.

A Snub.
A Snob.

charge to be again refused admittance. By the advice of an American gentleman, who accompanied us, we then went to the office of the *New York Herald*, interviewed one of the Editors, who most kindly listened to our tale, took down the salient points, and next morning we were amply revenged by an article Revenge. which must have shaken the Tombs and made the defunct gaolers writhe in their graves. The amiable Stokes has died out of notoriety, and nobody now seriously thinks he deserves to be hanged, yet if any man ever deliberately murdered another, our impression is that Stokes did when he shot the Colonel. Mrs. Mansfield, the lady about Mrs. M. whom the quarrel in a great measure arose, is leading a retired life in New York. Her photograph is to be bought for 1 dollar. She is a stout and rather comely woman, but her face does not suggest the thought that any two men would fight about her. Any gentleman with money burning the lining of his pocket can easily obtain relief at night: by applying to any policeman, he will be directed Alla Porta del Inferno. Pleasantly and socially The H—ll. conducted, he can lose his money to his heart's will, and when his purse is empty he will not be permitted, at least, to go without

Hush!　his supper. Space will not permit us to penetrate deeper into the varied pleasures of New York by gaslight. It is sufficient to say that no town on earth presents better facilities either for acquiring money or spending it. Money is made quickly and is spent profusely.

Telegrams.　You live in an atmosphere of telegrams. Every counting-house has its distance-defying instrument. The voice of gold is watched from hour to hour. Business is the pleasure of the day, the nightmare of the couch. It is but fair to mention any instance in this money-getting luxurious city, of any great public good arising out of large private

Mr. Stuart.　means. Stuart's stores are shown to every visitor. They swallow up Swan and Edgar, and make one mouthful of Marshall and Snelgrove. They represent the vast wealth and proud commercial position of one individual. But a still statelier building than this commends the name of Stuart to the

A Home.　public. It is a Home for Needlewomen, engaged in the trade which has founded his fortune. Erected at an enormous outlay its object is meritorious, and the founder has shown that he is not indifferent to the welfare of a class intimately connected with his own success. The maxim in vogue in America _{To the most much.} of "the greatest benefit for the greatest number," is not a favourite with the travelling minority who visit New York. The tramways that run along most of the _{Trams.} thoroughfares, impede the passage of private or hired carriages. The rails are very badly laid, and the jolting and suffering to axles is intolerable. The Fifth Avenue is alone exempted from the double line of rails. The cars are well horsed, and smoking is not permitted within them. Broadway is Pandemonium for many hours. It is too narrow for the increasing prosperity of the city. New York is rapidly running out of town, eastwards. This reminds us that we too must be getting out of it: we have been in it already too long for our purse, but not too long for its numerous attractions.

CHAPTER II.

WE now arrive at the match which, both
in its result and in its preliminaries, was distinguished above its fellows.

The Twelve had not been many hours in
Canada before they were met by a deputation
from Philadelphia. At Montreal the first
arrangements were made, and to the attention and kindness of Messrs. Cadwallader,
Outerbridge, and others of the committee, is
eminently due the satisfactory result afterwards obtained.

The Inter-national. In the first place an International match was agreed upon. The Twenty-two of Philadelphia were to be selected from the local clubs, and to consist of Americans. The match was fixed for Saturday, September 21, Monday and Tuesday, September 23 and 24.

The programme originally fixed was to include various kinds of amusement. The Philadelphians required a week, and it was with great regret that the Captain felt obliged to curtail the arrangements. An influential deputation had also met him from Boston, and it was found impracticable to arrange a longer stay at Philadelphia, and at the same time to do justice to the good folks of Massachusetts The Twelve left New York on Friday evening, September 20. Excellent accommodation was provided for them at the Continental Hotel in Philadelphia. The Continental.

The papers were full of the coming contest. The Press. One devoted itself to the personal history of the Twelve, but unfortunately had not taken the precaution of obtaining a correct list of the players. Hence the biographies of the Messrs. Walker, Thornton, Mitchell, and Yardley were brought prominently forward.

The information was tolerably correct, though
we are informed, for the first time, that the
"Messrs. Walkers, their sisters and dog,
could play against any Eleven in the world."
Alfred Lubbock is described as "taking the
place of wicket keep, in which position he is
inferior to none." This is indeed true. The
attributes of the Twenty-two were very
critically summed up, and it was enough to
strike terror into the stoutest heart to read of
"Joe Hargreaves as one of the strongest bats.

V. E., I. D. and Sisters and Dog.

Joe.

> Law—An enduring and conscientious
> bowler.
>
> Meade—A left-handed bowler with pecu-
> liar spin. He bowled 132 balls for 18 runs
> in the All-England Match of 1868, the
> very irregularity of his style proves
> effective.
>
> Charles Newhall—The fastest round-arm
> bowler in America, very straight with
> high delivery. A strong bat. Unusually
> heavy in the field.
>
> Dan Newhall—A thorough cricketer, bowls
> medium pace with his head.
>
> George Newhall—Has a long head. Ap-
> pointed Captain of the Twenty-two."

Saturday, Sept. 21.——There could be no Cricket
doubt about the interest taken in the match. 1st Day.
Immense crowds set towards the ground .The
road might have been to the Epsom Downs
on the morning of the Derby. The railroad
was a continuous train. On arriving at the
scene of action, one glance was sufficient to
tell that great attention had been paid to the
wickets. The soil is not the best. The
sun was intensely hot. Water had been
liberally bestowed. The ground belongs to
the German Town Cricket Club, and is
situated in a private demesne. It had been
enclosed by high pailings. Ropes and stakes
marked the outer ring. By 11.30 every
bough had a boy on it, every hayrick a tenant.
The band of brazen instruments piled up its The Brass
music on the roof of the Pavilion. The Grand Band.
Stand was rapidly filling with the fair
daughters of Penn.

The Captain lost the toss, and the Twenty-
two declared to go in. Harry Newhall and
Brewster, amidst the breathless attention of
all the spectators, went to the wickets, Rose
and Appleby bowling. To Appleby's bowling the Twelve were thus placed ;——Ottaway Places.

at the wicket; Edgar, long-stop; Grace, point; Fitzgerald, short-leg; Alfred, long-leg; Harris, cover-point; Haddow, mid-off; Hornby, mid-on; Rose, short-slip; Francis, cover-slip; Pickering, long-field. To the slows—Hornby dropped to long-leg; Pickering, Edgar, and Harris to the long-field; Francis cover-point. This arrangement was adhered to during the tour, with slight First Blood. alteration. Brewster drew first blood off Rose—a snick to leg, amidst thunders of applause. This soon changed to a lower key, as, on the first ball of Appleby, "Harry" retired, much chagrined, and Welsh, who looked confidence itself, was sent home with the next ball. You might have heard the hearts beating in the Grand Stand. Two wickets down for 2. Brewster soon followed suit—three wickets for 5. Bob Newhall made 4; and the cheers which greeted him at each run merely ushered on his knell, a ripper of Appleby's squandering his stumps. The Tormentor breathed blood to-day; he had now bowled 7 overs for 2 runs and 4 wickets. Cadwallader was overpowered by the Rose. "The mortality continued." Loper

Baird succumbed to the seductive slows, and Appleby administered a quietus to G. M. Newhall, shattering his wicket completely." The 5th, 6th, and 7th wickets fell for 11. Hargreaves "Joe" then appeared, amidst fluttering of scented rags in the Stand. He remained a quarter of an hour in company with Large (John). Joe yielded to "a gem of Appleby's;" eight for 19. Morgan then joined John; made a brilliant cut for three to the ropes. These two put a brighter look on the American mug. Each played carefully and well. The cricket was excellent all round. The Captain grafted Gilbert on A Graft. John Hopper. The change at once proved effective. Morgan was seduced by Gilbert's high-and-home-easy, and was cleverly stumped by the pallid Ottaway. Morgan only made 6, but he was deservedly cheered, as his defence was good and much wanted during the panic; nine for 30. Dan Newhall Dan. is a popular cuss, to judge by the hearty greeting he received on his appearance. An ironical cheer, however, followed him back home very shortly, as Gilbert bowled him from the second ball; ten for 30. Law

R

joined Large (John) whose term of office had
now expired. It had lasted an hour, during
which he made 14 runs. He had seen seven
of his compeers stricken down with unflinch-
ing face, and he was greeted with quite an
ovation upon his return to the pavilion ;
To Quote. eleven for 35. " Three first-class batsmen,"
to quote from a local, were thus disposed of for
cyphers. Charles Newhall had made 1 when
lunch was announced. Fourteen wickets had
fallen for 36 runs.

An excellent luncheon was provided.
After which Cooper Baird joined Charles
Newhall. Some tall hitting took place.
Baird was cleverly run out by Francis, whose
fielding in the match was superb at cover-
point. Hargreaves "Tom" fell into the
High, Ojibbeway's clutches. The O. was very
Home and
Easy. nippy to-day; sixteen for 42. Gilbert's high-
and-home style seemed to puzzle the Quaker
quite as much as Rosa's. Appleby, meanwhile, put in two successive stick-ticklers,
chawing up egregiously poor Charles Newhall and Sanderson — the 17th, 18th, and
19th wickets fell for 46. Magee couldn't
resist a dash a Gilbert's apparent half-

volley; a crash ensued; the stumps were in the embrace of the Red Indian. Magee went home without a murmur; twenty for 51. Young Sam Welsh now joined Hargreaves John. Sam. They enlivened the game vastly—Sam dashing out at Gilbert, and giving him Yankee all round the shop. John made two capital leg hits, and things were beginning to look ugly, when John and Sam got into two minds about a run which did not not require one to settle; and John was run out. His 11 John. was the innings, so far, of the day. Total 63.

If the applause had been hearty as each American champion walked to his wicket, equally so was the greeting that awaited each of the Twelve. Gilbert came in for the greatest measure; but to one and all there was the same kindly expression of welcome. Charles Newhall and Meade commenced the bowling. Gilbert and Ottoway, it was soon seen, were pegged to their crease. The field was active and well placed. An hour elapsed ere anything happened of importance. The score increased slowly—when a terrific roar announced the dissolution of the great man. He was bowled by Newhall for 14,

R 2

—he had had a little luck with this little lot. "The applause from all parts of the ground was terrific and deafening." Charles New-hall at that moment was a more popular hero **Horace.** than Horace Greeley. 1st wicket for 30. The O. soon followed. By a bad piece of judgment on his own part or the Monkey's, he was run out for 10, very carefully obtained; two for 32. Alfred joined the Nimble One. They ran everything in the semblance, ghostly or otherwise, of a run; and when stumps were drawn at 5.45, they were still in. Hornby, not out, 10; Alfred, not out, 6, and with extras. The total amounted to 48.

The Spectators. The attendance during the afternoon steadily increased. There was not a spare seat in the Grand Stand. Upwards of 7000 spectators were present. An honest English clique occupied one corner, and a gentle interchange of chaff with our American cousins was indulged in. The utmost good humour prevailed. The first experience of a genuine American match was very gratifying. The **Heat.** day had been hot, but tempered by a breeze. The night was cool, almost to frosty. The

Twelve were entertained in the evening by
Mr. Fisher, at his residence in the country, a
few miles from Germantown. A large party
had been invited to meet them. The cheer *Dinner.*
was of the best and the most. The Twelve
were very nearly losing it. They did lose
their way; and if somebody had not detected
the white teeth of a nigger shining in the
dark, the sable proprietor of which kindly
put them in the right track, the reed-birds,
the oysters, and other good things would
have gone down unsung in other gullets.
Mr. Fisher's house is replete with comfort *Mr. Fisher.*
and elegance. A well-stored library, and
walls hung with old family pictures, speak of
years that have rolled over successive generations under the same roof. Some fine
pieces of modern sculpture speak to the
cultivated taste and to the travelled experience which is an eminent characteristic
of the wealthy Philadelphian. The long
drive was well rewarded. The Twelve
were introduced to the *élite* of the neighbourhood; and, if no other reminiscence was
due to the evening than that of a pleasant
supper, it would still claim the honour and

the charm of our first introduction to General

Meade.

Sunday was intended as a day of rest. Practically it was not. Some of us did, indeed, go to church, and, under the influence of the powerful sun, did obtain a few moments' repose. Others were employed more

actively. A drive to Fairmount Park employed the afternoon. Philadelphia and its wife spends its Sunday in the park. It is a pleasant drive. The park is not artificial; it is nature reclaimed. It contains nearly 3,000 acres, and is three times larger than the Central Park of New York. It has always been a park; it is a park; it will be a park of the future, worthy of the increasing prosperity of its great town. The beautiful

Schuylkill runs by it. The Wissahickon waters it. It was, indeed, to preserve the purity of these waters that this noble Inclosure Act was passed. Philadelphia has earned the gratitude of posterity. All kinds of cunning compounds are concocted at the restaurant in the park. The Twelve were soon recognised, and many were the invitations to test the compounds. We met the fattest man of Philadelphia there. The Claimant has no claim to monstrosity beside him. There is a retired little house out of the track of the holiday-folk, whither a certain few of young Philadelphia resort on Sundays. Champagne and ice are the furniture, and a corkscrew is the only resident. Weeping willows of forest Residents. grandeur, and many other stately trees, cast their grateful shadows upon the garden. The Twelve enjoyed a rest here. Silence, broken only by the thirst-compelling pop, as Pop. the cork flew high into air from the creaming cham. The dust of the drive was forgotten; the heat was pardoned and almost thanked. The descendants of Penn have improved somewhat on the austere habits of their great father. As yet we had detected no trace of the Quaker; nor during our stay did we The come across a Quakeress. We saw many Quaker. pretty faces that no bonnet could spoil. But we were disappointed in our wish to see how far a pretty face can carry its assertion under an uncomely head-piece.

Monday, Sept. 23.—Before proceeding Cricket with to-day's play, we will quote a few 2nd day. passages from the Sunday papers. These

The Press. had teemed with accounts of Saturday's play. Each had some new feature; but they had one thing in common—they abused each other pretty roundly for "displaying the most complete ignorance of the game."

One paper abused the Twenty-two, declar-To Quote. ing their play "to be miserable, their efforts at runs getting the most feeble ever seen in a cricket-field. All the Newhalls were out of form, and batted badly." This is casti-gated in another report, which, in defence of the Twenty-two, says, "The reporter should have known that it is no disgrace to a bats-man to be bowled in the first over before he has gotten his eye accustomed to the ball. No judgment can be formed upon the play of the Newhalls, as they had no opportunity to face the ball." This is stretching a point in defence, the truth being that they were bowled out slick, and words cannot mend the manner. Another prophet says, "The score on Saturday indicates that the Britons will win easily in one innings."

Cricket. To resume. The ground was encircled by a deep throng at **12** noon, when Hornby and Alfred went to the wickets. Misfortunes began early. Alfred was run out, trying a second off a fine hit to cover point; three for 50. Hadow succeeded, and shortly after the Monkey received his death-warrant from Meade, who had changed ends; four for 51. The Hon. George appeared, "faced the bowling of Meade, scored one by a leg bye, and on the over forward play to leg, tallied only one." We don't quite follow this, but quote as printed. George made "a forward cut for one, and then a single by a sharp cut juggled by H. New-hall." George was well caught in the slips by Dan Newhall; five wickets for 56 runs. Hadow was gradually gaining confidence, and his commanding style was seen to advantage; runs came very slowly; both bowlers on the spot; another change in the ends took place, and the first ball of New-hall "took Hadow square in the stomach;" from this period the wicket began to play badly. Francisco meanwhile had "legged" and "slipped" a few notches; he was obliged to yield to Meade, who was bowling splendidly; six for 66. The band struck up a lively air when Appleby went to the

Marginal notes: Hadow, Fine form.

wickets, but the Unassuming was not ex-
cited. Hadow began to show his muscle,
some splendid drives to the off worth 4 each
only realized 1, owing to the smart return.
The Tormentor was not troublesome, he was

caught point for 2; seven for 86. Edgar's
turn now came; his style provoked remarks
in several papers. We read that "he took
a position as unusual as ungraceful, with his
feet far apart, after the fashion of some base
ball strikers, and with his bat almost per-
pendicularly placed." Another report has
it, that "this is the ruling style in Lubbock's section in England, and it is often
found very effective." "Bets were offered
that he would not get 10, as he could not
gather himself up in good season." The
event proved the correctness of the theory,
as he was speedily bowled for 0; eight for
88. The remaining batsman effected little.
The Captain carrying his bat out for 1;

Hadow had seen seven wickets fall; his
29 took him nearly two hours to put together; he went in with the score at 50,
and out, all told, at 105. It was a very fine
innings, and he was deservedly applauded

by the dense ring of spectators. The Philadelphians were justly proud of their exploit,
and the prospects of a good match revived;
an hour was devoted to lunch, and at one
o'clock, George Newhall and Hargreaves
John went in, the band striking up a solemn
tune. The Captain felt the importance of The Cap-
the moment; runs must be saved; catches tain's orders.
must be made; his instructions were con-
cise; he no longer button-holed his Rose, he A button
trusted to the high-home-and-easy Gilbert. hole.
Newhall made two fine cuts for 3, one
off Appleby, the other off Grace, his score
had reached 9 when he was bowled; one
for 10. These 9 runs were remembered in
the sequel; a bad miss by the Monkey at A bad miss.
long-leg having giving a life to Newhall
before he had scored one; the second, third,
fourth, and fifth wickets fell for 13. This
was as it should be, and the Captain felt relieved. Hargreaves John saw seven of his
comrades succumb to the various chances of
the game, he played a good innings of 7;
seven for 26. The bowling was well sustained, and the fielding brilliant; runs were
not amassed with freedom. The fair occu-

pants of the Grand Stand gave vent re-
Shrieks. repeatedly to little shrieks, as one after
another their champions retired crestfallen
to the pavilion; eighth and ninth wicket fell
Joe. for 29. Hargreaves Joe was bowled for 4,
and sought the consolation of his brethren;
eleven for 32. No stand was made till Clay
appeared, and runs came quicker. He made
several dashing strokes, aided by Dan New-
Another hall, who was badly missed by Edgar,
miss. another bitter souvenir in the future. "The
stylish did not cling to it." The crowd was
now becoming demonstrative, and cheer
after cheer greeted every hit. Clay was
" caught in the fluke by Hadow," having
with Newhall added 20 runs to the score;
To quote. sixteen for 61. R. Pesse, ' usually a
splendid batsman, free hitter, and good de-
fender," went to the wicket; "he had been
entered in the first innings for a blank
score." He was not in luck, he added
another round one to his gross total; seventeen for 62. Dan Newhall got hold of Gilbert and made 6 off him in one over. He
was stumped at last for 15 ; a fine dashing
innings, consisting of two 3's, three 2's, and

singles; eighteen for 70. Maiden overs now set in with great austerity. Cooper Baird " hit heavily at Grace's first ball, and was bowled " for 1; the twentieth wicket falling for 74. Sud. Law "blocked one ball, the next he was bowled." Such are the affecting records we have gleaned from the Dailies. The second innings resulted in 74 runs. This left 33 runs for the Twelve to get on Tuesday. Speculation was rife, and the following curious contrast was published in one paper. " In the match in 1868 between the All England Eleven and the Philadelphians, the Englishmen had 32 to win in the second innings, yet the Eleven only won by two wickets."

CHEERING THE PLAYERS.

We extract the following :—After the stumps were drawn, the crowd collected round the clubhouse, calling loudly for Grace, Ottoway, Hornby, and others of the Twelve. Cheer after cheer was given when Grace appeared, and nothing would quiet the crowd but the appearance of all the players on the balcony. Mr. FitzGerald, Captain of the Twelve, was then introduced to the crowd, and cheers were given for Gloucestershire, for Grace, and the British flag, when quiet was restored.

The Captain's address.

MR. R. A. FITZGERALD

made a neat little speech, in which he said that the Twelve were glad that they had come to Philadelphia, as they had seen the best ground and played the best game of the Tour; he was pleased to see so many English faces looking up to him, they had every appearance of having done well in America, and America doubtless owed something to them. He pleaded the excuse *Horace.* of the immortal Greeley, that he could not make a long speech before he had washed his face.

Great excitement prevailed in the English section of the crowd at this exciting phase of the game, and many were the exhortations to the Twelve "not to be beaten." The day had been superb, and the attendance remarkable of all classes of the citizens.

Cricket 3rd day. Tuesday, September 24.—Another bril-

o the
ouces-
flag,

e said
y had
on the
ime of
many
y had
ell in
owed
excuse
ld not
vashed

Eng-
xciting
e the
to be
, and
sses of

bril-

liant summer's day. Play commenced at a quarter past twelve; the Grand Stand was again filled, and the ring round the ground unbroken. 33 runs did not look like a match, but never was the old adage, that a match is not lost till it is won, better exemplified. The Twenty-two meant mischief; there was no mistaking the keen look, the business-like attitude of the field. Business.

A glance at the wickets made Gilbert remark that the few runs would take some getting, it had worn tolerably well, but the intense heat, and the ordeal it had gone The ordeal. through, had taken the colour out of it, and put a rough edge on it, which was much in favour of fast bowling.

Gilbert and Ottoway soon appeared. A general rustle of fans in the Grand Stand Rustle in proved the smothered excitement of the fair the Stand. occupants. Gilbert scored one run off Newhall's third ball, and the fourth found its way unchecked to Ottoway's middle stump. Roars of applause greeted the Roars. event. The sky was darkened with broad and narrow brims, billycocks, and headgear of every hue; one for 1. Hornby quickly, filled the gap, made one good hit for 3 to leg, when another roar announced his capture at short leg; two for 8. Alfred filled the vacant throne; runs were stolen rather than made; over after over was bowled without the batsmen leaving their wicket. The moments were worth pounds in a cricketer's life. Alfred had made 3, and Gilbert at last landed a 3 to leg; 15 runs had been obtained in three-quarters of an hour. Newhall's bowling rose dangerously high, and it was difficult to avoid his rib-roasters. Meade hammered away brilliantly, dead on the spot. Alfred was then caught and bowled; three for 15. Hadow approached amidst general acclamations. He at once opened an account, scoring three in his first over. Gilbert meanwhile had been " in luck." There was a case for the Umpire, which was awarded in his favour, and he narrowly missed capture amongst the slips. He had displayed great caution, but it was not destined for him to land the Twelve in triumph. A roar that might have made William Penn turn in his grave, suddenly told that the Leviathan was out.

Golden Moments.

Newhall Rib-roasting.

Hadow.

The Umpire.

A Scream.

'The Leviathan.

The flutter amongst the ladies was now as great as if they were sitting on a wasp's nest. The great man strode home; his seven had taken him nearly an hour; four for 18. George came in with a jaunty air, *George the Jaunty.* and with Hadow restored the aspect of the game, from the English point of view. The field was slightly shaken, hits at last penetrated the phalanx, and the return was less direct to the wicket, though no less sharp. The throwing-in was, as a rule, remarkably good in the match. The score had reached 29, and danger seemed to be averted, when *Out of Danger.* George was too impatient, and was caught off a mounter of Newhall's, at cover-point, for a most valuable 9; five for 29. Hadow soon followed him, bowled by Meade for 6; six for 29. The remaining four runs were fought out inch by inch. Francis went in "to do or die." He didn't—he died; seven for 29. There seemed a chance for the Quakers yet. Nobody could sit still in the *General Fidget.* Grand Stand. It was agony to answer a question. It was almost insulting to human nature to demand a light for a cigar. Appleby, the Unassuming, walked leisurely

s

in; on him the Captain relied, and not in
vain. Edgar had filled Francesco's cell,
and " as he stood in his peculiar attitude,
it seemed as if he must be bowled out by
Newhall before he was on his legs." " But
the said legs stood him in good stead, for a
leg bye off one of them was worth a pocket-
full of greenbacks, and 30 runs were up."
It must be mentioned that nearly half-an-
hour had elapsed without a run being
obtained. If the Captain had given orders
to prolong the excitement to the utmost
limits he could not have been better obeyed.
The end was now near. The Unaffected
let out at an over pitched ball of Newhall's
to the off, and four to the ropes was scored,
and the battle was won. The pent-up
excitement now broke loose. Shouts of
" well-bowled," " well-fielded, were met by
English counter-cheers of " well-played."
It was indeed a match that was worth the
winning, and it reflected little disgrace on
the defeated. If any mistake can be said
to have been made by the Captain of the
Twenty-two, it was in bringing in all his
men to save " one or two " runs; he should

have saved all chance of "fours," and he might thus have prolonged the game. It was scarcely possible that the Twelve would be beaten, although Fortune hung an unconscious time upon her scales. The protracted struggle was so far unfortunate, that it led to a hurried departure of the Twelve from the scene of their hardly-earned victory, in order to catch a train for Boston. The train was not caught, and the press was A Catch rather severe on the apparent discourtesy of missed. the Twelve in not remaining to acknowledge the last greetings of their antagonists. It was, however, solely and strictly in performance of their agreement with the cricketers of Boston, that the Twelve reluctantly left Philadelphia.

The reports at the close of the match were Reports. highly jubilant. Every paper teemed with accounts, and with morals drawn from the game. There is, doubtless, great praise due to the bowlers, who, though aided by the ground, and a smart field, contributed immensely to the exciting close. Newhall and Meade well deserve all that was printed of them by an admiring reporter. Hargreaves

s 2

" Joe " as wicket-keeper, once removed, did

good service. Prizes were distributed to Newhall and Meade for bowling, Large for batting, and Hargreaves Joe for fielding. F. Norley, who is in charge of the ground, deserves great credit for the pains he had taken.

We are glad to quote the following paragraph, which appeared in a leading paper :—

" Thus ended the first visit of the gentlemen of England to Germantown; and in closing this brief chronicle it behoves us, and is a pleasing duty, to express their sincere appreciation of the cordiality and kindness with which they were everywhere welcomed, of the great hospitality which they experienced in this city, and the goodfellowship which was accorded them, to tender their thanks for the same to the club with whom they were engaged, and to give vent to the hope that their first visit to Germantown may not be their last."

We are also glad to re-echo the following :

" The account of this great match cannot be complete without congratulation to the committee in charge of arrangements for their zeal in promoting the comfort of the spectators. Our especial thanks are due to Thomas McKean, Esq., J. D. Rodney, A. A. Outerbridge, and W. Vaux, Esqrs., for kind courtesies extended to us, and to all who visited the ground."

ENGLAND v. PHILADELPHIA.

TWENTY-TWO OF PHILADELPHIA.

Score

	1st inn.		2nd inn.
Brewster, b Appleby	4	c Rose, b Grace	0
H. Newhall, b Appleby	0	c Fitzgerald, b Grace	0
W. Welsh, b Appleby	0	b Appleby	1
R. Newhall, b Appleby	4	c Hornby, b Appleby	0
I. Large, h w, b Grace	18	c Appleby, b Grace	7
Cadwallader, h w, b Rose	2	b Grace	0
L. Baird, c Harris, b Rose	0	l b w, b Appleby	6
G. Newhall, b Appleby	0	b Appleby	9
Joe. Hargreaves, b Appleby	2	b Grace	4
W. Morgan, st Ottaway, b Grace	7	c Hadow, b Grace	1
D. Newhall, b. Grace	0	st Ottaway, b Grace	13
B. Law, c Rose, b Grace	0	not out	2
C. Newhall, b Appleby	3	l b w, b Appleby	0
Meade, c E. Lubbock, b Grace	0	b Appleby	0
R. Pease, h w, b Grace	0	b Appleby	0
C. Baird, run out	3	b Grace	1
Tom Hargreaves, st Ottaway, b Grace	0	st Ottaway, b Grace	2
R. Clay, b Grace	4	c Hadow, b Grace	13
John Hargreaves, run out	11	c and b Grace	7
Sanderson, b Appleby	0	b Grace	0
Magee, st Ottaway, b Grace	3	b Appleby	1
S. Welsh, not out	3	run out	0
Byes 1, leg byes 3	4	Byes	4
Total	—68	Total	—72

ENGLISH GENTLEMEN.

	1st inn.	2nd inn.
W. G. Grace, b C. Newhall	14	c Hargreaves, b C. Newhall.......... 7
Ottaway, run out	10	b C. Newhall......... 0
Hornby, b Meade	10	c R. Newhall, b Meade 4
A. Lubbock, run out	9	c and b C. Newhall 3
Hadow, c. Hargreaves, b Newhall	20	b Meade............... 6
G. Harris, c D. Newhall, b C. Newhall	3	c J. Hargreaves, b Meade............... 8
C. K. Francis, b Meade	5	b C. Newhall......... 0
Appleby, c Magee, b Meade	3	not out 4
E. Lubbock, c. J. Hargreaves, b Newhall	0	not out 0
W. M. Rose, c J. Hargreaves, b D. Newhall	0	
Pickering, b Newhall	7	
FitzGerald, not out	1	
Wides 3, byes 7, leg byes 4	14	Byes 1, leg byes 1 ... 2
Total	105	Total 34

We append the analysis of the bowling.

THE TWELVE.

FIRST INNINGS.

	Balls.	Runs.	Maidens.	Wickets.
Rose	64	16	6	2
Appleby	145	23	26	8
Grace	84	22	10	9

SECOND INNINGS.

Appleby	152	24	26	8
Grace	151	46	19	11

THE TWENTY-TWO.

FIRST INNINGS

	Balls.	Runs.	Maidens.	Wickets.
Newhall	212	45	26	6
Meade	200	44	28	3

SECOND INNINGS.

Newhall	73	24	8	4
Meade	72	8	13	3

2nd inn.
ives, b C.
ll............ 7
ull.......... 0
all, b Meade 4
  Newhall 3
.... 6
greaves, b
.... 8
ll.......... 0
.... 4

.... 0

yes 1 ... 2
         —
.... 34

wling.

Vickets.
.. 2
.. 8
. 9

. 8
11

okets.
6
3

4
3

Thirteen maiden overs were bowled at one time in succession. Great trouble had been taken in the selection of the Twenty-Two. They were drafted from the leading clubs of Philadelphia; the Young America Club furnishing eleven; the Germantown, six; the Philadelphia Club, five. The proportion of work done or omitted by the various representatives was critically reckoned. For instance, we read that the best fielding was done by the Germantown contingent, the brothers Hargreaves, as well as the worst, Cadwallader. The best bowling by the Young America, C. Newhall. We differ from this, as to our mind Meade is by far the best bowler; and on a good wicket, we do not think Newhall can hold a rushlight to him. To the bowling of Appleby the victory of the Twelve is eminently due. That the crowd thought likewise is proved by the loud calls for him to appear in the balcony. A local reports that "the innate modesty of this gentleman for a few moments deterred him from presenting himself, but the clamor grew so loud, that he ultimately consented to shoot, like a

[margin notes: Constituents. Appleby. Affecting.]

The blushing meteor. blushing, evanescent meteor, through the verandah."

We have entered fully into the fortunes of the field; we are anxious to do justice to our gallant antagonists; we were not prepared for the interest taken in the match by the spectators, nor were we aware of the hold that cricket has taken upon the youth of A surprise. Philadelphia. It was an agreeable surprise. From the cricket-field to the cupboard was the regular course, and the evening spent at The Union the Union League Club was one of the most Club. memorable during the tour. Upwards of 200 guests had been invited; the handsome rooms were well lighted, and an interesting series of portraits introduced the Twelve to many heroes of the late war. There was plenty of speechifying to a late hour. The evening entertainments are peculiar in one No seats. respect. There are no chairs; the good things are discussed standing. This is rather trying when you have been on your legs, and your legs have been on the move the greater part of the day. The Captain modestly asked for a chair, and requested The General. General Meade, who presided at the banquet, to follow his example, which he kindly did; but, with the exception of the cricketers, nobody sat down at the groaning board. The evening was cheerful; the most distinguished of the citizens were present. Toasts of the most genial character set in, and the Captain was called upon to reply to, or to propose, at least, a score of toasts. He could not miss such an opportunity of expressing the pleasure of his companions at making the personal acquaintance of American cricketers; he alluded gratefully to the services of the Philadelphia committee, which had been so instrumental in securing a happy result; he trusted that this visit would lead to many others, and he augured from the good cricket already exhibited that a love for the game would long be cherished, and that it would take root in the schools of the State, and bear its fruit upward ere many years were past, in an even-handed struggle with the best proficients of England.

A melancholy interest is attached to this evening, full as it is of pleasant memories. General Meade, who presided, is now no more; his son had taken a great part in the

[marginal note: The Captain up.]

[marginal note: Sad Memories.]

IMAGE EVALUATION
TEST TARGET (MT-3)

match. The General had won all hearts by his kind demeanour; his manly form and eagle eye distinguished him outwardly amongst his fellow men. It was our privilege to make his acquaintance, and to hear from his lips, as we walked together through the national gallery of the club, many anecdotes of the war, which came home to us with greater force in the martial words of the Hero of Gettysburg.

The Hero of Gettysburg.

Previously to appearing at the Union League Club, the Twelve had kept an engagement at Mr. Fox's Theatre, where stalls had been placed at their disposal. Upon the arrival of the Twelve, the band struck up "God save the Queen," and the audience cheered vociferously. The "Star Spangled Banner" was greeted with equal warmth by the visitors. We must conclude our account of Philadelphia with a brief review of the Official Handbook. It is an additional proof of the interest taken in the match that this book met with a large circulation. A copy of it, handsomely bound, was given to each of the Twelve, by Mr. Outerbridge, in memory of their visit.

Mr. Fox's Theatre.

Cheers.

The Official Handbook.

It was headed—

"PRICE 25 CENTS.

OFFICIAL HANDBOOK FOR

THE INTERNATIONAL CRICKET FÊTE

AT PHILADELPHIA, 1872,

omitting what everybody knows, and containing what everybody wants to know, including a score-sheet for spectators."

The title is not unambitious, but it carried out its programme. It was divided into three parts.

Part I.—Containing criticisms on the players, programme of play, preliminaries, &c.

Under the head of "American Players" appears the following:—"Philadelphia is the only place where the English Twelve will meet a local American Twenty-Two." Professionals and Englishmen have been excluded, with the view of making this a purely International contest. The following programmes appeared on every blank wall. They will prove the interest taken in the match :—

PROGRAMME OF THE MATCH.

Saturday.—Play will commence at 11.30,

and continue until sundown. A capacious grand stand has been erected, a restaurateur engaged, and the band from the navy yard will play at intervals. Telegraphs of the score will be posted, and the names of the English players will be exhibited on large canvas stripes as they take the bat. At the close of the day's play the Twelve will dine at a private entertainment. *Sunday* will be spent as a day of rest, with, perhaps, a drive through the park.

Monday.—Play will be resumed at 11 A.M. In the evening a private reception will be given at the Union League Club House, in Broad Street, in honour of the guests. *Tuesday* will be devoted to finishing the match.

ON THE GROUND.

There will be two entrances for spectators. The holders of checks will be shown to their seats by ushers.

Part II.—Scores of previous matches; Mr. Grace's innings; Curiosities of Cricket; Cricket Songs; The Daily Press on Cricket.

Part III.—Explanations for new Cricketers, with Diagrams; Miscellaneous Cricket

Chirps; Scores of Recent Matches; Blank Score-Sheets for Spectators, &c.

Directions how to reach the ground at Germantown were given in full.

> " Ye lovers of cricket, now lend me your ears,
> And I soon shall obtain your plaudits and cheers;
> I sing an Eleven, the gauntlet that hurled
> Of defiance, and challenged the rest of the world."

From poetry it descends to prose. In the first place explaining the distinction (if any) of " The Gentlemen Eleven." It would seem an affectation to dignify one class of cricketers with that appellation while another must be satisfied to be simply " players." But in England caste obtains, and a class of professional cricketers exists, as well as of " amateurs or gentlemen players." Thus dismissing a " vexata quæstio," it proceeds to draw freely upon Lillywhite's Guides for the morals and manners of the Twelve, and dips into the private histories of the Twenty-Two. It anticipates the forte of the Twenty-Two to be in fielding, its feeble spot in batting. The following gentlemen formed the committee of arrangements :—

C. E. Cadwallader.   C. Stuart Patterson.

F. C. Newhall.   Albert A. Outerbridge.

Chairman of Reception Committee:

J. Dickinson Sergeant.

In the regulations for the ground, we notice the prices of admission to be 50 cents. each day. Season ticket, admitting each day, 1 dol. Reserved seats on grand stand 50 cents.

The results of previous International Matches are set out in order, and it may be refreshing to learn that in 1859, on October 10—13, G. Parr's English Eleven obtained 126 and 29, with 3 wickets down, against the Philadelphia Twenty-Two, with an innings of 94 and 60.

Parr, Jackson, Wisden, Caffyn, and Carpenter bowled, Jackson obtaining 8 wickets, having bowled 236 balls for 37 runs in the first innings.

Wisden bowled 157 balls for 39 runs and 8 wickets in the second.

For the Philadelphians—

Mr. Senior bowled 105 balls for 20 runs and 5 wickets. The Eleven were victorious by 7 wickets.

In 1868, on October 3, Willsher's Eleven played a memorable match, resembling the amateurs in its close results.

The Philadelphians obtained 88 and 35 against the Eleven 92 and 36 with 8 wickets down.

For the Eleven Freeman bowled 168 balls for 15 runs and 14 wickets, Jarrant bowling 88 balls for 39 runs and 4 wickets.

In the second innings Freeman bowled 100 balls for 9 runs and 13 wickets, Griffith bowling 64 balls for 22 runs and 5 wickets.

For the Twenty-Two, C. Newhall bowled 116 balls for 48 runs and 6 wickets, Meade bowled 60 balls for 19 runs and 1 wicket.

In this match the first four wickets of the English Eleven fell in the first innings for 11 runs, and in the second innings for 17; eight wickets were disposed of for 32 runs.

The same Eleven played another match on October 10; the Twenty-Two were selected from the United States, and not confined to Philadelphia.

The Twenty-two obtained $\frac{47 \text{ and } 62}{109}$ against the Eleven $\frac{117 \text{ and } 64}{181}$.

In this match—

C. Newhall bowled 182 balls for 57 runs and 8 wickets.
,,   ,, 120 ,, 30 ,, 6 ,,
Meade   ,, 132 ,, 18 ,, 2 ,,
,,   ,,   94 ,, 22 ,, 4 ,,

FIRST INNINGS.

Freeman bowled 169 balls for 14 runs and 10 wickets.
Willsher ,, 176 ,, 18 ,, 7 ,,

SECOND INNINGS.

Freeman bowled 156 balls for 17 runs and 9 wickets.
Willsher ,, 136 ,, 22 ,, 6 ,,

W. G. Mr. Grace's performances are summed up, and we learn that scores of a century and upwards have only been obtained as yet in two instances in America. What an agreeable contrast this forms to our own satiated seats of spectators. Long may the bowling prove superior to the batting. A sparkling conceit, as it is termed, is extracted from the Evening Bulletin. It is the voice of the Cricket chirping to the cricketer in favour of the noble game; it summons young and old, gentle and simple to the ground, and if not

A quid. exactly sparkling, it is a merry conceit. Jerks in from short-leg is politely introduced in an appeal to the ladies. There is also a

William Shakspeare on Cricket. report of a cricket match by William Shakspeare (now first publisʰᵉᵈ).

The author professes to refute the general opinion that cricket was not known in the time of Queen Elizabeth, by many passages taken at random from the Bard of Avon. The Bard is supposed to be on the ground *The Bard.* and to be presented to the English Twelve, to whom he addressed these words—

> —— " And you, good yeomen,
> Whose limbs were made in England, show us here
> The mettle of your pasture," &c.
>
> *Henry V.*, act iii., sc. 1.

He is shown the cricket ball, upon which he remarks—

> " A carbuncle entire, as big as thou art,
> Were not so rich a jewel."
>
> *Coriolanus*, act i., sc. 4.

We scarcely think that this opinion would be shared by any but the most enthusiastic lovers of the game ; of Hadow, the Bard re- *Hadow.* marked—

> " How oddly he is suited ! I think he bo   t his doublet in Oxford, his round hose (O') in America, a..d his bonnet in Madame Louise's."   *Merchant of Venice*, act i., sc. 2.

Now Haddocks is a harlequin, and every *The Harle-* Oxonian will recognise the appropriate allu- *quin.*

T

sion to that fantastic costume. The Bard
however adds—

" Haddocks seems to be more noble in being fantastical—a
great man, I'll warrant."   *Winter's Tale*, act iv., sc. 3.

The spectators exhibiting nervousness at
the commencement of the game, William delivered the following lecture—

" Because you want the Grace that others have,
    You judge it straight a thing impossible
    To compass wonders."
                    Henry VI., part i., act v., sc. 4.

The Cap-
tain.

William nodded affably to the English
Captain, and said—

" Prepare you, General,
The enemy comes on in gallant show,
And something's to be done immediately."
                    Julius Cæsar, act v., sc. 1.

Farrands.

The umpire having quoted

" The play's the thing."
                    Hamlet, act ii., sc. 2.

And the batsman replying—

" Aye boy, ready."
                    Romeo and Juliet, act. i., sc. 5.

William exclaims—

" Make you ready your stiff bats;
Field, gentlemen of England, field boldly."
                    Richard III., act v., sc. 3.

Turning to Appleby, he whispered— Applepie.

"Now be a Freeman."
Julius Cæsar, act v., sc. 3.

The Bard made a few flattering remarks w. g. to Gilbert upon his appearing at the wicket, but the great man did not cotton to the Bard, for he muttered—

"Sir, praise me not ;
My work hath not yet warm'd me."
Coriolanus, act i., sc. 5.

The Captain is reported to have whispered The Captain. in Gilbert's ear—

"We must do something, and in the heat."
King Lear, act i., sc. 7.

—— "Dispatch
Those centuries to our aid."
Coriolanus, act i., sc. 7.

Wherupon the Leviathan opened his shoulders, and made

A hit, a very palpable hit."
Hamlet, act v., sc. 2.

An accident of a painful and dubious nature Edgar. having occurred to a player, an anxiou sweetheart whines to this effect—

"Is not that Edgar lying on the ground ?
He lies not like the living ! O, my heart !"
Julius Cæsar, act i., sc. 3.

Julius
Cæsar.

Julius Cæsar played at Philadelphia in 1859, and is constantly quoted.

The
Marmoset.

Monkey is described as the stealthy runner—

> "A snapper up of unconsidered trifles."
> *Winter's Tale*, act. iv., sc. 2.

Edgar, a very uncertain runner, is thus pourtrayed—

> "Stand, and go back.
> Back—I mean, go—back, that is the utmost of your having,
> Back." *Coriolanus*, act v., sc. 2.

Appleby is again introduced as a

> "Marvellous good neighbour, in sooth, and a very good bowler." *Love's Labour's Lost*, act v., sc. 2.

The youth-
ful George.

The youthful Harris is favourably mentioned as the favourite with the girls on the Grand Stand, for upon being asked who is their favourite—

> "Volumnia (replies) 'Honourable George.'"
> *Coriolanus*, act i., sc. 1.

We must conclude our remarks upon this lively article with the following soliloquies of the Captain, the Twenty-two, and the Committee.

The Captain sings out— The Cap-
tain.

> " Come, let us to the field,
> 'Tis three o'clock, and, comrades, yet ere night
> We shall try Fortune in a second fight."
> *Julius Cæsar*, act v., sc. 3.

Upon the conclusion of the match, the The
Twenty-
two.
Twenty-two, in chorus, howl—

> " Beaten, but not without honour ;
> In this glorious and well-foughten field,
> We kept together in our chivalry."
> *Henry V.*, act. 4, sc. 6.

The Committee chime in with the feeling The Com-
mittee.
words—

> " I will entertain them."
> *Julius Cæsar*, act v., sc. last.

Considering that the Official Handbook was the offspring of a few days' conception, it was marvellously well produced.

Before we quit the friendly soil of Pennsylvania, it would be unjust not to recognise the hearty co-operation of the public journals The Press. in the cause of cricket, and in favour of the English visit.

Under the head of International Amenities An Article. our paper has an article, in which it alludes to the cricketers as " Giving evidence of an international sympathy in the amenities of life, and though a visit of this nature may in itself be thought a small matter, yet 'many a little maketh a mickle,' in promoting a good understanding between the two countries."

Another. Under "Muscular Christianity" another journal speaks out boldly, "If we would take one step towards removing the occasion of such slurs on our American manhood, quoted above, we must encourage our youth to some manly exercises, and from all we know of cricket we can advise no better, 'Mens sana in corpore sano,' though 2000 years old, is a motto that we cannot improve upon."

Another article says : "If these more prominent cricket matches shall have the effect of encouraging the permanent adoption by our youth of a manly recreation which is admitted to be morally and physically healthful, as well as intensely enjoyable, the approaching visit of our English guests will not be without good results."

The Evening Telegraph on out-door sports. "Out-door sports" are well treated in the *Evening Telegraph.* Alluding to the approaching match in Philadelphia, the article goes on,—" Now is the time to re ze ow much we stand in need of somethin that will take us out into the fields occa nally and keep us there for a few hours, if only as inactive spectators. What we are suffering from is the want of out-door exercises and fresh air. To a very large number of our people the game of cricket, if they but knew it, would be a boon and also a pleasure, as the coming International Match will enable them to estimate. We hope that the coming of the famous gentlemen-players from England will revive all the old interest, and as a consequence bring new talent to our cricket-field in the future. We want our English friends to have a hearty welcome, and we want our people to see what a fine game cricket is."

Our last words are, that we received a hearty welcome, and we played a hearty match. Long may cricket continue to be played in the spirit which animated our kind friends at Germantown.

CHAPTER III.

Elegant
Extracts.
Prose.

" THE Boston Cricket Club and all cricketers in Massachusetts, where we have about a dozen clubs, wish to see you play at Boston. We shall esteem ourselves peculiarly unfortunate if you come through Boston and do not give us a day or two's cricket."

" We shall endeavour to do all we can to make your stay here agreeable, although the short time we have for preparation may prevent us from carrying out everything which we originally projected."

" It is perhaps needless to say how cordial your reception would be, but we should use every effort to make your stay enjoyable."

These extracts prove that the same friendly spirit animated the good people of Boston towards the English Cricketers. Time was the only difficulty.

Sept. 28 was the day fixed for sailing home. It was necessary to rob Peter to pay Paul. Philadelphia must be curtailed of some of her attractions, New York must abandon some of her many temptations, or Boston will not be satisfied.

Sacrilege.

It was sad indeed to slip away from Philadelphia, but not, as was ungenerously said in some quarters, in any want of grateful sentiment towards our entertainers there, it was strictly in accordance with our original plan. To see as much of America and Americans as we possibly could in the time.

The prolonged excitement of the match at Philadelphia led first to missing a train which would have conveyed the Twelve, travelling all night, to Boston in time to play on Sept. 25.

"The miss was as good as a mile," as good indeed as two hundred miles, for it hung the Twelve up to dry in New York for some hours, and it was not until the evening of

Proverb.

Sept. 25 that they were able to proceed to Boston.

The previous evening had been spent at Fifth Avenue. the Fifth Avenue Hotel in New York, a magnificent structure, crowded with fair and young nymphs, fresh from the briny attractions of Newport.

A long night's journey landed the Twelve at Boston on the morning of September 26. Heavy rain all night did not promise a good day's cricket—a promise kept to the full—a one day's match was arranged.

The original programme had included a Harvard College. drive to and breakfast at Harvard College. The Captain was compelled to abandon this, as his young friends were unkempt and unwashed, not to say hungry; their wants required immediate attention, and Harvard is several miles away from Boston. The Twelve were sorry not to acknowledge the University's kind proposals otherwise than by declining. Parker House received them— Parker House. a most comfortable and clean hotel. The chambermaids are remarkable, not only for good looks but for civility. It appeared miraculous to the wearied travellers, after

their experience of other handmaids in the ^{Maids.}
Land of Liberty, to find a bell answered, and
a belle bringing a bath in less than a quarter
of an hour after the demand. We owe these
damsels much more than we can at this
moment calculate or dare to own; an instance
of their peculiar merits must be recorded,
though a little out of date. Upon his return
home our William missed a packet of letters, ^{Our William.}
written—we will not say by whom, but of an
affectionate character. The loss would pro- ^{Love letters.}
bably never have been mentioned by him,
had he not been interrogated by the fair writer.
Imagine, if you can, the mutual delight with
which a packet was received, addressed, in
the first instance, to the Captain by the head
housemaid, containing the lost letters, and
marked "Unread." We were not convinced
of her truth after reading them ourselves, for
even we had great difficulty to part with
them.

September 26. The Captain had business ^{Cricket.}
in Boston, and in his absence Gilbert assumed
the lead, and made two great mistakes, first, ^{1st. fault.}
in consenting to play on such a ground;
second, in fixing the hour to draw stumps at ^{2nd. do.}

six p.m. In defence of the first, it may certainly be urged that not to have played would
have disappointed the Bostonians, but when
the state of the ground is considered, it is
open to question whether a good match had
not better be abandoned than allowed to
degenerate into a mud-lark. The Captain,
probably, would have adopted the same
course, but not without a struggle; he certainly would not have agreed to play as late
as agreed, and the result proved he would
have been wise.

Sawdust. Sawdust having been liberally carted upon
the spot, and a wicket having been selected,
the game commenced at 11.30. Gilbert
lost the toss. Mem : Every toss lost in the
States and won in Canada. It was a truly
ludicrous sight—long-stop up to his ancles
The swamp. in sawdust and mire, a swamp extending
around the ground, the few drabbled spectators clustering on any dry spot, the wickets
sodden with lean and lank grass; our William
and the Tormentor bowling, a wicket fell at
the first over of the former. It was much in
favour of the bowler, and the batsmen merely
went in for the purpose of a walk to the

wicket and back; four wickets fell for 8 runs. To sum up the sad history, nineteen wickets fell for 26. Then came in Linder, he swiped with vigour, and Gilbert, not taking the hint, allowed him to flirt with Rosa in a most improper manner. He should have interfered, even with his own high-home-and-easy; as it was, the plucky Bostonian landed 17, and carried his bat out amidst great applause, having seen 25 more added to this score. Total, 51. The Captain saw nothing of the above, and when he did arrive upon the scene a still more ludicrous spectacle awaited him; A surprise. eight wickets down for 39, of this meagre total, Gilbert had contributed 26. From what he could gather on the ground, the batsmen had played skittles, they were out of heart and Skittles. patience, had dashed into the mud, been stumped, run out, caught, and had committed every foolish crime that cricketers are capable of under any circumstances. It was scarcely credible, it was not (we are forced to own) creditable. Allowance may be made for the disheartening state of the ground, but that does not justify, in our mind, *not playing* the game. The game was *to stick, to time* the hits, *to be careful* in running—not one of the three specifics was adopted. Gilbert, in his 26, made two splendid hits out of the ground, these had been absurdly estimated at 4 each, a hit out of the ground was honestly worth 6. He was bowled by Eastwood, after being at the wickets 51 minutes—his score comprised two 4's, six 2's, and singles. The bowling of G. Wright and Eastwood had been well sustained, and the fielding was superior to any yet seen—Haigh being the best man yet met with behind the wicket. If ever a match required caution and not dash, this did; if ever a match fulfilled the necessary conditions, this didn't.

Lunch ? A luncheon was provided, not of a very *récherché* description—20 minutes only were lost at it. Edgar and the Tormentor at the wickets, the wicked one was rash, and paid for it. Haddock, Frances, and Appleby were all stumped for 7 runs between them. Rose and the Captain were run out, owing, in some Edgar on the straddle. measure, to the gentle Edgar, whose legs, once straddled on the deep ground, could not get out of it—47 runs off the bat, and 4 extras, A Tie. brought the total to a tie—51 all. In their

ne of the
t, in his
ground,
t 4 each,
worth 6.
being at
mprised
bowling
en well
erior to
man yet
a match
did ; if
ditions,

a very
y were
at the
d paid
y were
Rose
n some
s, once
ot get
extras,
their

second innings, the Twenty-two faced Gilbert and Appleby, the latter bowled splendidly, with a very bad foothold. Rosa was cashiered on spec. It turned out well, as Gilbert was difficult to play, and the total only reached 43. The innings commenced at 3.30, and concluded at 5 P.M. G. Wright made a splendid hit out of the ground in his score of 6. Eastwood also showed good form, the rest were defeated by the ground, and no opinion can possibly be formed of individual merit. The wickets were now a quagmire. The spectators were not numerous ; but, as many had come from a distance to view the contest, and all were as keen as Colman's mustard, Mustard. the Captain decided to continue, although the light was waning fast, and rain had begun to fall. There were only 44 to get. The bowlers were on their mettle, and the field, if possible, improved in activity. Gilbert and George were the first to appear to the bowling of G. Wright and Eastwood, George was splendidly caught and bowled, a fine hard hit, dashingly secured by the clever and civil George Wright. Gilbert found the mud too much even for him, and was also caught and

bowled by Eastwood for 5 ; two wickets down
for 7. Neither Monkey nor Haddocks had
profited by their lesson of the first innings,
Barnacles. and were returned members for Barnacles
without any opposition; four wickets down for 8.
Alfred was soon bowled by Eastwood; five for
11. • The light was now darkness. Francisco
went in full of fight, and made two magnificent hits in his little lot of 8, when he, too,
fell to Wright and Eastwood. Appleby, meanwhile, was playing with care. The juncture
was critical, not cricketal. The Captain consulted the Umpires as to continuing, but on
discovering that only ten minutes more play
was at stake, went in himself, remained two
overs, and finally received a full pitch on the
The Cap-
tain's toe. big toe, which, for all he knew, from all he
saw, might with equal pleasure have been
The last
ball. landed on his nose. It was the last ball
bowled in the American tour. The Umpire
cried time, the Tormentor and the Captain
carried their bats back to the dark room,
where their comrades were huddled together,
and in darkness and in damp was brought to
a close the last match of the series. 22 runs
had been made for the loss of six wickets, a

kets down
locks had
t innings,
Barnacles
down for 8.
d; five for
Francisco
) magnifi-
1 he, too,
by, mean-
e juncture
ptain con-
g, but on
more play
ained two
tch on the
om all he
have been
last ball
e Umpire
e Captain
ark room,
1 together,
orought to
. 22 runs
wickets, a

tie on the first innings being thus succeeded by half the wickets down for half the runs required, a funny match, the honours, if any, Honours even. strictly divided. The Twelve had only the weather to anathematize. Nothing could exceed the courtesy of the Bostonians, and cricketers would do well to lay to mind the lesson and example afforded by the spirited New Englanders. They did their best to win, and nearly won. We are of opinion that, with one or two exceptions, the Twelve did their best to lose, and nearly lost.

BOSTON.	1st inn.	2nd inn.	The Score.
Ward, hit wicket, b Appleby	3	run out	1
Leeson, b Rose	0	c Pickering, b Grace	2
Gorse, b Rose	0	c Francis, b Grace	1
Haigh, c Pickering, b Appleby	5	b Appleby	0
G. Wright, b Rose	0	c FitzGerald, b Appleby	6
Cruise, run out	1	c Appleby, b Grace	0
Eastwood	1	c Pickering, b Appleby	8
H. Wright, b Rose	3	c Harris, b Grace	0
Want, c Grace, b Rose	1	b Appleby	0
Perkins, c Francis, b Rose	1	st Ottoway, b Grace	2
McVey, b Rose	0	c Hadow, b Appleby	1
Mitchelson, b Appleby	1	c Pickering, b Grace	5
Wilkinson, b Appleby	0	c FitzGerald, b Grace	0
Sodon, st Ottoway, b Rose	1	st Ottoway, b Grace	2
Carpenter, b Appleby	0	c Francis, b Appleby	1
Barron, c Rose, b Appleby	7	st Ottoway, b Grace	0
Bate, b Rose	0	b Appleby	1
Davis, b Appleby	1	c FitzGerald, b Grace	0
King, b Appleby	1	not out	
Farley, c Grace, b Rose	6	c A. Lubbock, b Grace	1

U

BOSTON—*continued.*   1st inn.   2nd inn.

Thomas Linden, not out 17   st Ottoway, b Grace. 0

Leonard, st Ottoway, b Appleby .. 2   l b w, b Grace 2

                                          Byes, 4 ; leg-bye, 1... 5

         Total 51   Total 43

ENGLAND.   1st inn.   2nd inn.

Grace, b Eastwood 26   c and b Eastwood..... 5

Hornby, b G. Wright 0   b Eastwood 0

A. Lubbock, c Linden, b Eastwood 5   b Eastwood 3

Hadow, st Haigh, b Eastwood 1   b Eastwood 0

Harris, c Gorse, b G. Wright...... 3   c and b G. Wright ... 2

Francis, st Haigh, b G. Wright... 5   b Eastwood 8

Appleby, st Haigh, b G. Wright.. 1   not out 3

FitzGerald, run out.. .... 2 not out 0

E. Lubbock, not out................. 4

Rose, run out 0

Pickering, b Salon 0

Ottoway, b G. Wright 0

Extras 4   Bye 1

         Total........................ 51   Total 22

The game was not ended at sunset, and was drawn.

ANALYSIS OF BOWLING.

ENGLAND.—First Innings.

	Balls.	Runs.	Wickets.
Rose,	68 .... 37 10		
Appleby,	66 .... 14 9		

Second Innings.

| Grace, | 74 ... . 35 .... 13 | | |
| Appleby, | 72 .... 3 .... 7 | | |

BOSTON.—First Innings.

	Balls.	Runs.	Wickets.
G. Wright, 100 .... 24 5			
Eastwood, 100 .... 20 3			

Second Innings.

| G. Wright, 51 .... 11 .... 1 | | |
| Eastwood, 40 .... 10 .... 5 | | |

The thanks of the Twelve are eminently
due to Mr. Rockwell, for his exertions in their
behalf. The famous base-ball players, the
Brothers Wright, who had played in the New
York Twenty-two, are natives of Boston,
and took a prominent part in the match.
G. Wright presented each of the Twelve with
a base-ball. This game is well adapted to Base-ball.
the genius of the people. It is of comparatively short duration, it has few pauses, it is
constantly changing its aspect. There is no
sticking, no monotonous change of overs, all
is on the strike, everybody is on the bound.
It will hold its own in America, and cricket
can never expect to attain to its popularity.
From an English point of view it presents
little interest, there are no hard knocks on
the knuckles or shins, none of the excitement
that is engendered by a fast bowler on a quick
wicket. It demands quickness of foot and
eye, and above all it requires smartness and
precision of throwing. It develops fielding,
and it ought to teach men to open their
shoulders, for hard hitting is a *sine quâ non*
with a good base-ball player.

To sum it up, it is an improvement on our

v 2

old schoolboys' game of rounders, without,
however, the most attractive part to an
English schoolboy—the "corking." We can
see still, we are not sure that we cannot still
feel, the quiver of the fat boy's nether parts,
as the ball, well directed, buried itself in his
flesh. "Rounders" had attractions for youth,
we doubt if the improved game would amuse
the grown-up British public. Immense sums
are staked upon it in America, and a handsome income is realised by the celebrated
Red Stocking Boston Club. Cricket has to
contend against the business habits of Americans. They will not give the time necessary
for the game. They will snatch a few moments
from the counter for base-ball, and they would
do the same for cricket; but the same two
men may be in at the one game the whole
time they can devote to leisure, and they are
not charmed with monotony, even if it be
High Art. Whereas, at the other game, they
may see several sides out in the same time.
We believe this to be the true social position
of cricket in the States. Time is money here,
and there is no denying that much of that
valuable commodity is egregiously cut into

ribbons at cricket. Americans might learn much, if they chose, from our noble game : if it inculcates one thing, it preaches and practises patience, it enforces self-control, it eliminates the irascible, it displays the excellence of discipline, it is more eloquent than Father Mathew on temperance and sobriety. With all respect for base-ball and its disciples, we believe that it principally encourages the two' leading failings of American character—ultra-rapidity, quicksilver-sosity, or whatever else of lightning proclivity you like to call it, and ardent speculation.

At Boston, as at Philadelphia, invitations from the proprietors of the theatres were for-The drama. warded to the Twelve. The Boston Museum, by the kindness of Mr. Field, was open to them, and an excellent old comedy of Holcroft's, "The Road to Ruin," was admirably played. Mr. Booth, of the Boston Theatre, placed stalls also at their disposal.

Hadow, in the course of the day, was driven by a gentleman to Harvard University, where he met with great civility from the undergrads and dons in residence.

The Twelve in their tour through the

States were as busy as bees, they could but sip the honey in their hurried flight, but they treasure in the cells of their memory many sweet souvenirs of each place.

The club. The Somerset Club is one of the best in America, most comfortably and elegantly appointed, its members did all they could in the time at their disposal to introduce the Twelve to that inner sociality which distinguishes Boston. The last evening was almost sad—cricket-bags were closed for the last time, heads were now turned homewards, excepting Appleby's, he was bound to the far West, to the Pacific shore. The Eleven would plough the main without their great bowler, and to-night for the last time they all sat at the same board.

The modern Colon. The "discoverer of America," the hero of Alexandra Bay, has long been left out in the cold. Colonel Maude, V.C., C.B., had accompanied the Twelve throughout their tour. He had been their guide, philosopher, and friend in many a carouse. His philosophy was of the pleasantest, his guidance of value, his friendship of proved worth. It was unanimously agreed to present him with a slight mark of appreciation. The last dinner was selected for the occasion, the Captain's last speech was uttered in an attempt to do justice to it. A gold pencil-case with inscription, "Presented by the Gentlemen Cricketers of England to Col. Maude, V.C., C.B., 1872," *Presentation.* was handed to him. He was not allowed to return thanks. The tour was completed. The man that dared to make another speech would have been brained on the spot. Many was the parting glass, the long roll of cocktails was drained to the dregs; it was gratifying to hear but one consenting remark, that the tour had been successful, that the Eleven were well pleased.

A lurid glare in the sky betokened fire in *A fire.* the neighbourhood of the Parker House. All hurried to the spot, and a grand sight was presented, an enormous granite structure was in flames. Little dreaming of the awful catastrophe that lurked in the pauló post future of this fine town, we could not help remarking to a bystander in the crowd, as we noticed the activity and courage of the firemen, and the extraordinary power which they soon exerted over the destroying ele-

ment. "You are not likely to have a second
Chicago." "No, indeed," said the stranger,
"if any town can be safe from fire it is
Boston." Within a few weeks, as the
world knows, the most solid part of the town
was a crumbling ruin. The epidemic amongst
the horses had not yet been heard of. Fire
engines dashed through the crowd. What
appeared to us an alarming conflagration was
subdued with ease in a few hours. At 8.30 a.m.
on September 27, the Eleven left Boston *en
route* for Quebec. Heavy clouds dissolving
into rain hung over the White Mountains.
The line runs through some beautiful scenery,
the woods are donning their rich autumn
tints. Striking the Grand Trunk, over
which familiar line the Eleven were franked
by the kindness of Mr. Bridges, the State of
Maine law. Maine was entered. The horror of the
Cricketers on learning that no beverage except tea and coffee was to be obtained for
love or money at the refreshment stations
cannot be described. Thick pea soup washed
down with weak tea, mutton cutlets and
coffee, oysters and cold water might be had
for the asking.

second
anger,
e it is
s the
e town
iongst
Fire
What
n was
O A.M.
on *en*
lving
tains.
nery,
unn
over
iked
te of
the
ex-
for
ions
hed
and
had

Maine law is a fine thing in the main, but it is scarcely fair to impose its restrictions upon travellers passing through. It is one of the startling paradoxes that abound in America. That such a law can be passed in a dram-drinking community, that it can be observed in a nation of cocktails almost makes one believe that thirst is an artificial creation, and that whisky must have some higher aim than a human throat. The conductor of the train, who was quite as decided in his disapprobation of Maine law as ourselves, consoled us by a lesson in Euchre. This cap- Euchre. tivating game is very popular; Euchre and Poker may be called the national games of Poker. America. We did not clearly comprehend the game beyond an idea that it is profitable to the instructor, and expensive to the tyro. The journey continued through the night, and early on the morning of September 28 the travellers found themselves amidst the woods of Canada. In the first rays of the sun, glittering with the tears of departing night, the foliage of the woods is indescribably Autumn foliage. beautiful,—crimson, pink, magenta and every modern shade of rose, glowing amidst the

dark green pine or the still unchanged and
lighter verdure of the ash and oak.   The
maple is the glory of the Canadian autumn.
Gold and crimson vies with green on the
same bough.   Soon the mighty stream of St.
Lawrence is seen again.   Cape Diamond once
more presents its bold outline, and Quebec
greets again the pilgrims at its feet.   The
Eleven arrived at 10 A.M. and in the course
of an hour luggage and all were on board the
S.S. *Prussian.*   Mr. and Mrs. Patteson and a
few friends had travelled from Toronto to see
the last of the Eleven on Canadian shores.

It was with great regret that we heard of
the serious illness of Henley of the 60th
Rifles, who had played against us and been
a jovial comrade in the early part of the tour.
He was lying ill in Quebec; our time did
not permit us to land; the good ship was
impatient, steam was up; a word of com-
mand from the chief officer was quickly followed by the splash of the rope as it fell
from the tug, and with that splash was ended
our own connection with the pleasant country
of the West.

We did manage a cheer for our friends as

S.S. *Prussian.*

Mr.
Bennett.

ed and
The
itumn.
on the
of St.
l once
'uebec
The
:ourse
'd the
and a
:o see
es.
rd of
60th
been
tour.
did
was
om-
fol-
fell
ded
itry

; as

they gradually dropped back in our wake, but it was with a heavy heart we had seen the last of the hospitable friends who were the first to welcome us. *Sorrow.*

A few last words must find a place here. *Last words.* Our tour was ended, our faces were turned homewards, gently steaming on the placid waters of the St. Lawrence, the land growing fainter as each day saw us nearer the Atlantic. Before reaching the Straits of Belle Isle, before leaving behind us the shores of Labrador, and committing ourselves to the mercies of the ocean, let us hazard a conjec- *Hazard.* ture upon the results of our tour.

Firstly, to ourselves as cricketers the result *Firstly.* had been singularly successful: we had taken part in eight matches against odds; we had won seven and had made a drawn match of the eighth. Nothing can rob us of this roll of victory. Then comes the thought, Are the *Secondly.* victories worthy of the "Io Triumphe"? Will *A pæan.* the defeats of the Twenty-two work to their future advantage? The first thought admits of a little hesitation. The games, with one exception, Philadelphia, had been won with consummate ease, never at any moment was victory in doubt; is there, then, any reason for self-congratulation? To the outsider, who looks only at the scores and forms his opinion of the match accordingly, there is doubtless little on the surface to make him feel proud of his countrymen. The Captain can add something to the score : he is proud of his Eleven's achievements on this account; the matches were won by strict attention to orders, by discipline, not enforced but willingly displayed, by playing the game from first to last. It is no slight handicap to match any Eleven, on indifferent grounds, against a Twenty-two. The Canadian teams were certainly weak in batting, but their bowling was always good ; their fielding might have been better, but then there was no match without several fine fieldsmen, and runs were almost always hard to get. Runs *were* got by steady and careful play. Victory is of course largely due to the never-failing bat of W. G. Grace ; but to the fine fielding of the Eleven, and the splendid bowling of Appleby, coupled with the insinuating Rose, must the small scores of the opponents be attributed. The matches, in a word, proved

W. G.

the triumph of discipline over a confused mass. It is this triumph that we claim as Right or our own; not that we beat a series of might. Twenty-two, but that we owe our victory to the display of those qualities which distinguish good cricketers. That this is no vain-glorious assertion, was proved on two occasions,—once at Toronto symptoms of slackness set in, the opponents' score mounted accordingly; discipline restored, the average was kept within bounds. At Boston the Eleven were train-weary and disgusted, their *élan* was on the wane, their discipline was tottering—they nearly lost the match. The Canadian cricketers must not be judged merely by their small scores. They all did their best to make up for a small score by patience in the field and sustained efforts with the ball. They played a good game, if a losing one. The Twelve felt proud of their victory at the time, and we think they are entitled to their opinion. To New York and Philadelphia the same remarks apply. The Twenty-two of New York were perhaps the weakest team that was encountered, for their bowling was not so formidable, if the batting was a trifle superior. The palm certainly must be given to Philadelphia.

We come now to the second thought, Will our tour have any good result? We are not confident that we shall in any way have advanced the cause of cricket as against base-ball. We have before alluded to the reasons which give the latter game the call in American opinion. But we do believe, and the local papers bear us out, that a great stir was made by our advent, and that many returned to cricket who had abandoned it, and that some will take it up who have never tried it. We cannot expect that a new exhibition of first-class cricket will have any important or immediate result. No Canadian is likely to become a second W. G. if he lives to be a hundred and plays till past four score. But we trust that the root has been planted in the schools; that the boys who flocked upon the grounds will practise the game, and that the great public interest taken in our matches will provoke the authorities to direct the juvenile mind towards the noble game. It is possible that the Twelve may have committed many little social errors.

Rumours have reached our ears of acts of apparent want of civility on our part, for these we most humbly ask pardon. Our mistakes do admit of excuse; we had more to do in the time than we could do properly, and omissions must not be regarded in the same light as commissions. We trust that at any rate we did our best in the field to justify the invitation that was so generously extended to us.

Last words take long to utter. We have Farewell. said much but we feel more. In bidding farewell to Canada and the States, we shall only do justice to our own feelings when we place on record our deep conviction that a better knowledge of our own colony, a heartier appreciation of our American cousins will be due to the generous spirit which prompted the citizens, on both sides of the border, to invite the English Twelve to pitch their Wickets in the West.

The good ship *Prussian* pursued an even course across the Atlantic. The straits of Belle Isle were passed at 2.20 A.M. on the morning of *Oct.* 1st. The ship's log reads as follows :—

Sept. 29th, 300 miles; 30th, 275 miles. *Oct.* 1st, 280 miles; 2nd, 300 miles; 3rd, 270 miles; 4th, 275 miles; 5th, 280 miles; 6th, 301 miles; 7th, 258 miles.

Fine westerly breezes prevailed throughout the voyage; sails were set, and we bounded merrily towards home. Poor George was the only invalid. Marmalade and sardines were consumed in awful numbers of pots and tins; yarns were rife; and perhaps a story was never told more likely to make night hideous in a hammock than the following:—

An 'orrible tail.

"A report is current," so commenced the story-teller, "that a ghastly scene was witnessed at the death-bed of A—— B——, the late inmate of the lighthouse at Cape Race, the southern extremity of Newfoundland. Some ten years ago or more, Messrs. Allan lost a magnificent steamer, bound for Quebec, with full cargo and complement of passengers. Easterly winds had prevailed, and the steamer on a certain night must have been bowling along before the freshening breeze and approaching the coast hidden from view by gathering fog. That brave ship never was seen again; she had been sighted within a day's journey of Cape Race; a few broken boards, the unmistakable evidence of a wreck, were collected beneath the lighthouse amongst the rocks, of whose danger that lighthouse should have given warning. Had it failed on that night of troubled water to pierce the gloom? Could the shrieks, which the lighthouse men afterwards described as audible above the roar of the angry wind, have proceeded from the unfortunate beings on board that unhappy vessel? Only one thing was ever ascertained : it was the good ship —— that had driven on these rocks. Not one soul lived to tell how or when.

"The ten years rolled on, the memory of that night was preserved only by the friends of those beneath the sea; the lighthouse man lay on the bed of death; a secret weighed on his guilty mind; it left his lips, with the hue of death stealthily gathering over his brow. In his last agony, in almost his last words, he confessed to the fact of having on that night of horror, which now filled his mind, omitted to light the guardian lamp. He had been drinking and was overcome by sleep; he awoke to hear the shrieks of his victims,

x

but the secret of that night was never divulged till he sank beneath its weight."

All the stories told were not of this weird-like character; luckily not, as we were caught in a fog off the Irish coast, and for a few hours lay to, not knowing where we were. Hadow was the first to spy the revolving light on Instrahull. Our ship's head was pointing to Scotland. We were ten miles north of the light, and many miles out of our course. But we were out of the Atlantic without a gale of wind, and we could almost have run ashore gladly. At 7 A.M. Moville lay before us, and after a short delay, which the Honourable George took advantage of, to get his traps together and leave us, "The Ten" were soon steaming again down the Irish Channel—a charming day's sail. At midnight the bar of the Mersey was passed; at 1 A.M. the *Prussian* "stopped;" and at 3 A.M. on *Oct.* 8, the Chief Officer and a few of the Ten had a last glass together, to the memory of the American Tour.

Oct. 8.—Arrival of the English Cricketers at Liverpool. Dispersing of the same to the Four Winds of Heaven.

never di-
ight."
his weird-
we were
and for a
where we
spy the
)ur ship's
We were
iany miles
)ut of the
, and we
adly. At
d after a
le George
together
on steam-
-a charm-
)ar of the
Prussian
:t. 8, the
en had a
y of the

'ricketers
ae to the

GENERAL AND PERSONAL.

THIS concluding chapter will be an *olla
podrida*. It is intended to supply omissions,
and to give a little fresh information. It will
introduce some of the living poets of Canada,
in " Farewell Odes to the Cricketers." It will
give the Captain's last speech and his *best* —
because you will hear no more from him ; a
few scraps from Yankee papers perhaps ; in
fact, anything and everything that can be extracted from portfolio and waistcoat pockets,
or filched from a comrade's diary.

The following " Farewell Odes " were addressed to the Twelve before they left
Canada :—

Farewell, ye sons of England's favoured land,
Where peace and plenty flourish, hand-in-hand ;
Where'er you go, whatever realms to roam,
May you in safety reach your far-off home !

x 2

There may you guard your nation's wickets well,
By " hits" unerring as were those of " Tell " ;
And, lastly, may you win your final score,
Where "bats and balls" and " byes " are known no more.
                                        VETERAN.

The second Ode is less affecting, but of a
genial strain :—

THE GENTLEMEN CRICKETERS' TEAM.

A SONG.

(Respectfully dedicated to its subject.)

I've a toast to propose to you—so, Gentlemen, hand on
The Mumm, and the Cliquot, the Möet and Chandon :
The toast that I offer, with pleasure extreme,
Is the health of " The Gentlemen Cricketers' Team."

And first, here's the health of their Captain, FitzGerald,
Whose time-honoured name stands in need of no herald :
All know that he manages matches as well
As a match-making mother with daughters to sell.

Next, here's to the Chief of the ball-driving race,
A Giant in cricket, as well as a Grace :
Bat, bowler, or field, in himself he's a host,
All round, the best player that Britain can boast.

Here's to Hornby, who bears the cognomen of " Monkey,"
All muscle and nerve—never feeble or funky ;
For pluck, skill, and strength, he is hard to be beaten
By picked men from Winchester, Harrow, or Eton !

Here's the left-handed bowler, that Lancashire swell,
Whom Ottawa batsmen remember so well :
He bowled a whole innings (and bowled like great guns),
In *Apple-pie* order for—only three runs !

And here's to his *confrère*, spectacular Rose,
A rather quick bowler of dangerous " slows ":
And now to the Lubbocks, a brave pair of brothers,
Who rank with the Graces, the Walkers, and others.

Next, here's to four stars of the Oxford Eleven,
(With all due respect for the home-keeping Seven)
Here's to Harris and Ottoway, Francis and Hadow,
May Time ne'er decrease his Herculean shadow !

Here's to Pickering, lastly—his name is enough
To prove that he's made of good cricketing stuff—
Warm welcome, I'm sure, he will ever be shown,
For the sake of his Uncle, as well as his own !

So here's to them singly, or taken together—
A finer set never yet hunted the leather—
Once more, then, I pledge you, with pleasure extreme,
The health of " The Gentlemen Cricketers' Team."

In addition to the matches played, there Invitations.
were several invitations to the Twelve to
play elsewhere. A most cordial invitation
was given by the Cricketers of Detroit and
Chicago, and of Frederickton in Nova Scotia.
A match was also proposed by the Officers
quartered at Halifax. Time would not allow
of their fulfilment. Nothing strikes the
stranger more in his travels in the West
than the exuberance of the local papers;
they are racy and original beyond con-

ception; a bit free at times, but the country smacks of freedom. Births, deaths, and marriages are arranged under the graphic heads of " Cradle," " Altar," and " Tomb." Advertisements take the engaging form of an attractive or sensational story. We annex one or two specimens; they are from San Francisco, the Eldorado of journalism. Rooms are thus advertised:—" One of the most pathetic songs ever written is that entitled ' No Baby in the House.' We once roomed alongside a baby for two weeks, only a board partition between us. The little angel would begin to yell at exactly a quarter past one every night, and keep it up at intervals till daylight. We used to lie and imagine the pleasure—oh! the indescribable rapture—of clutching that darling's windpipe for about six minutes. The only thing that kept us from bursting through and committing some horrid deed was the thought of the awful end that sometimes awaits murderers in this State—the rope's end. So we removed *to the Galt House*, 623, *Market Street*, where we found '*Quiet well-furnished Rooms, and no Babies.*'"

The press.

Rooms.

We recommend the following to Messrs.
Jay and the Necropolis Funeral Company,
Limited :—

"Tom went home in a delightful state of Furnishing.
mind the night of the boat race; he had
been to Sacramento on business. His sweet
wife met him with a smile; he knocked her
down with the boot-jack; he pounded up
all his furniture into fragments about the
size of a piece of chalk. This done, he
picked up his wife and the rest of the rubbish and threw them out of window. With
her dying breath she gasped, 'Tom, promise
me you will not marry that red-haired Polly
Squibbs, and be sure you get your new
*furniture at Plum, Bell & Co.'s Establish-
ment.'* She then expired."

Business is indissolubly connected with Assurance.
life, it follows a man into his grave. Read
the following :—

" A lovely wife in town, on the death of Insurance.
her husband, sent the following thrilling
telegram to a distant friend. 'Dear John
is dead : loss fully covered by insurance.'"

Englishmen must be prepared for new
phrases in America; on the railroads nearly

every term in general use is distinct from those employed at home.

Phrases. The guard is a "conductor," luggage is "baggage," carriage is "car." Take your seats is translated "all aboard." "Please" has no equivalent in America. Rails are "trucks." The station is always a "dé-pot."

The favourite remark of ladies expressing delight or surprise is, "Oh, my!" At Boston one was constantly met with the ejaculation, "How!" pronounced "Heow."

The journals are not very particular, provided they can produce something sensational. To say that the press expresses public opinion is a libel on Americans. The mass of the people we believe to be moderate in their opinions; the general tone of the papers is extravagant. An outrageous attack appeared in the *New York Herald* upon the treatment The steerage passenger. of steerage passengers in Messrs. Allan's vessels. As we happened to cross in the very ship, *Sarmatian*, that formed the subject of several most excruciating columns, we are happy to give our evidence, which will contradict *in toto* the allegations of the correspondent. Amongst many other horrors he

alludes to the bad bread furnished to the Horrors of the middle passage.
steerage passengers. The bread complained
of was brought to our table one morning,
and by the request of the doctor, we tried it.
It was no better and no worse than that supplied at the doctor's table. It was not a
French roll, but it was bread fit to eat. The
greatest attention was paid to the passengers,
and we are confident that in no line is such
accommodation afforded as on board Messrs.
Allan's magnificent vessels.

Apropos of the *Sarmatian* and *Prussian*,
the Captain of the Twelve addressed a letter A letter.
to Messrs. Allan, which may be appended as
a parting illustration of the tour.

" Liverpool, Oct. 9, 1872.

" GENTLEMEN,

"On behalf of England's Amateur
Cricketers I beg to express our grateful recognition of your share in the success of our
expedition. The laurels we have won in
Canada will long be dear to us, but insepar-
ably connected with them will be the recol-
lection of the days spent on board your good
ships *Sarmatian* and *Prussian*. I am happy
to add our tribute to the well-established

fame of the Allan Line. In conclusion, permit me to return our thanks to the officers,
to whose kindness and good fellowship we
owe many pleasant hours; and last, but not
least, to all those who administered so effi-
ciently to the wants of the saloon and the
comforts of the cabin.

" I am, Gentlemen,

" Yours, &c.,

" R. A. FITZGERALD,

"Captain of the Twelve."

A reply.   The following reply was received to the
above :—

" SIR,

    " We have to acknowledge receipt of
your favour of yesterday's date, and are
much gratified to learn that you can express
yourself so warmly with respect to the pleasures experienced on board the steamers of
our line.

    " We highly appreciate the spirit which
prompts you to take notice of any little attention which may have been specially bestowed upon yourself and friends, and will

take care to convey your acknowledgments to the proper quarter.

"We are, Sir,

"Yours faithfully,

"ALLAN, BROTHERS & Co.

"Liverpool.

"Pray accept also our congratulations on the successful results of your efforts abroad."

The Twelve were not much gratified upon landing in England, to find the object of their expedition and the good taste of their Captain and the managers in America severely questioned. They rose like one man at the objectionable article, and in order that the British public might be put in possession of all the facts, and in justice to the hosts and antagonists on the other side, the following article was published by the kindness of the Editor, in the world-wide columns of *Bell's Life*. As the article enters fully into the origin and terms of the expedition, we invite attention to it.

VISIT OF THE ENGLISH CRICKETERS
TO AMERICA.

(From Bell's Life in London.)

The return of the English amateurs from America has elicited an unreflecting and invidious spirit of criticism in certain quarters. A wrong impression of the objects and results of the trip is thereby promulgated. A deliberate slur is passed upon the hospitality and resources of the Canadians; the enterprise of our gallant representatives is carped at, and the good taste of the promoters on each side is questioned. We cannot imagine anything more distasteful to our friends in Canada than the tone of such an article. In justice more especially to them, and at the same time to place our own Twelve in a proper light for public opinion, we propose to analyse the objections taken to the expedition. We will admit, in common with one hostile section, that curiosity to see Mr. Grace and his companions actually in the flesh may be laid to the charge of the managers on the other side, and it is pos-

ETERS

rs from
and in-
uarters.
l results
A deli-
lity and
terprise
ped at,
on each
ne any-
nds in
article.
and at
lve in a
propose
e expe-
ith one
ee Mr.
in the
of the
is pos-

sible that the Secretary of the Marylebone Club, who may be taken as the manager on this side, in accepting this invitation, was somewhat influenced by a desire to see a new country, and to eke out a novel holiday. But we cannot admit that there is any want of taste or anything that reflects discredit, even if the above-mentioned reasons were the principal objects in view on either side. Whether these were or were *not* the principal objects in view, it will be our business to determine.

The first question that presents itself is, Will the cause of cricket be furthered by this expedition? Out of this will arise another question. Were the arrangements entered into between the respective parties worthy of the cause, or satisfactory to the great body of amateurs who watched with interest the proceedings of their representatives? Before we analyse these questions, it will be necessary to refer to the great stride in popular favour taken by the noble game of late years. It requires no power of speech, no strength of argument, to prove the increasing popularity of cricket amongst all classes in England. The scene presented by Lord's ground at the University and School's match, with its arena year by year diminished, to accommodate the outer circle of visitors; the apparition of a new cricket ground in Pimlico, with its own long list of matches, presenting replicas of the great matches played elsewhere, the attendance at the Oval at a stirring county match, the columns of the sporting papers—all attest beyond any doubt the development of the game.

It is beside our mark to inquire whether the excellence of either batsmen or bowler has advanced in equal proportion to the development of the game. The *laudator temporis acti* clings stoutly to the Redgate and F   r, the Charles Taylor and Alfred M   .t his happy youth. We will not dispute the point with him, nor attempt to explain why centuries are as common with us as twenties were with him. Why matches are so often left unfinished? Why lobs are looked to as lights to the ship in distress? Whether catches now-a-days are not more often missed than made? Whether, in a

sented
y and
y year
circle
cricket
list of
great
ince at
h, the
attest
of the

hether
bowler
to the
udator
edgate
Alfred
ot dis-
npt to
n with
latches
bs are
stress?
t more
, in a

word, the cricket of to-day is not diluted rather than developed? In the midst of all these queries stands out one prominent object. It is admitted by the oldest admirers of the game that for patience and judgment, for strength of play, and precision of placing the ball, there has never been the equal of Mr. W. G. Grace. He has arisen as a phenomenon in the game. Against all bowling, and on all grounds, he has left his mark. All who are acquainted with our metropolitan grounds cannot have failed to notice the anxiety of the public on its arrival on the ground to ascertain which side had won the toss. On learning that Mr. Grace's side is going to the wicket, the public to a man remain; should it be otherwise, a large majority apply for their "pass," and return some hours later on the chance of seeing the "Leviathan" in. Here, doubtless, lies the mainspring of the Canadian invitation. The first advances were made in the summer of 1870. Some English officers quartered in Canada endeavoured to persuade an English Eleven to visit the Dominion. The arrangements from various causes came to

nothing, but the germ then planted did not
wither.   Cricket owes its present position in
Canada in a great measure to the untiring
exertions of British officers.   Conspicuous
amongst them were Captain Tyron and his
gallant companions of the Rifle Brigade.
They diffused life into the game; and established grounds where the bear and the
opossum lately held their midnight revels.
The enlightened policy of Home Government withdrew the gallant advocates of the
willow, the croquet mallet, and the light
fantastic; smiles fled from fair faces,—the red
man was seen no more; with his departure,
sports of all kinds declined for a season.
The Canadian proper has to struggle with
the forces of nature, he has a great and un-
developed country before him; steam, the
genius of civilisation, is every day opening
up new sources of wealth to him; a thrill of
public enterprise at this moment pervades
every department; his hands are too busy,
either with the pen or the axe, to devote
many moments to the practice of the willow.
Still, in the intervals of business, on such
days when the sun's more tempered rays

did not
ition in
ntiring
picuous
and his
Brigade.
id esta-
nd the
revels.
Govern-
s of the
e light
-the red
parture,
season.
gle with
and un-
am, the
opening
thrill of
pervades
oo busy,
) devote
willow.
on such
ed rays

permit of exposure, a few enthusiasts keep
the embers alive. At Montreal new blood
from England and Scotland continually brings
news of the game and its English exponents;
at Toronto, the home of the game, the true
English spirit has never died: it has flickered
and fallen, but to rise revigorated from its
ashes. The same may be said of London
and of Hamilton—Quebec alone belongs to
the past, but it would require very little to
revive even there the love for the game.

We have now arrived at the second stage
of our analysis. We have endeavoured to
establish the existence of a sound cricket
basis throughout the Dominion; it remains
to inquire whether the expedition is likely to
further the cause of cricket, and whether the
means adopted were worthy of the cause.
The cause depended on the " hour and the
man." Had the "hour come?" We think
it had in 1872. Where was "the man?"
He came to the front in the person of Mr.
Patteson of Toronto. The necessary arrangements were hundred-headed; he undertook
to look the hydra in its mouth, and dare, if
need be, the British Lion in his den. He

Y

came over to England in July, 1871, and
interviewed the B. L., represented hirsuti-
cally by the Secretary of the M.C.C., at Lord's
Ground. As the arrangements here entered
into have formed the subject of hostile criticism, it will be well to briefly state them :—
Mr. Patteson, on the part of the Canadians,
invited an English Eleven to Canada, at the
same time mentioning that all expenses
would be defrayed by a general fund, towards
which he had received the most liberal promises. It was expressly stipulated that Mr.
Grace should be one of the Eleven. " The
invitation," to quote Mr. Patteson, "proceeded
from the Dominion, and all classes were
united in wishing success to the negotiations.
The project had not originated in any spirit
of speculation, but proceeded from a genuine
love of the game." An offer thus handsomely conveyed appeared to the M.C.C.
Secretary worthy of serious consideration.
He took the proper course of consulting the
authorities of his club, and in the course of
the winter sounded the leading amateurs ;
from one and all he received in the first instance a favourable reply. In the spring of

1872 a skeleton list was forwarded to Canada, and on hearing from Mr. Patteson that the selection had given great satisfaction to the promoters on his side of the Atlantic, the Secretary committed himself, body and soul, to the expedition. We need not enter into the collateral question, whether the team, as eventually selected, represented properly the Amateurs of England. It is sufficient to say that it was a formidable team, and that several departures from the original list unavoidably occurred,—sudden indisposition preventing some, dread of sea-sickness deterring another. Disappointment is the natural incident in the life of a cricket manager. Cricket is one of our public institutions, and it owes its proud position in a great measure to the unrestricted criticism that has followed it step by step. The changes that from time to time have been made in its laws have been religiously watched and minutely questioned. All cricketers must be grateful to the jealous watch that is established over their favourite pastime, and thankful for the healthy tone, inseparable, as it would appear, from the very game, that pervades the press regarding it.

But we think that in connection with the subject of our inquiry a wrong impression prevails in some minds. We demur to the taunt conveyed by the assertion that the invitation proceeded from a " comparatively poor dependency," and was accepted by eleven gentlemen " of the richest country in the world." We consider the remark to be not only offensive to the Canadian hosts, but unjust to the English guests. There is just sufficient truth in it to pass muster with a superficial inquirer. The Marylebone Club itself is certainly rich enough to pay the expenses of an eleven to Timbuctoo or Otaheiti. We are not writing with their banker's book before us, but we are by no means certain that the Eleven selected were *not* able to pay their own expenses, or, at least, that an eleven equally able to hold their own against odds could *not* have been found to whom the expenses of the journey would have been no objection. It has been more than hinted that the love of the game was merged in an inordinate desire to banquet and carouse at the expense of the " poor dependency," that first-class cricketers can take no pleasure in playing with raw antagonists, and, in fact, the whole affair reflects but little credit on the good taste of the promoters. We have a proper respect for pride, and can imagine that a rich man may be averse to a feeling of obligation to his inferiors in wealth or position, but we consider that the parallel is overdrawn in this case. To our mind there is no pride involved, no bad taste displayed in an invitation handsomely couched, and generously accepted. Cricket admits of no distinctions, it is the sport of all sports which affords an open platform to all classes. We have but to consider the invitation and its object to dispel any idea of bad taste or false delicacy. The first proposal came from Canada, the terms were suggested by Canadians, the cricketers of England were *invited* by their brothers of the willow in Canada. The *object* was to resuscitate the embers where the glow still lingered, and to kindle the fire where it was yet latent. A perusal of the Canadian papers during the matches is sufficient to prove the interest taken in them by artisan and mechanic of the busy town, as well as by the hardy backwoodsman and settler of the forest. We are assured on good authority, that though the batting opposed to them was weak, the English team had to contend against excellent bowling, and far from moderate fielding. We are inclined to give the English visitors credit for more than a paltry ambition to secure a victory which would cost them little and should please them less. We believe that they accepted the invitation in the spirit in which it was offered. We dare to look beyond the cricketfield. We are at least hopeful that their visit will not only promote the cause of cricket, but will tend towards dispelling the ignorance and prejudices of many at home in respect to Canada. It is scarcely to be denied that the advent of an English Eleven, of acknowledged proficiency in the various departments of the game, must have a beneficial effect upon less skilful exponents. It may not be possible to create a second Grace or another Alfred Lubbock, but much can be learned from the patience of an Ottoway or brilliancy of Hornby. More to be appreciated than any individual lesson is the great and general example of discipline, which places a picked

issured on
itting op-
lish team
vling, and
e inclined
for more
a victory
ild please
accepted
h it was
cricket-
ieir visit
cricket,
norance
spect to
that the
vledged
s of the
ion less
sible to
Alfred
om the
ncy of
in any
eneral
picked

Eleven at such advantage when opposed to
odds—discipline that is not enforced but
willingly displayed. We may judge already
to some extent of the success of this expedition. We are told that on no field did
any dispute arise between the contending
parties. We may safely argue from this that
the Canadians were willing to accept the
gospel introduced by the apostles of the
game. There was no dispute as to time;
there was no unnecessary delay. Can we
say the same even on our best managed
grounds at home? We should not have
been surprised to hear of differences, not unknown to us here, arising out of umpires'
decisions. The silence of the Canadian historian speaks volumes on this head. If any
doubt can exist still as to the success of the
expedition from a cricketing point of view,
we think that from a social or political one
it cannot but demand our sympathies. The
Canadians have no great reason to be satisfied with the policy that has distinguished
the conduct of the Home Government towards them of late years. They are not
pleased at the withdrawal of the soldiers;

they are not quite certain that, out of *respect*
to their neighbours, their own claims upon the
Mother Country are not to some extent ignored.
They are particularly sensitive on all points
affecting their loyalty to the Queen, and devo-
tion to British institutions. They believe that
ignorance on some points and prejudice on
others prevail in England, which tend to
separate rather than to knit together the
Mother Country and her colony. They desire,
above everything, that Englishmen should
see the Dominion before they pronounce
judgment on its resources. They are sanguine
that a great future is in store for them, and
their only want for the present is the hearty
co-operation of English hands and hearts, to
assist them in the great work of bringing
the far-West within the pale of civilisation.
We must, therefore, draw attention to the
fact that the young Englishmen were not
suffered to draw their comparisons from the
cricket field alone. The special object in
view was to introduce them to the leading
inhabitants of each town, and to make them
acquainted, as well as could be in so hurried
a visit, with the principal features of each

district. No effort was spared on the part of the hosts, and we cannot think so poorly of the guests as to suppose that they would leave the hospitable board with no better result than a satiated appetite. On the contrary, we are informed that the visitors took great interest in all they saw, and that they on several occasions expressed their grateful sense of the attention shown to them and the pleasure afforded to them. We must not omit to mention one special instance, which will illustrate our political view of the expedition. Col. Cumberland, an influential resident at Toronto, organised a large party, and after providing special train and steamer, entertained his visitors at Allandale, on the shores of Lake Simcoe. The route is destined to take its place in Canadian history.

Allandale is a station whose elegance of design confronts the forest in its primeval solitude. The railway, opened thus far, will convey little to the English mind under the letters G. N. R. But to his English guests the colonel explained the great part which that line is intended to play in the future of Canada. It is the artery of the West, along which will throb, ere many years are over, the pulse of the Pacific and Atlantic shores. In their journey through the bush the visitors could estimate the resources of the lumber trade. They could wonder at the surprising fertility of the scanty clearings, the struggle of the backwoodsman with the forces of nature, the track of the fire, that spread destruction for miles, but which left behind it hopes for the settler in the charred stump and tottering trunk. It was remarked *en route* that the Englishmen were not only cricketers but emigration commissioners. We accept the latter title with pleasure for them, their eyes and ears may yet make some return to Canada for the hospitality she gave them. At the University it may well be presumed that those members of the Canadian team, *in statu pupillari*, will not hide their candle under a bushel. They may be allowed the privilege of travellers, to adorn their tale, but we shall be disappointed if they do not spread amongst their companions a desire to visit Canada and a better knowledge of its loyal inhabitants. If only curiosity is aroused by this excursion of

are over,
c shores.
the visi-
s of the
r at the
:ings, the
he forces
t spread
t behind
d stump
irked *en*
1ot only
ers. We
or them,
ce some
he gave
well be
e Cana-
1ot hide
may be
o adorn
inted if
panions
· know-
f only
sion ot

cricketers we maintain that its results will be advantageous; for the promotion of cricket it will have done much, for the better acquaintance with our most attached colony it will have done more. If there be any still susceptible enough to disparage the expedition, either by dislike of the terms on which it was started, or by dissatisfaction at its results, we can only record our conviction that an offer so made should never be rejected, and that nothing could contribute more to a good understanding between the inhabitants of both countries than a visit of gentlemen, on pleasure bent and on information bound.

We cannot dismiss our subject without allusion to our American cousins. They played an important part in the expedition. They not only contributed handsomely to the general fund, but they vied with the Canadians in providing the best attainable cricket, and the most hearty welcome to their guests. The spirit in which the visitors were received, at Philadelphia especially, illustrates very forcibly our political argument. International amenities were the burden of their song, and the advantages to be derived by young America from their contact with English exponents of the game were urged by the press of all shades. The Americans have equal difficulties of climate and business to contend against; but there exists at Philadelphia and at Boston a strong undercurrent of enterprise that will not let the game expire. At New York a healthy English element alone preserves it. The most closely-contested match took place at Philadelphia, as that at Boston cannot be called a match, owing to the saturation of the ground by heavy rains. But one feeling pervaded the whole cricket community, to show the Englishmen that a love of the game does exist in America, and that its preservation and maintenance would be secured by periodical visits of this nature from our side of the Atlantic. We can in conclusion only express a hope that many years will not elapse ere the expedition be repeated. We feel certain that the cricketers to come will re-echo the sentiment of Mr. Fitzgerald and his companions, that from Quebec to Philadelphia they passed as strangers, but to part as friends.

ntages to
om their
the game
es. The
f climate
but there
a strong
l not let
a healthy
it. The
place at
annot be
iration of
ne feeling
unity, to
e of the
that its
d be se-
cure from
in con-
ny years
be re-
ricketers
of Mr.
iat from
ssed as

CONCLUSION.

THE end is at hand. We have attempted
to describe faithfully our impressions of
America. We lay down our pen with a
feeling of relief. We have discharged, to
the best of our ability, our debt to the
Canadians and the cricketers of the States.
We scarcely hope that we have been able to
carry with us many readers step by step
through our tour. Our exploits appeal to a
small section of our countrymen, but we
believe we had the wishes of all for our
success.

The Captain's task is almost done; it
remains only for him to acknowledge most
gratefully the services of each of his Eleven;
each did his part well; each contributed to

the general success. The services of the umpires and scorers at the several matches must not be overlooked. There was no dispute, and no difficulty at any place. The thanks of the Twelve are eminently due to them, as they fill an invidious post, and have much laid to their charge that they deserve not. Farrands gave general satisfaction, and his conduct at all times was worthy of the high character which distinguishes the ground players of the Marylebone Cricket Club. It does not often fall to the lot of any leader, from the head of an Eleven to the general of an army, to conduct any expedition without some cause of complaint on the one side or the other. The Captain can truthfully say, that, from Quebec to Philadelphia, his Eleven were of one accord with himself; and to the united good feeling and harmony that prevailed he attributes the great success of the expedition.

He will long remember their faithful trust in him; may they never regret that they followed him across the Atlantic, and may the first visit of Amateur Cricketers lead to others of a similar nature; so that the link

ces of the
al matches
was no dis-
place. The
ntly due to
st, and have
hey deserve
faction, and
orthy of the
s the ground
et Club. It
any leader,
the general
ition without
e one side or
uthfully say,
a, his Eleven
; and to the
ny that pre-
uccess of the

faithful trust
ret that they
tic, and may
ceters lead to
that the link

that connects this country with the Dominion
and the great Republic may, by such friendly
contests, " lengthen long, and grow old."

Farewell, Brethren of the Willow!

> " O dulces, comitum, valete, cœtus
> Longè quos simul à domo profectos
> Diversè variæ viæ reportant."
>
> *Catull.* xlvi., v. 9.

THE END.

BRADBURY, AGNEW, & CO., PRINTERS, WHITEFRIARS, LONDON.

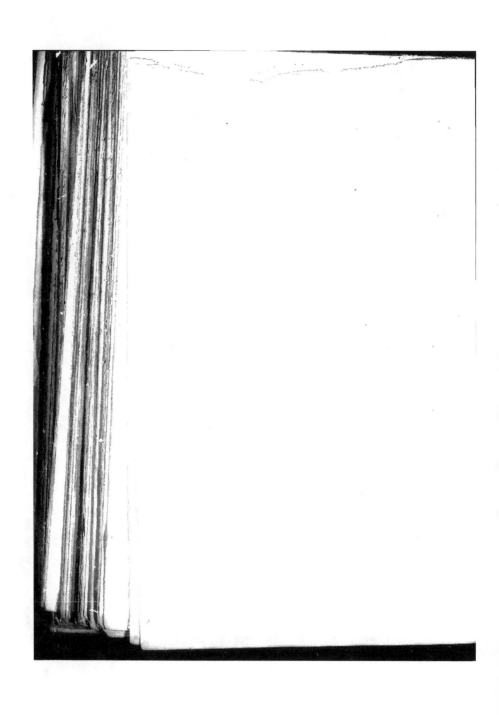

TINSLEY BROTHERS' LIST OF NEW BOOKS.

Foreign Biographies. By Wm. Maccall. 2 vols. 8vo.

Unorthodox London; or Phases of Religious Life in the Metropolis. By the Rev. C. Maurice, D.D., formerly Fellow of the University of Durham. 1 vol. 8vo, 14s.

Unexplored Syria. By Capt. Burton, F.R.G.S., and Mr. C. F. Tyrwhitt Drake, F.R.G.S., &c. With a New Map of Syria, Illustrations, Inscriptions, the 'Hamah Stones,' &c. 2 vols. 8vo, 32s.

"The work before us is no common book of travels. It is rather a series of elaborate, and at the same time luminous, descriptions of the various sites visited and explored by the authors, either together or singly, and of the discoveries made there by them. . . . The present joint production of Captain Burton and Mr. Tyrwhitt Drake is therefore most opportune, on account of the material additions it makes to our acquaintance with a region which, notwithstanding the deep interest it excites, is still but imperfectly explored."—*Athenæum.*

"While these magnificent volumes, with their original plans and sketches by Mr. Drake, the unrivalled map of Northern Syria, and the luxurious print, are triumphs of typography, they are at the same time enduring monuments of the energy and enterprise of our countrymen."—*John Bull.*

"The book must be pronounced to be valuable for its information."—*Spectator.*

The Recollections and Reflections of J. R. Planché (*Somerset Herald*). A Professional Autobiography. 2 vols. 8vo, 25s.

"Besides illustrations of social and dramatic life, of literature, and of authors, Mr. Planché gives us record of travels, incidents of his *other* professional life as a herald, and reflections on most matters which have come under his notice. We have only now to leave Mr. Planché and his book to an appreciating public. There are few men who have amused and delighted the public as long as he has done; and perhaps there has never been a dramatic writer who has been so distinguished as he has been for uniting the utmost amount of wit and humour with refinement of expression and perfect purity of sentiment."—*Athenæum.*

"We have here two goodly octavo volumes full of amusing and often instructive gossip. To the portions of his book which will chiefly interest the general reader we have scarcely adverted at all, simply because we know not how to deal with them. So many and so good are the anecdotes he relates, that two or three could not be taken from the rest by any process more critical than the toss of a halfpenny."—*Saturday Review.*

The Life and Times of Margaret of Anjou. By Mrs. Hookham. 2 vols. 8vo, 30s.

"Let Mrs. Hookham's history be as largely circulated as possible, and earnestly read in every home."—*Bell's Weekly Messenger.*

"The collection of the materials has evidently been a laborious task; the composition is careful and conscientious throughout, and it contains a great deal that is valuable and highly interesting."—*Pall Mall Gazette.*

William with the Ring: a Romance in Rhyme. By J. R. Planché, author of "The Recollections and Reflections of J. R. Planché," &c. 1 vol. crown 8vo, 6s.

"We are sure that it must have been a pleasure to Mr. Planché to write this graceful poem, the pages of which he has coloured like a painted window with his antique lore; and we are equally sure that it will be a pleasure to his friends, who are many more people than he knows by name, to read it."—*Times.*

TINSLEY BROTHERS, 8 CATHERINE STREET, STRAND.

History of France under the Bourbons, 1589-1830.
By CHARLES DUKE YONGE, Regius Professor, Queen's College, Belfast. In 4 vols. 8vo. Vols. I. and II. contain the Reigns of Henry IV., Louis XIII. and XIV.; Vols. III. and IV. contain the Reigns of Louis XV. and XVI. 3*l.*

The Regency of Anne of Austria, Queen of France,
Mother of Louis XIV. From Published and Unpublished Sources. With Portrait. By Miss FREER. 2 vols. 8vo, 30*s.*

The Married Life of Anne of Austria, Queen of
France, Mother of Louis XIV.; and the History of Don Sebastian, King of Portugal. Historical Studies. From numerous Unpublished Sources. By MARTHA WALKER FREER. 2 vols. 8vo, 30*s.*

Zanzibar. By CAPTAIN R. F. BURTON, author of
"A Mission to Geléle," "Explorations of the Highlands of the Brazil," "Abeokuta," "My Wanderings in West Africa," &c. 2 vols. 8vo, 30*s.*

Explorations of the Highlands of the Brazil; with
a full account of the Gold and Diamond Mines; also, Canoeing down Fifteen Hundred Miles of the great River, Sao Francisco, from Sabará to the Sea. In 2 vols. 8vo, with Map and Illustrations, 30*s.*

Wit and Wisdom from West Africa; or a Book of
Proverbial Philosophy, Idioms, Enigmas, and Laconisms. Compiled by RICHARD F. BURTON, author of "A Mission to Dahomé," "A Pilgrimage to El-Medinah and Meccah," &c. 1 vol. 8vo, 12*s.* 6*d.*

Memoirs of the Life and Reign of George III.
With Original Letters of the King and Other Unpublished MSS. By J. HENEAGE JESSE, author of "The Court of England under the Stuarts," &c. 3 vols. 8vo. £2 2*s.* Second Edition.

The Newspaper Press: its Origin, Progress, and
Present Position. By JAMES GRANT, author of "Random Recollections," "The Great Metropolis," &c., and late Editor of the *Morning Advertiser.* 2 vols. 8vo, 30*s.*

Baron Grimbosh: Doctor of Philosophy and some-
time Governor of Barataria. A Record of his Experiences, written by himself in Exile, and Published by Authority. 1 vol. 8vo, 10*s.* 6*d.*

The Court of Anna Carafa: an Historical Narra-
tive. By MRS. ST. JOHN. 1 vol. 8vo, 12*s.*

The Public Life of Lord Macaulay. By FREDERICK
ARNOLD, B.A. of Christ Church, Oxford. Post 8vo, 7*s.* 6*d.*

TINSLEY BROTHERS, 8 CATHERINE STREET, STRAND.

89–1830.
College, Bel-
gns of Henry
n the Reigns

f France,
shed Sources.

Queen of
on Sebastian,
s Unpublished
30s.

author of
of the Brazil,"
vols. 8vo, 30s.

azil; with
Janoeing down
'ancisco, from
strations, 30s.

a Book of
ns. Compiled
Dahomé," "A
vo, 12s. 6d.

eorge III.
shed MSS. By
and under the

ngress, and
ndom Recollec-
of the *Morning*

and som -
riences, written
ol. 8vo, 10s. 6d.

ical Narra-

· FREDERICK
7s. 6d.

, STRAND.

Lives of the Kembles. By PERCY FITZGERALD,
author of the "Life of David Garrick," &c. 2 vols. 8vo, 30s.

The Life of David Garrick. From Original Family
Papers, and numerous Published and Unpublished Sources. By
PERCY FITZGERALD, M.A. 2 vols, 8vo, with Portraits. 36s.

The Life of Edmund Kean. From various Pub-
lished and Original Sources. By F. W. HAWKINS. 2 vols. 8vo, 30s.

Our Living Poets: an Essay in Criticism. By
H. BUXTON FORMAN. 1 vol., 12s.

Memoirs of Sir George Sinclair, Bart., of Ulbster.
By JAMES GRANT, author of "The Great Metropolis," "The Religious Tendencies of the Times," &c. 1 vol. 8vo. With Portrait. 16s.

Memories of My Time; being Personal Remini-
scences of Eminent Men. By GEORGE HODDER. 1 vol. 8vo, 16s.

Biographies and Portraits of some Celebrated
People. By ALPHONSE DE LAMARTINE. 2 vols. 8vo, 25s.

Under the Sun. By GEORGE AUGUSTUS SALA, author
of "My Diary in America," &c. 1 vol. 8vo, 15s.

The History of Monaco. By H. PEMBERTON. 1 vol.
8vo, 12s.

The Great Country: Impressions of America. By
GEORGE ROSE, M.A. (ARTHUR SKETCHLEY). 1 vol. 8vo, 15s.

My Diary in America in the Midst of War. By
GEORGE AUGUSTUS SALA. 2 vols. 8vo, 30s.

Notes and Sketches of the Paris Exhibition. By
GEORGE AUGUSTUS SALA. 8vo, 15s.

From Waterloo to the Peninsula. By GEORGE
AUGUSTUS SALA. 2 vols. 8vo, 24s.

Rome and Venice, with other Wanderings in Italy,
in 1866–7. By GEORGE AUGUSTUS SALA. 8vo, 16s.

Paris after Two Sieges. Notes of a Visit during
the Armistice and immediately after the Suppression of the Commune.
By WILLIAM WOODALL. 1 vol. 2s. 6d.

Judicial Dramas: Romances of French Criminal
Law. By HENRY SPICER. 1 vol. 8vo, 15s.

The Retention of India. By ALEXANDER HALLIDAY.
1 vol. 7s. 6d.

TINSLEY BROTHERS, 8 CATHERINE STREET, STRAND.

Letters on International Relations before and during the War of 1870. By the *Times* Correspondent at Berlin. Reprinted, by permission, from the *Times*, with considerable Additions. 2 vols. 8vo, 36s.

The Story of the Diamond Necklace. By HENRY VIZETELLY. Illustrated with an exact representation of the Diamond Necklace, and a Portrait of the Countess de la Motte, engraved on steel. 2 vols. post 8vo, 25s. Second Edition.

English Photographs. By an American. 1 vol. 8vo, 12s.

Travels in Central Africa, and Exploration of the Western Nile Tributaries. By Mr. and Mrs. PETHERICK. With Maps, Portraits, and numerous Illustrations. 2 vols. 8vo, 25s.

From Calcutta to the Snowy Range. By an OLD INDIAN. With numerous coloured Illustrations. 1 vol. 8vo, 14s.

Stray Leaves of Science and Folk-lore. By J. SCOFFERN, M.B. Lond. 1 vol. 8vo, 12s.

Three Hundred Years of a Norman House. With Genealogical Miscellanies. By JAMES HANNAY, author of "A Course of English Literature," "Satire and Satirists," &c. 1 vol. 12s.

The Religious Life of London. By J. EWING RITCHIE, author of the "Night Side of London," &c. 1 vol. 8vo, 12s.

Religious Thought in Germany. By the *Times* Correspondent at Berlin. Reprinted from the *Times*. 1 vol. 8vo, 12s.

Mornings of the Recess in 1861-4. Being a Series of Literary and Biographical Papers, reprinted from the *Times*, by permission, and revised by the Author. 2 vols. 21s.

The Schleswig-Holstein War. By EDWARD DICEY, author of "Rome in 1860." 2 vols. 16s.

The Battle-fields of 1866. By EDWARD DICEY, author of "Rome in 1860," &c. 12s.

From Sedan to Saarbrück, viâ Verdun, Gravelotte, and Metz. By an Officer of the Royal Artillery. In one vol. 7s. 6d.

British Senators; or Political Sketches, Past and Present. By J. EWING RITCHIE. 1 vol. post 8vo, 10s. 6d.

Prohibitory Legislation in the United States. By JUSTIN McCARTHY. 1 vol., 2s. 6d.

The Idol in Horeb. Evidence that the Golden Image at Mount Sinai was a Cone and not a Calf. With Three Appendices. By CHARLES T. BEKE, Ph.D. 1 vol., 5s.

TINSLEY BROTHERS, 8 CATHERINE STREET, STRAND.

Ten Years in Sarawak. By CHARLES BROOKE, the
" Tuanmudah" of Sarawak. With an Introduction by H. H. the Rajah
Sir JAMES BROOKE; and numerous Illustrations. 2 vols. 8vo, 25s.

Peasant Life in Sweden. By L. LLOYD, author
of " The Game Birds of Sweden," " Scandinavian Adventures," &c.
With Illustrations. 1 vol. 8vo, 18s.

Hog Hunting in the East, and other Sports. By
Captain J. NEWALL, author of " The Eastern Hunters." With numerous Illustrations. 1 vol. 8vo, 21s.

The Eastern Hunters. By Captain JAMES NEWALL.
1 vol. 8vo, with numerous Illustrations. 16s.

Fish Hatching; and the Artificial Culture of Fish.
By FRANK BUCKLAND. With 5 Illustrations. 1 vol. crown 8vo, 5s.

Incidents in my Life. By D. D. Home. In 1
vol. crown 8vo, 10s. 6d. *Second Series.*

Con Amore; or, Critical Chapters. By JUSTIN
MCCARTHY, author of " The Waterdale Neighbours." Post 8vo, 12s.

The Cruise of the Humming Bird, being a Yacht Cruise
around the West Coast of Ireland. By MARK HUTTON. In 1 vol. 14s.

Murmurings in the May and Summer of Manhood:
O'Ruark's Bride, or the Blood-spark in the Emerald ; and Man's Mission a Pilgrimage to Glory's Goal. By EDMUND FALCONER. 1 vol., 5s.

Poems. By EDMUND FALCONER. 1 vol., 5s.

Dante's Divina Commedia. Translated into English in the Metre and Triple Rhyme of the Original. By Mrs. RAM-
SAY. 3 vols. 18s.

The Gaming Table, its Votaries and Victims, in all
Countries and Times, especially in England and France. By ANDREW
STEINMETZ, Barrister-at-Law. 2 vols. 8vo, 30s.

Principles of Comedy and Dramatic Effect. By
PERCY FITZGERALD, author of " The Life of Garrick," &c. 8vo, 12s.

A Winter Tour in Spain. By the Author of " Al-
together Wrong." 8vo, illustrated, 15s.

Life Beneath the Waves; and a Description of the
Brighton Aquarium, with numerous Illustrations. 1 vol., 2s. 6d.

The Rose of Jericho; from the French; called by
the German " Weinachts-Rose," or " Christmas Rose. Edited by the
Hon. Mrs. NORTON, Author of " Old Sir Douglas," &c. 2s. 6d.

The Bells: a Romantic Story. Adapted from the
French of MM. ERCKMANN-CHATRIAN. 1s.

TINSLEY BROTHERS, 8 CATHERINE STREET, STRAND.

TINSLEY BROTHERS'
CHEAP EDITIONS OF POPULAR NOVELS.

The Golden Lion of Grampere. By ANTHONY TROLLOPE, author of " Ralph the Heir," " Can You Forgive Her?" &c. 6s.

Sword and Gown. By the author of " Guy Livingstone," &c. 5s.

Brakespeare. By the author of " Sword and Gown," " Guy Livingstone," &c. 6s.

Old Margaret. By HENRY KINGSLEY, author of " Geoffry Hamlyn," " Hetty," &c. 6s.

The Harveys. By HENRY KINGSLEY, author of " Mademoiselle Mathilde," " Old Margaret," &c. 6s.

Barren Honour. By the author of " Guy Livingstone." 6s.

A Life's Assize. By Mrs. J. H. RIDDELL, author of " Too Much Alone," " City and Suburb," " George Geith," &c. 6s.

A Righted Wrong. By EDMUND YATES. 6s.

Anteros. By the author of " Maurice Dering," " Guy Livingstone," &c. 6s.

Stretton. By HENRY KINGSLEY, author of " Geoffry Hamlyn," &c. 6s.

Maurice Dering. By the author of " Sans Merci," " Guy Livingstone," &c. 6s.

Guy Livingstone. By the author of " Sword and Gown," " Barren Honour," &c. 6s.

The Rock Ahead. By EDMUND YATES. 6s.

The Adventures of Dr. Brady. By W. H. RUSSELL, LL.D. 6s.

Black Sheep. By EDMUND YATES, author of " The Rock Ahead," &c. 6s.

Sans Merci. By the author of " Anteros," " Border and Bastille," &c. 6s.

Border and Bastille. By the author of " Sword and Gown," " Brakespeare," &c. 6s.

Not Wisely, but Too Well. By the author of " Cometh up as a Flower." 6s.

Miss Forrester. By the author of " Archie Lovell," &c. 6s.

Recommended to Mercy. By the author of " Sink or Swim ?" 6s.

Lizzie Lorton of Greyrigg. By Mrs. LYNN LINTON, author of " Sowing the Wind," &c. 6s.

The Seven Sons of Mammon. By G. A. SALA, author of " After Breakfast," &c. 6s.

Maxwell Drewitt. By Mrs. J. H. RIDDELL, author of " Too Much Alone," " A Life's Assize," &c. 6s.

Faces for Fortunes. By AUGUSTUS MAYHEW. 6s.

TINSLEY BROTHERS' NEW NOVELS

AT EVERY LIBRARY.

Boscobel: a Tale of the Year 1651. By WILLI
HARRISON AINSWORTH, author of "Rookwood," "The Tower of I
don," &c. With Illustrations. 3 vols.

At His Gates. By Mrs. OLIPHANT, author of "Ch
nicles of Carlingford," &c. 3 vols.

The Vicar's Daughter: a New Story. By GEOR
MACDONALD, author of "Annals of a Quiet Neighbourhood," "
Seaboard Parish," &c. 3 vols.

A Waiting Race. By EDMUND YATES, author
"Broken to Harness," "Black Sheep," &c. 3 vols.

Valentin: a Story of Sedan. By HENRY KINGSLE
author of "Ravenshoe," "Geoffry Hamlyn," &c. 2 vols.

Two Worlds of Fashion. By CALTHORPE STRANG

The Pace that Kills: a New Novel. 3 vols.

A Woman's Triumph. By Lady HARDY. 3 vol

Erma's Engagement: a New Novel. By the Auth
of "Blanche Seymour," &c. 3 vols.

Dower and Curse. By JOHN LANE FORD, author
"Charles Stennie," &c. 3 vols.

Autobiography of a Cornish Rector. By the la
JAMES HAMLEY TREGENNA. 2 vols.

The Scarborough Belle. By ALIC CHARLOTJ
SAMPSON. 3 vols.

Puppets Dallying. By ARTHUR LILLIE, author
"Out of the Meshes," "King of Topsy Turvy," &c. 3 vols.

Under the Greenwood Tree. A Rural Painting
the Dutch School. By the Author of "Desperate Remedies," &
2 vols.

Coming Home to Roost. By GERALD GRANT.
vols.

Midnight Webs. By G. M. FENN, author of "Tl
Sapphire Cross," &c. 1 vol. fancy cloth binding, 10s. 6d.

Sorties from "Gib" in quest of Sensation and Se:
timent. By E. DYNE FENTON, late Captain 86th Regiment. 1 v
post 8vo, 10s. 6d.

TINSLEY BROTHERS, 8 CATHERINE STREET, STRAND.

l. By WILLIAM
l," " The Tower of Lon-

author of "Chro-

ry. By GEORGE
Neighbourhood," " The

YATES, author of
l vols.

[ENRY KINGSLEY,
&c. 2 vols.

THORPE STRANGE.
l. 3 vols.

HARDY. 3 vols.

. By the Author

FORD, author of

r. By the late

LIC CHARLOTTE

ILLIE, author of
" &c. 3 vols.

ural Painting of
sperate Remedies," &c.

RALD GRANT. 3

author of " Tho
ng, 10s. 6d.

nsation and Sen-
86th Regiment. 1 vol.

REET, STRAND.

The Pilgrim and the Shrine, or Passages from the
Life and Correspondence of Herbert Ainslie, B.A. Cantab. 3 vols.

Oberon's Spell. By EDEN ST. LEONARDS. 3 vols.

Under which King. By B. W. JOHNSTON, M.P.
1 vol.

Under the Red Dragon. By JAMES GRANT, author
of "The Romance of War," " Only an Ensign," &c. 3 vols.

Hornby Mills; and other Stories. By HENRY
KINGSLEY, author of " Ravenshoe," " Mademoiselle Mathilde,"
" Geoffry Hamlyn," &c. 2 vols.

Grainger's Thorn. By THOS. WRIGHT (the " Jour-
neyman Engineer"), author of " The Bane of a Life," " Some Habits
and Customs of the Working Classes," &c. 3 vols.

Church and Wife: a Question of Celibacy. By
ROBERT ST. JOHN CORBET, author of " The Canon's Daughters,"
3 vols.

Not Easily Jealous: a New Novel. 3 vols.

Rough but True. By ST. CLARE. 1 vol.

Christopher Dudley. By MARY BRIDGMAN, author
of ' Robert Lynne,' &c. 3 vols.

Love and Treason. By W. FREELAND. 3 vols.

Tender Tyrants. By JOSEPH VEREY. 3 vols.

Loyal: a New Novel. By M. A. GODFREY. 3 vols.

Fatal Sacrifice: a New Novel.

Old Margaret. By HENRY KINGSLEY, author of
" Ravenshoe," " Geoffry Hamlyn," &c. 2 vols.

Bide Time and Tide. By J. T. NEWALL, author of
" The Gage of Honour," " The Eastern Hunters," &c. 3 vols.

The Scandinavian Ring. By JOHN POMEROY. 3 vols.

The Harveys. By HENRY KINGSLEY, author ot
" Old Margaret," " Hetty," " Geoffry Hamlyn," &c. 2 vols.

Henry Ancrum: a Tale of the last War in New
Zealand. 2 vols.

She was Young, and He was Old. By the Author
of " Lover and Husband." 3 vols.

A Ready-made Family : or the Life and Adventures
of Julian Leep's Cherub. A Story. 3 vols.

TINSLEY BROTHERS, 8 CATHERINE STREET, STRAND.

Cecil's Tryst.   By the Author of " Lost Sir Ma
ingberd," &c.   3 vols.

Denison's Wife.   By Mrs. ALEXANDER FRAS
author of "Not while She lives," "Faithless; or the Loves of
Period," &c.   2 vols.

Wide of the Mark.   By the Author of " Reco
mended to Mercy," "Taken upon Trust," &c.   3 vols.

Title and Estate.   By F. LANCASTER.   3 vols.

Hollowhill Farm.   By JOHN EDWARDSON.   3 vo

The Sapphire Cross: a Tale of Two Generatic
By G. M. FENN, author of "Bent, not Broken," &c.   3 vols.

Edith.   By C. A. LEE.   2 vols.

Lady Judith.   By JUSTIN MCCARTHY, author
"My Enemy's Daughter," "The Waterdale Neighbours," &c.   3

Only an Ensign.   By JAMES GRANT, author of "
Romance of War," "Lady Wedderburn's Wish," &c.   3 vols.

Old as the Hills.   By DOUGLAS MOREY FORD.   3 v

Not Wooed, but Won.   By the Author of "L
Sir Massingberd," "Found Dead," &c.   3 vols.

My Heroine.   1 vol.

Sundered Lives.   By WYBERT REEVE, author of
Comedies of "Won at Last," "Not so Bad after all," &c.   3 vol

The Nomads of the North: a Tale of Lapland.
J. LOVEL HADWEN.   1 vol.

Family Pride.   By the Author of " Olive Varco
"Simple as a Dove," &c.   3 vols.

Fair Passions; or the Setting of the Pearls.   By
Hon. Mrs. PIGOTT CARLETON.   3 vols.

Harry Disney: an Autobiography.   Edited
ATHOLL DE WALDEN.   3 vols.

Desperate Remedies.   3 vols.

The Foster Sisters.   By EDMOND BRENAN LOUGHN
3 vols.

Only a Commoner.   By HENRY MORFORD.   3 v

Madame la Marquise.   By the Author of " Da
Singleton," "What Money Can't Do," &c.   3 vols.

Clara Delamaine.   By A. W. CUNNINGHAM.   3 v

TINSLEY BROTHERS, 8 CATHERINE STREET, STRAND

9 781376 129830